EVERY
SHOT
COUNTS

EVERY SHOT COUNTS

**USING THE REVOLUTIONARY
STROKES GAINED APPROACH TO
IMPROVE YOUR GOLF PERFORMANCE
AND STRATEGY**

MARK BROADIE

GOTHAM BOOKS

GOTHAM BOOKS
Published by the Penguin Group
Penguin Group (USA) LLC
375 Hudson Street
New York, New York 10014

USA | Canada | UK | Ireland | Australia | New Zealand | India | South Africa | China
penguin.com
A Penguin Random House Company

LIBRARY OF CONGRESS CATALOGING-IN-PUBLICATION DATA
Broadie, Mark Nathan.
  Every shot counts : using the revolutionary strokes gained approach to improve your golf
performance and strategy / Mark Broadie.
     pages cm
   ISBN 978-1-592-40750-7 (hardback)
  1. Swing (Golf) 2. Golf—Statistical methods. I. Title.
   GV979.S9B76 2014
   796.352′3—dc23
                              2013037178

Printed in the United States of America
10 9 8 7 6 5 4 3 2 1

Set in Univers, Trade Gothic Extended, and Melior
Designed by BTDNYC

To Nancy, Christopher, and Daniel, who all liked "foozled"

———————————————————————————

CONTENTS

PART II

GOLF STRATEGY

FOREWORD

SEAN FOLEY

Coach of Hunter Mahan, Edoardo Molinari, Justin Rose,
Lee Westwood, Tiger Woods, and other PGA Tour pros

The first time I became familiar with Mark Broadie's work was when I browsed the PGA Tour website one day and saw this thing that said "Strokes Gained Putting." Golf isn't a team sport, it's an individual sport, so using statistics to help improve a player's perception of himself, or to figure out what he needs to spend time working on, was fascinating. Using these stats, we see how a guy putted today, and how it helped him gain or lose strokes against his competitors. I thought: This is kind of a noble idea.

My next step was to wonder if the numbers could be used to evaluate driving and iron play. It wasn't long until I reached out to Mark. I'm not really a math guy, but as he sent me the strokes gained stats, I started noticing a massive difference. A guy could be number one in total driving, when under Broadie's strokes gained driving he is number 27. At first I thought that was strange, but then it was obvious: The stats showed that the old adage "drive for show, putt for dough" just isn't true when it comes down to these guys' earning revenue.

The thing is that the math doesn't lie. Strokes gained driving shows that distance is more valuable than accuracy. You look at strokes gained driving, look at the top five guys, and the one thing they all have in common is that they bomb it. They hit it forever. Sometimes these guys don't hit many fairways. Obviously their misses are going to be exaggerated compared to a guy with a slower swing speed. Still, Bubba Watson or Dustin Johnson or Tiger Woods or Rory McIlroy coming out of the rough with a 9-iron, they have an advantage over most players hitting a 5-iron out of the fairway, because they're closer to the hole.

We'd always been taught that the important thing is hitting it in the fairway and hitting it on the green, but my intuition had told me long iron shots were important. Everyone's always telling me, "Your guys should be practicing a lot more wedges," but I just don't see them hitting many 80-yard wedge shots in a round. I've always wanted my guys practicing a lot of 190- to 230-yard shots. And here were the strokes gained numbers to support that.

It becomes obvious how important it is to spend your time in the right place. Typically it's easy to practice what you like and what you're good at. I'm not against working on your strength, because if something is a strength you want to keep it that way. But it's also important to work on your weakness. In the past, guys would fight me on that, but it's tough to resist when you see the numbers right out in front of you.

The numbers approach also helps me tell my guys, "Look, you're in this to win tournaments, you're in this to earn money, so you need to use more of your time doing what the numbers say you need to work on, not just whatever you feel like doing." And they have to agree. They see the numbers and they're just, like, "Yeah, I get it."

Another way it works is psychological. Justin Rose once told me, "My wedge play has to get better. I'm not happy with it, we have to work more on it." I said, "That's funny, because Mark Broadie has you as number one on the PGA Tour in wedge play." As soon as he saw that, he played with more confidence, standing over a shot thinking, "Man, I'm the best, this is a great opportunity," rather than, "I'm not really comfortable with this."

There's not a psychologist in the world who could do a better job convincing a guy that he's good than those numbers. They are just too reasonable, there's too much logic.

I'm going to lift every rock possible to figure out how to maximize these guys' earnings and world rankings, and that's why I value Mark's information. Because why would I guess about what I can measure? So much of what we believe in life comes from what we've been told over and over, and we never really question it. The value of the numbers approach for a coach is that it's not belief, it's fact.

Traditional golf stats today are like a plane that's circling the airport until it runs out of gas. It's going to either land or crash. People are in a comfort zone, and they're not willing to go through the pain or doubt that goes with developing a new way of thinking. But at some point, Mark's approach will become how people determine golf performance. They're just going to have to accept it, because it makes too much sense.

This approach gives me an opportunity to help guys become better players. On the PGA Tour I've watched guys spend hours practicing skills that are just 6% of their score, whereas my guys are on the range hitting 4-irons until their hands bleed. Even with the young kids I coach, our goal has become smashing it as hard as we can. I've changed them to workouts that do more for acquisition of power and velocity than what I'd previously done. If the kids can hit it far, they can learn to hit it straight later.

Mark Broadie's findings are very important to competitive players, more than anyone even understands yet. My getting a guy to make a little change in his technique is going to have less effect than getting him to recognize the truth in the numbers in front of him. For people who want to become better golfers, and for young golfers and college players, even if it flies in the face of what they've been taught, the numbers approach is the way to go.

INTRODUCTION

How do you make your golf decisions? Many of us stand over the ball and decide based on our feelings at the moment. Feeling confident: Go for the pin. Made a mess of the last hole: Play it safe. Our decisions are often made on hunches. But what if you could base your decisions on something more convincing, on data and solid analysis? As Charles Dickens wrote in *Great Expectations*: "Take nothing on its looks; take everything on evidence. There's no better rule."

As golfers, we often make poor decisions. We decide to thread our ball through a narrow opening only to see our shot ricochet deeper into the woods. We attack a pin only to see our hopes of a birdie vanish as the ball settles into a bad lie in the bunker. In many situations it's not easy to tell a good decision from a bad one. Is it better to lay up to a comfortable distance of 90 or 100 yards or to hit it farther, leaving 20 or 30 yards to the hole? On a five-foot breaking putt, is it better to die it in the hole, or jam it to take away most of the break?

Each golf decision involves a trade-off between risk and reward. Aiming at a hole tucked on the edge of a green increases the risk of hitting into a bunker, but the reward is the increased chance of knocking it close and converting a birdie opportunity. In many cases it is not obvious how to balance these risk-reward factors to produce the lowest score.

To evaluate the best overall golf strategy, one not influenced by the outcome of a few shots, requires a lot of data. More than ten years ago, when I set out on a quest to learn what makes golfers tick, I searched everywhere for this data, this evidence, but I couldn't find it in any golf instruction books or golf magazines. I decided I needed to gather it myself.

I wanted to dissect the game to better understand golfers' strategies and performance. A mountain of detailed golf shot data, I knew, would allow me to analyze different strategies and performance outcomes, to gain new insights on how best to play the game.

The problem with traditional stats

One reason I couldn't find the evidence I needed at first was that traditional golf stats did not provide the right kind of information. What does it take to drop 10 strokes from your golf score? How much is 20 yards of extra driving distance worth? What separates the best pro golfers from merely average pro golfers? Traditional golf stats can't answer these questions.

Pat Goss, coach of Luke Donald and head coach of the Northwestern University golf team, believes in the power of golf analytics. Yet he doesn't have the golfers on his team record their traditional stats. Why? Because traditional golf stats just aren't informative enough to make it worth the time and effort. In a single round of golf, with one golfer taking 31 putts and another 28 putts, the 31-putt round might represent the better putting performance after considering where the putts started on the green. How useful is it to know your greens in regulation if you can't tell whether missed greens were the result of poor driving or subpar approach shots?

I had an idea that developing new stats would help in my quest to understand the game of golf, but to make any progress in developing more informative stats, I needed to have data. Better data. And a lot of it.

At the time, there was little or no usable data on amateur golfers, and professional data was limited to traditional golf stats. The PGA Tour collected data, but most of the information was based on counting: number of strokes, putts per round, fairways hit. In the era of paper and pencil, this was the best that could be done on a large scale. But what I really needed for my analysis was detailed, shot-level data.

The information I needed on individual shots included: how far they travel, what direction they go, and where they end up relative to the hole. I needed to know the starting and ending location of shots, whether they started in the fairway, rough, sand, or fescue; whether shots were obstructed by trees; whether putts were uphill or downhill; and whether they broke right-to-left or left-to-right. So in 2001, I began work on a computer program called Golfmetrics to collect, store, and analyze golf data.

The first step is to create a map of the course, which can now be done using Google Earth. Then, on the course, a golfer records each shot by marking an X in a paper yardage book that contains an image of the hole. After the round, the shots are manually entered into a computer, a 20-minute process that is daunting for most golfers. (In the future, my hope is that the whole process will be made easier with a mobile app, so that data can be entered at the touch of a button when a golfer is standing next to the ball. When the golfer finishes the round and touches another button, the app will provide detailed feedback and analysis.)

After a few years, and thanks to countless hours of programming and data input effort, the Golfmetrics database contained more than 100,000 shots from more than 200 golfers ranging in age from eight to 70-plus years. The golfers whose shots were recorded in the system included LPGA Tour pros, club pros, college golfers, and male and female amateur golfers with scores ranging from the 60s to the 140s (yes, those were really painful to enter). With such a sizable amount of data, I could start analyzing and studying golf performance, and trends started becoming apparent.

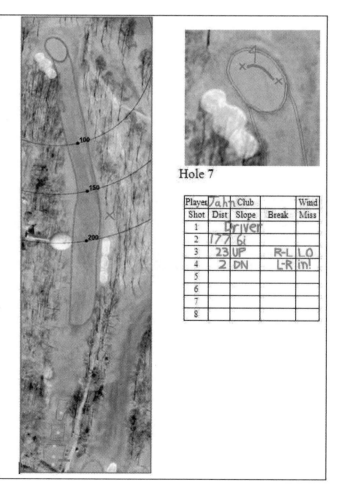

Hole 7

Player	Jahn	Club		Wind
Shot	Dist	Slope	Break	Miss
1	Driver			
2	177	6i		
3	23	UP	R-L	LO
4	2	DN	L-R	in!
5				
6				
7				
8				

A sample page from a Golfmetrics yardage book. My friend Jahn Levins's drive finished in the right rough, 177 yards from the hole. He hit a 6-iron onto the green. His 23-foot uphill, right-to-left-breaking putt missed on the low side of the hole. He sank the downhill, left-to-right two-footer for par. When a shot location is entered into Golfmetrics, the program automatically distinguishes fairway, rough, sand, and green locations, computes shot distances and shot angles, and much more.

While the original Golfmetrics database contained mainly amateur data, I needed professional data to be able to compare the play of amateurs to that of pros. I knew that some pros recorded their shot data. Charlie Coody, winner of the 1971 Masters, kept a chart of all the shots he hit in competition. Ron Green wrote that Coody used it "to study the trends in his game and determine where he needs work." In the 1990s and 2000s Annika Sörenstam charted "every shot of every round so as to identify her weaknesses."

Of course, I didn't have access to their data, and I needed data for as many pros as possible.

Unbeknownst to me, at the same time I was creating Golfmetrics, the PGA Tour was developing its own shot-level data collection system, called ShotLink. Beginning in 2003, the PGA Tour recorded detailed information on every golf shot at its tournaments, using laser technology and about 350 volunteers per tournament. To collect ShotLink data, golf ball locations on the green were measured within a two-inch accuracy, and off-green locations were measured within one-yard accuracy. Between 2003 and 2012, the ShotLink database, powered by PGA Tour technology partner CDW, gathered information on more than 10 million shots, a vast store of information and just what I needed to analyze and assess the performance of the best golfers in the world.

My son Daniel manning a ShotLink laser behind a green

Managing the data collection inside the PGA Tour's ShotLink trailer

This was a massive, expensive, and forward-looking undertaking by the PGA Tour. Why did they do it? Officials from the PGA Tour wanted an updated scoreboard system, an improved fan experience at tournaments, and better information for their media partners. Unlike baseball, basketball, and other sports, golf had relatively little in the way of stats information to offer fans. ShotLink data was a quantum improvement.

For a researcher like me, having access to this data is like exploring a cave filled with treasure. There's something new and interesting wherever you look. What fraction of putts does a PGA Tour golfer sink from 15 feet? Half? 30%? You can figure out from the ShotLink data that the PGA Tour average is 23%. If you watch golf on TV, it appears that pros sink putts from all over the planet with great regularity. But TV distorts our view because successful putts are shown repeatedly, while missed putts rarely make the highlight reel.

How could this information help? If you're a pro standing over a 15-foot putt, knowing whether you are better or worse than the tour average isn't going to help you sink the putt. But if you spend too much of your practice time trying to achieve an unrealistic goal of a 40% success rate on 15-foot putts, you're probably wasting a lot of valuable time.

Strokes gained: a better measure of golf performance

This mountain of shot-level golf data—information about where shots start and end—wasn't useful by itself. New ways to analyze it were needed. Building on ideas developed at the dawn of the computer age, especially with a tool called *dynamic programming,* I developed a method to analyze golf performance that is now called *strokes gained.* The strokes gained method makes it possible to analyze a player's game as a whole. It allows putting skill to be measured more accurately than by just counting putts. It allows driving skill to be measured better than it had been using fairways hit or driving distance. And most important, it allows putting, short game, and long-game skills to be compared directly with each other.

This thinking for golf was similar to the approach that Bill James used in his sabermetrics revolution with baseball stats, popularized in the book and movie *Moneyball*. In baseball, batting average had long been the main stat used to measure proficiency at the plate. James showed that another stat, on-base plus slugging percentage (OPS), was a better predictor of a batter's contribution to runs scored, and therefore of a player's value to his team.

Another sabermetrics stat is ultimate zone rating (UZR), which Sig Mejdal, director of baseball analytics for the Houston Astros, pointed out to me as an example of how similar sabermetrics and strokes gained can be. In baseball, the UZR stat measures the average number of runs saved by a defensive play relative to an average fielder. In golf, strokes gained measures the decrease in average strokes to hole out relative to an average golfer. Both stats measure performance as progress to a goal: scoring runs in baseball and holing out in golf. The similarity in the two stats stems from their common ancestry in the realm of dynamic programming.

Dynamic programming is a systematic approach to thinking ahead. The concept also extends to other sports. "Skate to where the puck's going to be, not to where it has been" was the advice hockey great Wayne Gretzky got from his father. Dynamic programming allows you to figure out the optimal path through multiple stages of connected problems. Choosing the best path to navigate through multiple shots on a golf hole is one dynamic programming challenge. The optimal decision on a tee shot depends on what can happen on the tee shot, and what decision and outcomes can happen on the second shot, and so on. Golf is, in effect, a dynamic program in which the objective is to minimize your golf score by making the best decision on each shot. This viewpoint leads naturally to the strokes gained performance measure, in which progress to the hole is measured, not in yards, but in the decrease in the average strokes to hole out.

I implemented the strokes gained approach for putts and off-green shots in the Golfmetrics system in 2005. In 2008, I published the first strokes gained results, comparing professional and amateur play across a variety of shots. I reported strokes gained results for putts, short-game shots, and long-game shots, though I used the term "shot value" at the time. Building on the same concept, a group of three researchers from MIT, Doug Fearing, Jason Acimovic, and Steve Graves, ranked putters on the PGA Tour. Their paper was published in 2011 and in it they coined the term "strokes gained."

In 2010, the PGA Tour was looking for a new putting stat, because it recognized the flaws in the three main putting stats that it was using: putts per round, putts per green in regulation, and average length of holed putts. Together, the group from MIT, the PGA Tour, and I worked on the design and details of the Tour's strokes gained putting implementation. The PGA Tour rolled out strokes gained putting in May 2011, its first new core stat in fifteen years, and strokes gained quickly became accepted and used as their primary stat for measuring putting.

Some will argue that strokes gained putting and other strokes gained stats don't take into account the psychological aspects of the game or the pressure of performing down the stretch. My response is that if you want to analyze an intangible such as putting performance under pressure, it is still better to use strokes gained putting, a more accurate measure of putting performance, than simply counting putts.

Every Shot Counts explains the idea behind strokes gained. The book also gives results for a whole family of strokes gained stats that allow both pros and amateurs to analyze skill in driving, approach shots, short game, and putting. These four large shot categories are further broken down to provide more detailed analysis and understanding of golf performance.

Every Stroke Counts takes apart the games of PGA Tour pros to see how they win tournaments. Tiger Woods is the best golfer of his era, if not in all of golf history, but there is considerable debate about whether it is his putting, scrambling ability, or long game that explains his success. The strokes gained method allows putting, short game, and long-game skills to be compared directly with each other on a scientifically sound basis, unaffected by preconceived beliefs or hidden biases. It allows us to find the true secret of Tiger Woods's success.

A scientific approach to golf strategy

Using data to understand golf performance is just the beginning, for golf is a game of both decisions and strategy. Have you played golf with a friend who regularly beats you by four or five shots, even though you hit your drives similar distances and have comparable short games and putting? Your physical skills are similar, but your friend wins because he has the better strategy. He plays the game better.

Golf is notoriously difficult to analyze. Sometimes a bad strategy works out. Sometimes a good strategy—one that should have the best chance of success—doesn't pay off.

James Hahn was attempting to get his PGA Tour card when he faced a decision on his second shot on a par-five. Hahn thought he could clear the water and reach the green in two but his caddie and good friend, Dong Yi, wanted to lay up. In a hilarious moment on the course, they resolved their difference of opinion by playing rock-paper-scissors. Hahn's scissors beat Yi's paper. James told me, "I definitely had enough club to clear the water. The ball landed just over but rolled back in." He did get up and down for par.

Every Shot Counts will show how you can shoot lower scores by making many better decisions on the golf course. It won't teach you how to improve your swing, but it will explain how to lower your handicap with your current swing through smarter play. Learn the lessons in this book and you will find strokes falling off your score.

As golf writer Bill Pennington observed, "It is undoubtedly true that the average golfer is an exceedingly poor gauge of what really ails his or her performance." To remedy this, chapter 9 contains a number of games and drills that can be used to track your skills through time and benchmark your performance against PGA Tour pros as well as groups of amateurs. You'll learn new ways to identify your strengths and weaknesses. Taking lessons and practicing to improve the weakest parts of your game is a much faster way to lower your score than beating balls on the range. The results of this effort can make you a better golfer.

What do pros and coaches think about golf stats?

Allow me to share some of the conversations I've had with pros and coaches on the subject of traditional golf stats and strokes gained analysis. When I first met with Robert Karlsson, he said to me, "I want to warn you that I'm not a big fan of golf stats." I appreciated his candor, understood why he said it, and moreover, I agreed with him. It's not surprising that many players, coaches, and fans were skeptical about golf stats, because the traditional stats—putts per round, fairways hit, greens in regulation, and others—can be confusing, uninformative, and even misleading. But I strongly believe in the power of good stats.

Since early 2011, I've worked with Luke Donald and his coach Pat Goss to analyze Luke's game. Pat, who majored in economics at Northwestern, said, "I have always worked hard at evaluating Luke's game statistically, and developing measurable and tangible practices around those statistics. My brain is definitely wired that way!" He compared our work to former Cardinals' baseball manager Tony La Russa. "All Tony La Russa tries to do is cheat the odds," Pat said. "Use a guy that bats .270 against lefties instead of someone who bats .240. Over the course of a year, that will add up to some runs. If Luke can become a 2.5% better short-game player, he'll get more balls up and down over the course of a season."

Colin Swatton and Justin Poynter are two coaches with an analytical bent similar to that of Pat Goss. Colin, who coaches Jason Day and Greg Chalmers, prepares quarterly stats reports for his players, which he uses to monitor their progress and to set goals. Justin Poynter, coach of J. J. Henry and Hunter Haas, also believes in the power of golf analytics. For their junior golfers, both Colin and Justin use points-based skills tests to identify strengths and weaknesses and to set practice plans.

Spend a few minutes discussing golf with Sean Foley, coach of Tiger Woods, Justin Rose, and Hunter Mahan, and you'll be treated to launch angles, spin rates, a bit of geometry, physics, philosophy, and some amusing stories. Foley, Goss, Swatton, and Poynter are some of the most analytically minded coaches in the game.

Many pro golfers, not just their coaches, believe in the value of analyzing stats. When a mutual friend, Tom Dundon, connected me with Bo Van Pelt, I asked Bo whether he cared about his stats. Yes, he was very interested, he said, and he gave a great reason. He explained that he had a family, his time was valuable, and he wanted to be able to get the most out of his practice sessions.

My good friend Edoardo Molinari understood strokes gained in a flash. Because he plays primarily on the European Tour, where they have only basic stats, he wrote his own computer program to calculate strokes gained (putting to good use his master's degree in engineering). He tracks strokes gained for all parts of his game, not just putting. He asks me better questions about statistics than I get from doctoral students in my business school classes. A few years ago, informed by patterns he saw in the stats he collected, Edoardo changed his swing. The changes paid off, culminating in two tournament wins in 2010.

Edoardo is, I'll admit, an exception—a golfer-mathematician. Still, many pros do want to see a statistical analysis of their game, and many ask cogent questions about how the results are calculated and what they mean. But most pros can't explain the details of strokes gained putting. "Not even a little bit," D. A. Points told golf writer Adam Schupak. And that's understandable, if they've never seen an explanation of how strokes gained putting works.

At its core, strokes gained is a simple and powerful concept that most golfers "get" after a few minutes of explanation. One of the beautiful aspects of strokes gained is that the results are understandable even if you don't know exactly how they are calculated. If a pro gained four strokes on the field, with a three-stroke gain from putting and a one-stroke gain from off-green strokes, you can immediately see that putting explains most of the pro's good score. Compare that with two traditional golf stats. If a pro took 29 putts and hit 12 greens in regulation, what does that imply about his round? It's not so obvious.

MOST PROS HAVE CONFIDENCE in strokes gained putting, even though they might not know all of its inner workings. Why? Because they see that the rankings and results make sense. It passes the "smell test." Webb Simpson said, "The new putting stat, strokes gained, is so great, because it's really a nonbiased stat."

There's a huge variation among pros with regard to their opinion about strokes gained or any golf stats. Forget about stats, even today there are a few pros who don't use yardage books, a practice first made popular by Deane Beman and then Jack Nicklaus in the 1960s and 1970s. There might always be a few pros who succeed without the help of coaches, yardage books, or stats.

Golf stats, even informative ones, by themselves don't make better golfers, yet touring pros compete against the best golfers in the world and are looking for an edge. They are constantly striving to improve. Even some pros who don't care to look at their stats want their coaches to study them. They'd rather use their coaches as an information filter, and that's fine. Many of the requests and questions that I get are from coaches. In some cases, a coach observes a flaw in a player's game, but a player is skeptical. Strokes gained can provide, and has provided, objective and quantitative support for the coach's observation.

Even more exciting to me is the use of golf data to analyze golf strategy. You'll see some examples of how the analysis works in the second part of the book. I've done strategic analyses of a number of holes on the PGA Tour for pros, and I give examples of this approach in chapter 8. Peter Hanson said my analysis saved him four or five strokes in one tournament. I'm sure he was exaggerating, but it does indicate the potential impact of this scientific approach to the analysis of golf strategy.

About the author and research methods

My research and teaching as a professor at Columbia Business School is focused mainly on quantitative finance: the measurement and management of financial risk and the construction of financial portfolios to achieve maximum investment goals. My hobby is playing golf and I've enjoyed playing the game since high school. At my home course, Pelham Country Club in New York, I won the club championship once and the senior club championship twice. I currently carry a four handicap and I've had the good fortune to hit three holes-in-one. While I'm not a complete hack, compared to any pro and to many amateurs, my golf playing credentials are slim, so you won't get any advice from me about how to swing a golf club.

Every Shot Counts isn't a book about golf mechanics. It's about using data to better understand golf performance and golf strategy. I started this project because the same methods I use in my academic and consulting work are the ideal tools for analyzing golf. I realized I could combine my professional and personal passions and help other golfers benefit from analysis techniques inspired by the world of finance.

Since 2003, I've been a member of the United States Golf Association's Handicap Research Team (HRT). The HRT is the group that created the current handicapping system, the slope system that was officially incorporated into USGA handicaps in 1987. The HRT still maintains, tweaks, and improves the system.

There are similarities between golf handicapping and performance assessment. A central issue in handicapping is determining how much of a golfer's score is due to skill and how much is due to course difficulty. A score of 75 on a wide-open 5,800-yard course isn't at all comparable to the same score on a 7,300-yard course with narrow fairways and numerous water hazards. Course and slope ratings, which measure the difficulty of a course for scratch and bogey golfers, are the way the USGA creates handicaps that are portable between courses.

Many of the tools that I use for studying golf are the same ones I use for analyzing financial problems: statistics, simulation, optimization, and dynamic programming. Statistical analysis is useful in developing and analyzing golf stats. It helps us to understand whether a result is significant or just a fluke.

Simulation is a method that uses computers, through models, to mimic the behavior of real-world systems. It is now familiar to many because video games are, in effect, simulation models with varying degrees of realism. Simulation is useful for analyzing situations that don't occur in the data. I can simulate the shots of a golfer with a driver that goes 20 yards farther to see how much his score would go down. Or test with simulation techniques whether, as has been suggested numerous times throughout the years, golf places too much emphasis on putting. What would happen if the diameter of the hole was doubled? Who would benefit more, good putters or poor putters? I can simulate thousands of rounds played on course with a larger hole and tell you the answer.

Optimization is used to find the best decision among a number of alternatives. It can be used to find the best portfolio for a hedge fund or the best route for delivering goods to the market, and it can be used to find the best strategy for a golfer to achieve the lowest score. Golf is a series of risk-reward trade-offs. Should I be conservative or aggressive on this shot? What strategy will lead to my lowest score? Optimization is like a smart caddy, who can search through a range of possible decisions, assess the cost or benefit of each, and then recommend the best choice.

Dynamic programming is essentially a mathematical way to work through multistage problems and help you to plan ahead.

The PGA Tour's ShotLink system and my Golfmetrics program have provided the data we need, the raw stockpile of material containing hidden golf secrets waiting to be discovered. Statistics, simulation, optimization, and dynamic programming are the right tools for doing the digging. The ingredients are in place for uncovering the secrets of the game of golf. Shot-level data together with strokes gained analysis allow us to answer questions about golf performance and golf strategy that we couldn't answer just a few years ago. Some of the answers are surprising and run counter to conventional wisdom, while others reinforce our intuition and give us new perspectives on this age-old game we love. The information in this book is not based on opinions or educated guesses, but on evidence from mathematical analysis using real data collected from a wide range of amateur and professional golfers. *Every Shot Counts* is the culmination of years of program development and analysis of this treasure trove of data. Let's get started!

EVERY
SHOT
COUNTS

PART I

GOLF PERFORMANCE

CHAPTER 1

PUTTING IS OVERRATED:
Why Conventional Wisdom Gets It Wrong

Golf's most sacred truism is that putting is the key to scoring. Why was Tiger Woods the best player in the world for many years? "Because he's the best putter," said nine-time major-winner Gary Player. "I think by now every player on tour is aware that the biggest reason Tiger is the best is because he putts the best," said 2006 U.S. Open winner Geoff Ogilvy.

"Drive for show and putt for dough," is a saying attributed to the great South African golfer Bobby Locke, who won four British Opens from 1949 to 1957.

The importance-of-putting idea is as old as golf itself. Celebrated golf writer Bernard Darwin, grandson of Charles Darwin, wrote in 1912 that putting's "supreme importance no one with even the smallest experience of golf will be disposed to deny." John Henry Taylor, who won five British Opens between 1894 and 1913, wrote that "more matches are lost or won upon the green than upon any other portion of the course." In the first instruction book ever published by a professional golfer, Willie Park Jr., British Open winner of 1887 and 1889, wrote, "Putting is therefore probably the most important part of the game, as no player who putts indifferently can ever hope to excel, however proficient he may be in driving and approaching." Park is also famous for saying, "A man who can putt is a match for anyone."

For more than two centuries, the mistaken idea that putting is the key to scoring has been the settled wisdom of experts and nonexperts alike. In an 1805 book about the beauty of Scotland, before greens were even called greens, author Robert Forsyth declared that the shot near the hole, or "putting as it is called," was "of the greatest importance."

We also used to believe that the universe revolved around a stationary Earth. Just because an idea has been repeated and accepted through the years doesn't make it true.

Why do golfers attach such outsize importance to putting? How does this thinking about the importance of putting square with the evidence? Let's look at five claims people make to support the idea that putting is the beating heart of golf. Then, let's consider why each one falls short of the truth.

Five ideas that overvalue putting

1. **You can make up for a poor drive, but you can't get back a missed putt.**

You hit a perfect drive in the fairway and then follow with an approach into the sand, a wedge onto the green, and a missed par putt. Your playing companion drives into the trees, chips back to the fairway, and then follows with an up-and-down for par. Your missed putt cost a stroke. His holed putt saved a stroke. The observation appears to be literally true: Your companion *did* recover from a poor drive, and your bogey *was* the result of a missed putt for which there was no recourse.

But wait. Mathematically speaking, it can't be that the missed putt cost one stroke and the holed putt saved one stroke. The difference in scores between you and your companion was only one stroke, not two. The "missed-putt-cost-a-stroke" and "holed-putt-saved-a-stroke" explanations are compelling, but flawed. Double counting overemphasizes the importance of putting.

These explanations incorrectly attribute each golfer's score to a single shot. Your bogey wasn't due solely to the missed putt. It resulted from a less-than-stellar approach shot as well, and happened in spite of a better-than-average drive. Your companion's par also resulted from more than one circumstance, though it was partially due to his putt as well as to his superior approach shot, which made up for his poor drive.

The final score on a hole typically results from the accumulation of *fractional* gains and losses on each stroke; only occasionally is it due to a single shot. So although it may be literally true that you can make up for a bad drive but not for a missed putt, this observation overvalues the importance of putting and wrongly discounts other parts of the game.

2. Putting affects confidence and confidence affects scores.

Poor putters may lack skills; they don't get up and down as often as better putters, for instance. In addition, their lack of confidence may also influence their scoring. Poor putters might feel more pressure on approach shots, because they don't have confidence in their ability to recover from a missed green. A missed putt can bring on tension and despair and lead to worse results on the next hole. Golf psychologists make their living, in part, by training golfers to minimize these negative spillover effects.

The opposite can happen as well. Getting up and down for par, sinking a long birdie putt, or making a series of short putts can give a golfer confidence that spreads to the rest of his game. Irish golf champion Pádraig Harrington summed it up by saying, "You can hit three bad golf shots onto a par-four, and if you hole a ten-footer for par, you forget about the three bad shots. If you hit two good shots and you three-putt it, all of a sudden you lose your confidence in your swing for some reason."

The effect of shot outcomes on confidence, and confidence on shots, isn't limited to putting. Some golfers may gain confidence from booming a drive down the middle of the fairway. Knocking an approach shot to within one foot of the hole sure takes the pressure off the putt. Who's to say that putting performance isn't affected by the confidence transferred from other shots?

The indirect effects, both positive and negative, of one shot on another may be real, but scientists have not yet developed ways to quantify the mental aspects of the game and their impact on performance. In contrast, shot data can effectively be used to quantify the effects of putting on scoring. A quantitative approach to improving your golf game, then, will set aside questions of confidence in favor of looking at the data.

3. Pivotal putts are the heart of golf history.

Anecdotal evidence abounds that history revolves around the putt. "Maybe, yes, sir!" announcer Verne Lundquist said as 46-year-old Jack Nicklaus raised his putter and his 18-foot birdie putt dropped at the 17th hole on the way to his iconic 1986 Masters victory. At the 72nd hole of the 2008 U.S. Open, Tiger Woods needed to make a birdie putt to force a playoff with Rocco Mediate. The 12-foot putt bobbled on the uneven Poa annua grass on the way to the hole, then just caught the edge and fell in. Tiger went on to win the playoff the next day to bring his major count to 14.

In 1970, Doug Sanders was in his stance ready to stroke his three-foot putt to win the British Open when he saw a little pebble in his line. He reached down to remove it, then returned to his stance, and for another few seconds he glanced at the hole and then the ball. Finally he pulled the trigger and missed the putt to the right, the ball never touching the hole. Sanders lost in a playoff the next day to Jack Nicklaus. He's been haunted by that missed putt every day since.

On the last hole of the 1946 Masters, Ben Hogan was 12 feet away from victory and two putts away from a playoff. His gentle putt missed and rolled two and a half feet by the hole. Taking his time, Hogan then missed the comebacker to lose to unheralded Herman Keiser.

Do these examples prove that putting is more important than other parts of the game? Or do they instead prove that confirmation bias is alive and well?

Confirmation bias refers to the tendency of people to selectively gather or remember information that supports a preconceived idea, while discounting contrary information. British philosopher and mathematician Bertrand Russell wrote, "If a man is offered a fact which goes against his instincts, he will scrutinize it closely, and unless the evidence is overwhelming, he will refuse to believe it. If, on the other hand, he is offered something which affords a reason for acting in accordance to his instincts, he will accept it even on the slightest evidence."

As easy as it is to find examples of putts that decided the outcome of major tournaments, the list of important off-green shots is equally impressive.

In the last round of the 1972 U.S. Open at Pebble Beach, Jack Nicklaus hit a 1-iron into a howling wind at the treacherous 218-yard par-three 17th hole. The ball landed one foot from the cup, hit the flagstick, and stopped five inches from the hole. The birdie sealed the 11th of his eventual 18 major victories.

Twenty-two years earlier, Ben Hogan was standing in the fairway of the 72nd hole of the U.S. Open at Merion, needing a par to join a playoff with Lloyd Mangrum and George Fazio. Hogan had recovered from a near-fatal car crash just over a year earlier, and his legs were aching from walking his 36th hole of the day. He pulled a 1-iron from his bag and hit his shot into a stiff breeze onto the green some 40 feet from the hole, with a photographer recording the iconic image for posterity. He two-putted for par and then won in the 18-hole playoff the next day.

In the captivating book *Bobby's Open*, Steven Reid identifies the almost impossible 175-yard shot made by the great Bobby Jones on the 17th hole of the last round of the 1926 British Open as pivotal in the tournament. Jones landed the blind shot over wasteland onto the green, and went on to win the first of his three British Opens. Many view that miraculous shot as the defining one in his legendary career. As Bernard Darwin once wrote, "A teaspoonful too much sand might have meant irretrievable ruin."

As fun as it is to revisit golf history's greatest putting moments, a handful of cherry-picked examples does not make for good data. For every critical shot or putt near the end of the tournament, there were many successful strokes each golfer took earlier. Which putt or shot is pivotal in a round or tournament? Are putts more important to scoring than other shots? To determine the relative importance of putting requires an unbiased examination of all shots that compose a golfer's score. The importance of putting can't be judged by looking only at putting, or only at winners, or by examining anecdotal evidence that focuses only on a handful of shots.

4. The sheer number of strokes taken on the green proves their importance.

The putter is the one club that every golfer uses on virtually every hole. A golfer may go an entire round without hitting a sand shot, so how important can sand play be relative to putting? Most golfers use their driver 10 to 14 times per round, but use their putters 25 to 40 times per round. Putting has to be more important than driving and sand play, conventional wisdom says, if only because of the number of shots involved.

Bobby Jones called putting "a curious sort of game within a game." He explained, "There is no need to labor its importance in golf. Nearly half the shots played by any expert performer are on the putting surface. Sometimes more than half. I recall with mournful distinctness my last round in the 1926 British Open championship when I used, or misused, 39 shots on the putting surface, and employed only 35 other shots." Jones won the tournament by two strokes.

Shot count statistics can be misleading. PGA Tour pros average 29 putts per round, with an average score of 71, so putts represent about 40% of their strokes. The number of strokes and the importance of strokes, however, can be very different. Nine of those 29 putts occur within two and a half feet of the hole (where pros make over 99.5%), so putts outside of two and a half feet represent 30% of their strokes. Putts make up 30% of high-handicap golfer shots and only about 20% if you exclude putts inside two and a half feet.

These gimmes illustrate a fundamental point: Not all shots are equally important. Two-foot putts aren't as important as 10-foot putts. Why? Because almost all golfers make almost all two-foot putts, so they don't explain much of the scoring differences among golfers. Ten-foot putts matter because some golfers make more of these putts than others. It's not the sheer number of putts that matters, nor the number of drives or sand shots. Shots are important if they lead to scoring differences.

- ### A detour into Fairyland
  Imagine that you lived in Driver-Fairyland, a magical world where every drive travels 300 yards and finishes in the middle of the fairway. You confidently stride to the tee of every long hole knowing that you will

hit a straight, towering drive unaffected by the wind, your score on the previous hole, or how well you slept last night. Unfortunately, the rest of your foursome also hits 300-yard drives that finish in the fairway. And so do your wife, your 10-year-old daughter, and everyone who plays golf in Driver-Fairyland. The exhilaration you feel in booming your drives is quickly replaced by boredom, since the driving magic is shared by everyone.

In Driver-Fairyland, golfers don't need to tee it up and hit their drives, since driving doesn't determine the outcome of any match. Eventually the residents decide to save time, and they start playing the long holes from the same spot in the middle of the fairway. In Driver-Fairyland, it doesn't matter whether there are five or fourteen holes that require a driver. The number of drives on the Driver-Fairyland course doesn't matter at all. Which golfer shoots the lowest score depends entirely on shots other than drives.

Now imagine living in Putter-Fairyland, a place where all golfers take two putts to hole out, no matter where they start on the green. Instead of carrying putters and actually putting the ball, golfers simply add two strokes to their total after reaching the green. When all golfers are equally skilled putters, strokes on the green contribute nothing to scoring differences among golfers. In Putter-Fairyland, putts don't affect scores. Putter-Fairyland golfers' scores depend entirely on shots other than putts.

Coming back from Fairyland to reality, we can see that putting isn't necessarily any more important than other parts of the game. In Driver-Fairyland, driving doesn't matter, and in Putter-Fairyland, putting doesn't matter. In the real world, two-foot putts hardly matter because nearly everybody makes them. Neither putts nor drives can be said to be the more important kind of shot based on the number of shots alone.

5. Skilled putters who botch long shots still win tournaments.

Lucas Glover had been winless since his 2009 U.S. Open victory, and had missed three consecutive cuts leading up to the 2011 Wells Fargo championship at Quail Hollow. But in that tournament, Glover tied his Clemson buddy Jonathan Byrd at 15 under par in regulation play and then won on the first playoff hole. After his win, Lucas said, "I knew Thursday I was going to have a great putting week. You know, you just get those feelings and seeing the line very well." Glover finished the tournament ranked first among in-the-money finishers in putting, but 25th in driving distance. His woeful driving accuracy record tied for 49th place: Glover hit just 46% of the possible fairways for the week. Clearly, he felt that his good putting made up for a multitude of sins.

On the other hand, in 2004 Vijay Singh won nine events on the PGA Tour with little help from his putting. At the Shell Houston Open in April of that year, Singh won with a score of 11 under par. He was ranked first in driving distance and third in driving accuracy, but a lowly 55th in putting. Similarly, in 2009 Sean O'Hair won the Quail Hollow Championship in spite of a putting rank of 67 out of 74 golfers who made the cut.

Contrary to popular belief, winning and ranking high in putting don't always go together. In some cases, such as Lucas Glover's 2011 win at Quail Hollow, putting seems to reign supreme, but in plenty of other cases victories are won in spite of relatively poor putting. What conclusions can we draw? At the least, putting is not the only shot that counts in the game of golf. We need to look at data from a large number of tournaments to see what patterns emerge.

What do ranks tell us?

When you compare the ranks of tournament winners for various shot types in recent PGA Tour tournaments, it is tempting to conclude that putting is twice as important as either driving distance or driving accuracy. That interpretation would be wrong. Scores, not ranks, determine winners. A high rank in putting or any other single part of the game does not make you win. If a golfer wins a tournament and ranks first in sand saves, with one sand save in one attempt, that doesn't mean that sand play was the key to victory. If a golfer wins a tournament and ranks first in putting, driving distance, driving accuracy, and sand saves, how can you tell which part of the game contributed the most to his win?

From 2004 through 2012 on the PGA Tour, tournament winners averaged a fairly high putting rank of 14. In contrast, the average driving distance rank of tournament winners was 26, and the average driving accuracy rank was 28. Winning and putting rank went together more than winning and driving distance rank, and also more than winning and driving accuracy rank. Winners were ranked in the top 10 in putting in about 60% of tournaments, but winners were ranked in the top 10 in only about 30% of tournaments for both driving distance and driving accuracy.

Analysis of the same tournaments shows that tournament finish positions were also highly correlated with a lesser-known statistic: "greens in regulation." Greens in regulation (GIR) is a stat that measures tee-to-green performance. A golfer who hits the green on a par-three hole in one stroke is said to have hit a GIR. A GIR is recorded if a golfer hits the green on a par-four hole in two (or fewer) strokes or hits the green on a par-five hole in three (or fewer) strokes. The "regulation" number of strokes to hit a green is determined by taking the par of a hole and subtracting two, which represents the nominal number of putts. Since the GIR stat depends only on the number of strokes to reach the green, it is a measure of ball striking, and not putting.

The average GIR rank of tournament winners between 2004 and 2012 was 14. Winners were ranked in the top 10 in greens in regulation in about 60% of tournaments. Putting and GIR results for tournament winners were almost identical. In the week they win, tournament winners tend to putt well and hit the ball well. Winners also tend to rank above average in both driving distance and driving accuracy, even if not as high as their ranks in putting and GIR.

Table 1.1. Analysis of PGA Tour tournament winners from 2004 to 2012. Putting refers to the PGA Tour's main putting stat, strokes gained putting. Ranks are relative to all golfers who earn prize money (i.e., those who make the cut).

	Putting	Driving distance	Driving accuracy	Greens in regulation (GIR)
Average winner rank	14	26	28	14
Fraction of winners in top 10	58%	32%	31%	58%

Ranks are useful because the raw statistics are sometimes inscrutable and difficult to understand without context. Quick—if a PGA Tour golfer's average proximity to the hole is 33 feet, is that good or bad? If a PGA Tour golfer's putts per green in regulation is 1.79, is that high or low? Stats alone don't tell us. In fact, an analysis of 2011 data shows that an average proximity to the hole of 33 feet was quite good: A golfer with that stat would have been ranked at number 10 that year, one of the best on tour. On the other hand, a PGA Tour golfer with 1.79 putts per green in regulation was not doing very well, far below the tour average with a rank of 125.

Ranks are a good way to measure golfers' performance against each other *within* categories, but they still do not help us to measure *across* categories. From ranks alone you can't tell whether it is better to be first in driving distance or first in sand saves. Using ranks, we've seen that winning and putting are highly correlated, but so are winning and greens in regulation. We cannot tell, using ranks, whether putting or off-green play is more closely connected with winning tournaments.

In order to quantify the importance to winning of putting (as well as driving, sand saves, and all different types of golf shots), we need a statistic that can measure all shots on the same scale. The statistic I developed for this purpose, as we will learn in coming chapters, is called *strokes gained.*

Conclusion: putting is only part of the picture

Many of the observations in this chapter about putting seem persuasive because they are true. It is true that you can't get back a missed putt, that confidence can affect results, that there have been pivotal putts in tournament history, and that putts account for a large fraction of all golf shots. The elements of truth in these observations are partly why so many people believe, incorrectly, that putting is more important than any other part of the game of golf.

Why is faith in the supremacy of putting misguided? The last putt on a hole has a certain finality, but we can mathematically prove that over the course of a round, putting is not necessarily more important than the shots that came before it. If an 800-meter race comes down to a homestretch sprint between two runners, that doesn't mean the first 750 meters aren't important. In golf, the outcome of a tournament might come down to a putting duel on the last hole, but the finalists' other shots separated them from the field and were critical in determining who is the last one standing.

An out-of-bounds drive can lose a hole in match play before a putt ever has a chance to matter. The number of shots in a shot category has some relation to importance, but number and importance are not equivalent concepts. Golfers average about nine to 10 gimme putts per round, but these aren't as important as a smaller number of greenside sand shots, because skill differences in bunker play lead to bigger scoring differences than skill differences in gimme putts.

Winners tend to rank high in putting, but they rank high in other stats as well. Ranks are useful because they can be easier to comprehend than raw stats, but ranks still don't allow us to evaluate a golfer's whole game, because you can't make rank comparisons across categories. Ranks cannot tell us the relative importance of putting compared with other shot types. Anecdotes that bolster people's misconceptions about putting are no substitute for a systematic analysis of the golf data that are available today. Any good data wonk will see that in order to conduct such an analysis, we have to find a consistent way to measure skill throughout the game across all types of strokes.

19th Hole Summary

- Since the beginning of golf itself, people have overestimated the importance of putting.

- The overemphasis on putting is partly due to an approach based on hunches rather than on data, and partly due to cherry-picking some bits of data while ignoring others.

- A stroke lost by a wild drive is as important to your score as a stroke lost by missing a putt.

- A quantitative approach to understanding golf can help get rid of superstition.

- Since most golfers make nearly all their putts inside two feet, short putts do not explain much of the scoring differences between them.

- The importance of putting can't be judged by looking only at putting, or by looking only at winners, or by examining anecdotal evidence that focuses only on a handful of shots.

- Ranking helps compare one golfer to another within a shot category, but not across the whole game.

CHAPTER 2

NUMBERS TALK: Quantifying the Importance of Putting

Going back in golf history, there has always been a small band of putting skeptics who have stood up to the putting-is-all mainstream. In his 1913 book *First Steps to Golf*, George Brown wrote, "Putting is thought by many players to be the most important part of the game. My own opinion is that its importance is greatly overestimated, and that the advantage which a player who can putt well has over a player who cannot putt is not so great as the advantage a good Brassy player has over a man whose Brassy never leaves his bag." Bobby Jones wrote that "excellence in driving and iron play receives its reward as certainly as putting." More recently, when *New York Times* writer Bill Pennington asked several expert golf instructors to name the most important shot in golf for amateurs, Jim Hardy, 2007 PGA teacher of the year, answered, "The most valuable shot in golf is the tee shot. Because most players are not just missing the fairway off the tee, they are barely keeping the ball on the planet." Teachers Randy Smith and Jim Flick agreed with Hardy. Another great teacher, Butch Harmon, bucked both the driver and putter camps, arguing that the wedge is "the biggest stroke-saving shot" for amateur golfers.

What is common to all of these opinions is a lack of supporting data and analysis. With a careful look at the data, using meaningful measures of golfer performance, we can quantify the relative importance of putting compared to other kinds of strokes. We'll examine the role of putting compared with other strokes in winning on the PGA Tour, and we'll also see which strokes lead to the separation between pros and amateurs.

First, let's look again at the 2004 to 2012 PGA Tour data, this time at the number of putts taken by tournament winners. Not surprisingly, winners almost always take fewer putts than nonwinners. On the PGA Tour between 2004 and 2012, tournament winners averaged 27.5 putts per round while the field averaged 29. Winners took, on average, 1.5 fewer putts per round than the field.

Can the data tell us whether 1.5 putts constitutes a big difference? To answer that, let's look at the total number of strokes—not only putts but also drives and approach shots and all others as well—that separated the winners from the field. The data show:

- Tournament winners averaged 67.4 strokes per round.
- The field averaged 71.1 strokes per round.
- Winners of tournaments beat the field by an average of 3.7 strokes per round (71.1 minus 67.4).

The 1.5 fewer putts taken by winners compared to the field accounts for 40% of the 3.7 fewer overall strokes that separate winners from the field. The remaining 60% must be caused by skill differences in shots other than putts, that is, by off-green shots. This simple calculation reveals that off-green shots explain more of the difference in scores between winners and the field than putting can.

We can quantify the contribution of putting skill more accurately than by just counting putts. Tournament winners, on average, start their first putt on each green slightly closer to the hole than their competitors do (for example, because they hit their approach shots closer to the hole). So we would expect the winners to take fewer putts, even if their putting ability was identical to the average of the field. The strokes gained putting stat takes this putt-distance effect into account and provides a more accurate measure of putting skill. The methodology, explained in chapter 3, shows that from 2004 to 2012, tournament winners gained 1.3 strokes relative to the field due to putting, slightly less than the value obtained from counting putts.

Putting's contribution to victory (PCV) is defined to be the winners' putts gained on the field divided by the number of strokes by which the winner beat the field. To find out how much tournament winners gained while putting relative to their number of total strokes, let's look again at the scores of all players on the PGA Tour between 2004 and 2012.

- Winners of tournaments beat the field by an average of 3.7 strokes per round.
- Winners gained 1.3 strokes relative to the field due to putting.

• Dividing the winners' strokes gained putting (1.3 strokes) by the winners' advantage over the field in all strokes (3.7), we see that the average putting contribution to victory is 35%.

This calculation tells us that putts are less important to the victories of tournament winners than other types of shots. Putting contributed 35%, on average, to victories on the PGA Tour, while off-green shots accounted for 65%.

> Putting contributed 35%, on average, to victories on the PGA Tour, while off-green shots accounted for 65%.

The 35% contribution of putting to victory is an average over many tournaments. Putting contributed much more to some victories than others. Figure 2.1 presents a chart of PCV results for each of the 315 tournaments in the 2004–2012 sample. Table 2.1 shows the top, middle, and bottom PGA Tour tournaments from 2004 to 2012 ranked by PCV. The middle of the table contains typical tournaments, where the putting contribution to victory is close to the average. For example, in Ernie Els's 2004 win at the Memorial, he beat the field by 5.20 strokes per round with 1.76 strokes due to superior putting. His putting contribution to victory was 34% (1.76/5.20), close to the 35% average contribution of putting.

In many victories, putting contributed far more than the 35% average. Excellent putting is the key to the victories at the top of Table 2.1. Topping the list is Bill Haas, who won the 2011 TOUR Championship beating the field by 1.79 strokes per round while gaining 2.05 putts on the field. His putting contribution to victory was 114%. A value greater than 100% occurs when the winner's off-green play is *worse* than the field. Haas lost 0.26 strokes per round to the field in his off-green play. Not shown in the table, but twelfth on the list, is our old friend Lucas Glover with his 2011 win at Quail Hollow, where putting contributed 72% of the strokes in his victory, more than double the average. Glover had 36 one-putt greens in 72 holes.

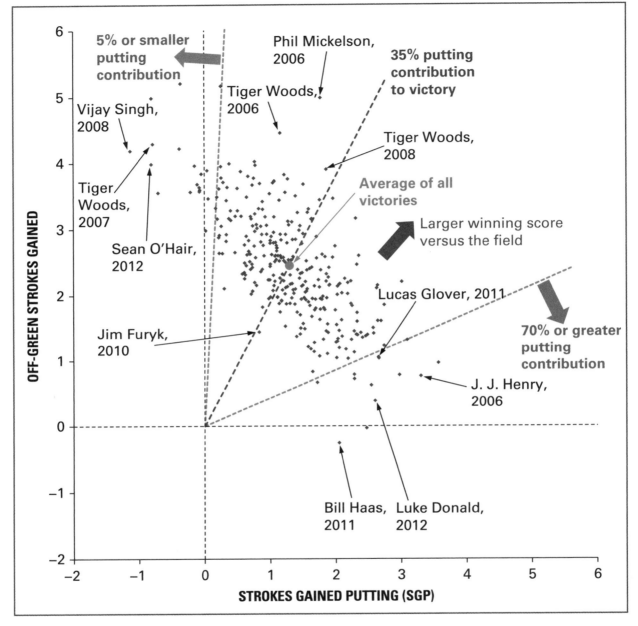

Figure 2.1. Winners' off-green strokes gained per round plotted against strokes gained putting per round (SGP). Off-green strokes gained is the winner's score versus the field (SVF) minus strokes gained putting (SGP). The putting contribution to victory is the ratio SGP/SVF. The average putting contribution to victory for these 315 victories was 35%.

Winning in spite of putting

At the bottom of Table 2.1 are golfers who are living proof that tournaments can be won without any help at all from putting. Pulling up the rear, so to speak, is Vijay Singh's 2008 win at the World Golf Championship-Bridgestone. His putting contribution to victory (PCV) was -37%. The negative value indicates that he won while putting significantly worse than the field. This could only happen with superb play from the tee to the green. Overall, Singh lost 1.1 strokes per round to the field with his putting, while scoring 3.1 strokes better than the field. That means he gained a whopping 4.2 strokes per round on the field with amazing drives and other tee-to-green shots.

Let's look in more detail at Singh's putting during the statistically historical 2008 tournament. In the first round, he three-putted from 10 feet. In the second round, he three-putted from 40 feet, due to a missed four-footer. In the third round on hole 12, he three-putted from 30 feet, missing a five-footer. Then on hole 17, he chipped to two feet and missed the putt. On hole 11 of the final round, Singh three-putted from 38 feet, missing a six-foot second putt. He proceeded to miss a six-footer for par on hole 13. On hole 16 he missed a five-foot birdie putt. Asked why he had been practicing short putts, Singh said, "Because I miss a lot of those. I'm very, very uncomfortable with four- and five-footers . . . I tried to hit it as close as possible so I didn't leave myself a putt." On the 17th hole, he had four and a half feet remaining after leaving a 27-footer short. He sank it for par. Then on the 18th hole, he needed two putts from 29 feet to win the tournament. "I had a good line, and I said, just cozy it down there. If it goes in, fine. Don't leave yourself a four-footer. I left myself a four-footer." But he sank it to win by one, while at the same time setting the PCV bar for winning in spite of lousy putting. No golfer in the ShotLink era has won while putting worse.

Winning while putting worse than the field (with a negative PCV) occurred 14 times in the sample of 315 PGA Tour tournaments played between 2004 and 2012, or 4% of the time. Vijay Singh accounted for five of those wins. Winning with off-green play worse than the field (PCVs greater than 100%) was much rarer. It occurred only twice in the sample, or 0.6% of the time, and both of these were small-field events with only 30 or 31 competitors. The numbers show that it's possible to win with below-average putting, but victories almost never happen with below-average ball striking.

Table 2.1. Selected PGA Tour tournament winners ranked by putting contribution to victory. Results from 315 PGA Tour tournament winners from 2004 to 2012. Putting performance is measured by strokes gained putting (SGP) per round. Winning performance is measured by the winner's average score versus the field (SVF) per round. The putting contribution to victory is the ratio SGP/SVF. Off-green strokes gained is the score versus the field (SVF) minus strokes gained putting (SGP). The top eight golfers won because of their putting. The middle eight are representative of typical putting contributions to victory. The bottom eight golfers won in spite of their putting.

Rank	Player name	Year	Event	Strokes gained putting (SGP)	Off-green strokes gained	Winning score versus field (SVF)	Putting contribution to victory (SGP/SVF)
1	Bill Haas	2011	TOUR Championship	2.05	-0.26	1.79	114%
2	Daniel Chopra	2008	Mercedes-Benz	2.47	-0.03	2.44	101%
3	Luke Donald	2012	Transitions	2.60	0.38	2.98	87%
4	J. J. Henry	2006	Buick Championship	3.30	0.76	4.06	81%
5	Matt Kuchar	2009	Turning Stone Resort	2.54	0.63	3.17	80%
6	Vijay Singh	2006	Barclays Classic	2.97	0.78	3.75	79%
7	Ben Curtis	2006	Booz Allen	3.57	0.96	4.53	79%
8	Wes Short Jr.	2005	Michelin	2.28	0.72	3.01	76%
154	Vijay Singh	2004	Chrysler Championship	1.63	3.15	4.78	34%
155	Rory Sabbatini	2009	Byron Nelson	1.50	2.93	4.43	34%
156	Adam Scott	2006	TOUR Championship	1.19	2.32	3.51	34%
157	Ernie Els	2004	Memorial	1.76	3.44	5.20	34%
158	Fred Funk	2004	Southern Farm Bureau	1.15	2.26	3.42	34%
159	Geoff Ogilvy	2005	Chrysler Tucson	1.00	1.98	2.98	34%
160	John Senden	2006	John Deere Classic	1.28	2.54	3.82	33%
161	Joey Sindelar	2004	Wachovia	1.04	2.08	3.12	33%
308	Mark Hensby	2004	John Deere Classic	-0.22	3.57	3.35	-7%
309	Vijay Singh	2004	Deutsche Bank	-0.37	5.21	4.84	-8%
310	Jason Dufner	2012	Byron Nelson	-0.39	4.22	3.84	-10%
311	Steve Flesch	2007	Reno-Tahoe Open	-0.81	4.99	4.18	-19%
312	Tiger Woods	2007	WGC-CA	-0.79	4.29	3.50	-23%
313	Sergio Garcia	2004	Byron Nelson	-0.71	3.55	2.84	-25%
314	Sean O'Hair	2009	Quail Hollow	-0.82	3.99	3.17	-26%
315	Vijay Singh	2008	WGC-Bridgestone	-1.14	4.19	3.05	-37%

Tournament winners play better than the best golfers in the world when they win. They usually do most everything well in those weeks. They putt better, drive better, hit more accurate approaches, and get up and down more often compared to the field. But the often-heard claim that Tiger Woods wins because of his putting is not borne out by the data. The numbers show that Woods is actually in the bottom quarter of golfers ranked by putting contribution to victory. His putting only contributed an average of 28% to his 24 victories in the sample. This is significantly less than winners' overall average PCV of 35%. In his victories, Tiger gained 1.14 putts per round on the field, but he gained 2.94 strokes per round on the field with his tee-to-green play.

Just as there are many ways to shoot a low score, some golfers win *because* of their putting and others win *in spite* of their putting. Table 2.2 shows the putting contribution to victory of golfers with three or more wins. At the top of the list is Matt Kuchar, whose putting was the key to his three victories. Ben Curtis, Bill Haas, Stewart Cink, and Luke Donald are other golfers whose putting has been key to their victories. At the bottom of the list are golfers who win with stellar tee-to-green play, including Vijay Singh, Bubba Watson, Sergio Garcia, and Sean O'Hair.

The two golfers with the most victories in the sample are Phil Mickelson and Vijay Singh. Phil Mickelson's putting contributed an average of 27% to his 11 victories in the sample. Vijay Singh, as we learned earlier, won while putting much worse than his fellow winners, with an average PCV of 20% in his 17 victories. Looking at the numbers for the big three of Tiger, Phil, and Vijay—the three golfers with the most victories in the sample—all performed in the bottom quartile of putting performance relative to other tournament winners. Putting contributed just 25% to the top three golfers' victories in our sample, significantly less than the overall average PCV among winners of 35%.

Table 2.2. Putting contribution to victory of golfers. Results ranked by putting contribution to victory and only include golfers with three or more wins in PGA Tour tournaments from 2004 to 2012.

Rank	Player name	Number of wins	Strokes gained putting (SGP)	Off-green strokes gained	Winning score versus field (SVF)	Putting contribution to victory (SGP/SVF)
1	Matt Kuchar	3	2.17	1.12	3.29	66%
2	Ben Curtis	3	2.67	1.53	4.20	64%
3	Bill Haas	3	1.84	1.12	2.96	62%
4	Stewart Cink	3	2.15	1.45	3.60	60%
5	Luke Donald	3	1.96	1.52	3.48	56%
6	Hunter Mahan	4	1.77	1.86	3.63	49%
7	Aaron Baddeley	3	1.94	2.06	4.00	48%
8	Bart Bryant	3	1.71	2.09	3.80	45%
9	Ben Crane	3	1.56	1.97	3.52	44%
10	Stuart Appleby	5	1.65	2.18	3.83	43%
11	K. J. Choi	6	1.61	2.15	3.76	43%
12	Geoff Ogilvy	4	1.28	1.76	3.04	42%
13	Brandt Snedeker	3	1.40	1.93	3.33	42%
14	Justin Rose	4	1.60	2.24	3.84	42%
15	Jim Furyk	7	1.52	2.18	3.70	41%
16	Carl Pettersson	5	1.57	2.31	3.88	41%
17	Mark Wilson	3	1.30	1.95	3.24	40%
18	Jonathan Byrd	4	1.28	2.07	3.35	38%
19	Anthony Kim	3	1.43	2.45	3.88	37%
20	Adam Scott	7	1.47	2.69	4.15	35%
21	Ryan Palmer	3	1.17	2.15	3.32	35%
22	Kenny Perry	7	1.34	2.57	3.91	34%
23	David Toms	3	1.61	3.10	4.71	34%
24	Stephen Ames	4	1.26	2.54	3.79	33%
25	Camilo Villegas	3	1.18	2.40	3.58	33%
26	Zach Johnson	7	1.24	2.65	3.89	32%
27	Ernie Els	5	1.17	2.81	3.98	29%
28	Steve Flesch	3	1.06	2.61	3.67	29%
29	Steve Stricker	9	1.10	2.76	3.86	29%
30	Nick Watney	4	1.08	2.73	3.81	28%
31	Tiger Woods	24	1.14	2.94	4.09	28%
32	Justin Leonard	3	1.15	3.01	4.16	28%
33	Phil Mickelson	11	1.10	3.02	4.12	27%
34	Rory Sabbatini	4	1.04	2.88	3.92	26%
35	Dustin Johnson	4	0.76	2.73	3.49	22%
36	Heath Slocum	4	0.67	2.72	3.39	20%
37	Vijay Singh	17	0.77	3.15	3.92	20%
38	Bubba Watson	3	0.44	3.22	3.66	12%
39	Sergio Garcia	4	0.36	2.98	3.34	11%
40	Sean O'Hair	4	0.26	2.94	3.19	8%

Tiger Woods's 2008 win at Bay Hill

One of Tiger Woods's most dramatic wins was at the 2008 Arnold Palmer Invitational at Bay Hill. He needed a birdie on the difficult final hole to win the tournament. He hit a 290-yard drive in the fairway, followed by a 165-yard 5-iron into the wind to set up the crucial putt. He drained the 24-foot putt to win the tournament for the fifth time.

Tiger is regarded by many as the best clutch putter of all time. Most golf fans have seen the replay of his winning putt at this tournament, but few remember that he three-putted from inside seven feet on the tenth hole of the final round. If he had merely two-putted on the tenth hole, he could have won the tournament with a simple two-putt on the last hole. Tiger missed all of his putts over 20 feet—20 in total—before sinking his final putt.

In order to understand the role of putting in his victory, we need to look at the strokes gained from all of his shots in the tournament and compare them with his strokes gained from putting. Tiger finished the tournament at 10 under par and gained 3.4 strokes per round on the field during the tournament. He gained 1.0 strokes per round with his putting and he ranked 18th out of 120 golfers in the tournament in putting. He gained 2.4 strokes on the field with his off-green shots. Tiger's putting contributed 29% of his total strokes gained. Putting played an important, but not dominant, role in his win.

Quantifying the importance of putting for pros in all tournaments

In the same way that we determine the contribution of putting to any PGA Tour victory, we can determine the contribution of putting to any PGA Tour golfer's score relative to the field. As shown in Table 2.3, from 2004 to 2012 Luke Donald's average score was 1.8 strokes better than an average PGA Tour field. He putted 0.7 strokes better than the field during this time. Putting contributed 39% (0.7/1.8) to Luke Donald's scoring advantage. I define *putting contribution to scores* (PCS) to be strokes gained putting per round divided by the total strokes gained per round relative to the field.

Just as golfers come in all shapes and sizes, there are many ways to excel at golf. From 2004 to 2012, K. J. Choi beat the field by an average of one stroke per round. He gained 0.2 strokes versus the field with his

Table 2.3. Putting contribution to scores (PCS) for pros: top 40 golfers in total strokes gained on the PGA Tour from 2004 through 2012. Ranks are out of 240 golfers with at least 200 rounds during 2004–2012 (also included is Rory McIlroy with only 120 rounds). Total strokes gained per round is the golfer's average score relative to the field. Off-green strokes per round is obtained by subtracting strokes gained putting per round from total strokes gained per round.

Golfer	Rank			Strokes gained per round			PCS
	Total	Off-green	Putt	Total	Off-green	Putt	
Tiger Woods	1	1	3	2.79	2.16	0.63	23%
Jim Furyk	2	7	19	1.84	1.44	0.40	22%
Luke Donald	3	10	1	1.82	1.11	0.71	39%
Phil Mickelson	4	3	86	1.70	1.57	0.14	8%
Rory McIlroy*	5	3	153	1.66	1.72	-0.07	-4%
Vijay Singh	5	2	193	1.58	1.76	-0.18	-11%
Ernie Els	6	4	164	1.43	1.52	-0.08	-6%
Sergio Garcia	7	5	156	1.43	1.50	-0.07	-5%
Steve Stricker	8	26	13	1.34	0.85	0.49	37%
Adam Scott	9	6	178	1.33	1.45	-0.12	-9%
Zach Johnson	10	31	16	1.24	0.79	0.45	36%
Pádraig Harrington	11	18	50	1.17	0.93	0.23	20%
David Toms	12	16	62	1.15	0.95	0.20	18%
Justin Rose	13	8	140	1.15	1.18	-0.03	-2%
Retief Goosen	14	23	45	1.13	0.88	0.26	23%
Stewart Cink	15	50	12	1.09	0.59	0.50	46%
Geoff Ogilvy	16	36	34	1.05	0.71	0.34	32%
K. J. Choi	17	28	64	1.02	0.82	0.20	20%
Rickie Fowler	18	27	77	1.02	0.85	0.17	17%
Robert Allenby	19	9	191	1.00	1.17	-0.18	-18%
Tim Clark	20	30	60	0.99	0.79	0.21	21%
Kenny Perry	21	11	180	0.98	1.11	-0.12	-13%
Bo Van Pelt	22	32	79	0.95	0.78	0.17	17%
Scott Verplank	23	17	130	0.94	0.95	0.00	0%
Lee Westwood	24	14	160	0.92	1.00	-0.08	-8%
Dustin Johnson	25	13	165	0.92	1.01	-0.09	-10%
Webb Simpson	26	70	22	0.90	0.51	0.39	43%
Paul Casey	27	49	42	0.88	0.59	0.29	33%
Bubba Watson	28	15	176	0.88	1.00	-0.12	-13%
Jason Day	29	74	24	0.87	0.49	0.39	44%
Brandt Snedeker	30	93	10	0.87	0.31	0.56	64%
Rory Sabbatini	31	22	146	0.85	0.89	-0.04	-5%
Matt Kuchar	32	66	38	0.85	0.52	0.33	39%
John Senden	33	21	152	0.83	0.89	-0.07	-8%
Charles Howell III	34	43	78	0.81	0.64	0.17	21%
Ben Crane	35	110	9	0.80	0.24	0.56	70%
Anthony Kim	36	51	58	0.80	0.59	0.21	27%
Nick Watney	37	38	91	0.79	0.68	0.11	14%
Davis Love III	38	25	159	0.78	0.86	-0.07	-9%
Arron Oberholser	39	40	88	0.78	0.66	0.12	16%
Ian Poulter	40	54	59	0.78	0.57	0.21	27%
Top 40 average	20	29	87	1.13	0.95	0.17	15%

putting. Choi's PCS is 20%: Putting contributed 0.2 strokes of his one-stroke total gain versus the field. In the same time period, Robert Allenby also beat the field by an average of one stroke per round. He lost 0.2 strokes versus the field with his putting. Allenby's PCS is -18%. Put another way, if Allenby was an average tour putter, then he would have gained 1.2 strokes per round rather than 1.0 strokes per round.

Table 2.3 shows PCS values for the top 40 golfers ranked by their average score relative to the field (also called total strokes gained). The contribution of putting to a golfer's scoring advantage varies substantially from one golfer to the next, but when we look at a group of golfers, a clear conclusion emerges. Across the top 40 golfers, putting contributed 15% to their total scoring advantage, while off-green shots contributed the remaining 85%.

> In 2004–2012 across all tournaments, putting contributed only 15% to the top 40 golfers' scoring advantage, while off-green shots accounted for 85%.

For other groups of pro golfers, the contribution of putting is similar: 15% for the top 20 golfers, 13% for the top 10 golfers, and 17% for the top 100 golfers. For the bottom 100 golfers, putting contributes 18% to the total loss of strokes relative to the field. We'll see later that when we compare amateurs to pros and good amateurs to poor amateurs, putting contributes between 12% and 18% of the difference in scores.

The contribution of putting to scoring varies considerably from one round of golf to the next. Even over many rounds, there is considerable variation from one golfer to another. If putting is a golfer's strong suit, it might contribute 50% or more (see Brandt Snedeker and Ben Crane). If putting is a relative weakness, it might contribute negatively to a golfer's score (see Kenny Perry and Robert Allenby). Between two groups of golfers (say, the best pros and average pros or good amateurs versus poor amateurs), putting contributes an average of 15% to the difference in scores.

If putting contributes 15% to scoring, then how can it contribute 35% to victories? Most every week a different golfer is victorious. Tournament winners are a diverse group of golfers who win by virtue of playing at an elevated level compared to their normal games. Putting contributes more to the elevated play of winners than it contributes to the top golfers' performance in all of their tournament play.

Let's look at a couple of examples. In Phil Mickelson's victories, he gained 4.1 strokes per round versus the field, with 1.1 strokes, or 27%, coming from putting. Taking all of his rounds from 2004 to 2012 together, Phil gained 1.7 strokes per round versus the field, with 0.1 strokes, or less than 10%, coming from putting. In his victories, Phil elevated his entire game by 2.4 strokes per round, while he elevated his putting by one stroke per round. In Vijay Singh's victories, he gained 3.9 strokes per round versus the field, with 0.8 strokes, or 20%, coming from putting. Taking all of his rounds from 2004 to 2012 together, Vijay gained 1.6 strokes per round versus the field, while losing 0.2 strokes per round putting. In his victories, Vijay elevated his entire game by 2.3 strokes per round, while he elevated his putting by one stroke per round. These two golfers illustrate the finding that putting contributes a larger proportion to scoring during tournament wins than during normal play. Figure 2.2 shows the overall contribution of putting for the top 40 golfers in all of their rounds from 2004 to 2012, and tournament winners' performance during their wins. Figure 2.3 shows details of putting contributions for individual golfers and victories.

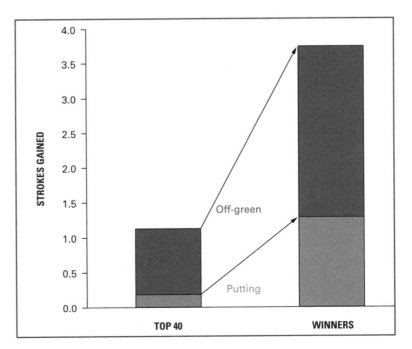

Figure 2.2. Putting contribution of the top 40 golfers and tournament winners: off-green strokes gained per round and strokes gained putting per round for the top 40 golfers in 2004–2012 and tournament winners in the same time period. Putting contributed 15% to the scoring advantage of the top 40 golfers and 35% to the scoring advantage of tournament winners.

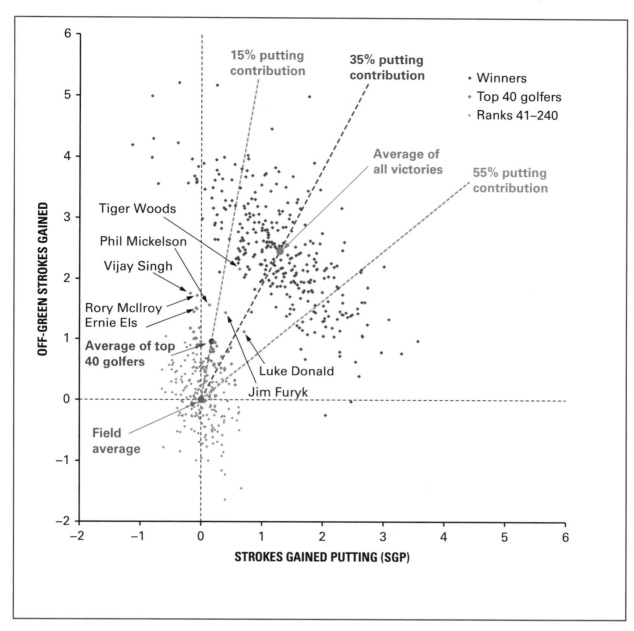

Figure 2.3. Tournament winners and 240 golfers in 2004–2012: off-green strokes gained per round plotted against strokes gained putting per round (SGP). The 240 red and green diamonds represent career average results of individual golfers with at least 200 rounds played in 2004–2012 (plus Rory McIlroy with 120 rounds). The red diamonds represent golfers ranked 1 through 40 and the green diamonds correspond to ranks 41 through 240. The blue diamonds represent the results of tournament winners in the week of their victory. Tiger Woods gained 2.8 strokes per round from 2004 to 2012, with 2.2 strokes from off-green shots and 0.6 from putting. He is the closest to the average 3.7 strokes gained per round for all victories. The chart shows many victories where putting contributed 55% or more, but only two golfers in the top 40 had putting contributions of 55% or more. The average putting contribution for these 315 victories was 35%. The average putting contribution for the top 40 golfers was 15%.

Quantifying the importance of putting for amateurs

Analyzing the performance of pros is fun, but how much of that translates to the performance of amateurs? How much of the difference in scores between amateurs and pros can be explained by putting?

Let's look at the putting and scoring performance of two groups of amateur golfers: golfers with an average score of 80 (80-golfers) and golfers with an average score of 100 (100-golfers). The average score difference between the two groups is 20 strokes. How much of those 20 strokes can be explained by putting? Using Golfmetrics amateur data, we find that 80-golfers gain an average of three putts per round relative to 100-golfers' average. Putting contributes 15% (3 strokes out of 20) of the score difference between 80- and 100-golfers. Put another way, 85% of the difference in scores between 80- and 100-golfers comes from skill differences in off-green shots.

A broader look at the data reveals that putting contributes 15% of the scoring difference between any two groups of typical amateur golfers with average scores between 75 and 125. The contribution of putting to scores can be quite different for any two individual golfers, just as the pro results vary from one golfer to the next and from one tournament to the next. If a particular golfer with an average score of 100 putts as well as a golfer with an average score of 80, then putting explains 0% of the difference in their scores.

The putting contribution to scores calculation emphasizes that differences in putting performance should be compared to differences in scores. If we traveled back to Putter-Fairyland, where all golfers take two putts to hole out no matter where they start on the green, and if we ran the PCS calculation on all the golfers there, the putting contribution to scores would be zero, exactly as it should be.

Between the best pros and average pros, between pros and amateurs, and between good amateurs and poor amateurs, the numbers show that putting contributes about 15% to the difference in scores. Tee-to-green shots explain the remaining 85% of score differences. How much of the 85% is due to driving? Approach shots? Wedge shots? The answers are coming up. But first we look at a better way to measure putting performance than simply counting putts.

19th Hole Summary

• I define shots to be "important" if they lead to scoring differences. A player hits more putts than drives or sand shots in a typical round of golf, but that does not mean putting is more important.

• Between 2004 and 2012, PGA Tour pros' putting contributed an average of 35% to victories, a stat known as putting's contribution to victory, or PCV.

• Putting's contribution to scoring is a larger proportion (35%) when you look at golfers' tournament wins, and a smaller proportion (15%) when you compare top golfers' performance in all their tournament play.

• Between almost any two groups—the best pros and average pros, pros and amateurs, or good amateurs and poor amateurs—the numbers show that putting contributes about 15% to the difference in scores. Tee-to-green shots explain the remaining 85% of score differences.

• Putting is important, but golf is not a glorified putting contest.

CHAPTER 3

STROKES GAINED PUTTING: A Better Measure of Putting Performance

Golfers know a great shot when they see one. The explosion from a bunker to tap-in range. The low hook that escapes from the trees and finishes on the green. The downhill double-breaking 30-footer that finds the bottom of the cup. The towering drive that cuts the corner of a dogleg and finds the fairway. At the same time, awful shots are painfully obvious. The 40-yard wedge skulled over the green. The fat fairway wood that dies after barely 50 yards. The short iron shot that finds the drink. The two-foot putt left short of the hole.

While the most awesome and most awful shots are easy to identify, it isn't so clear how to compare a drive that travels 20 extra yards with an approach that finishes five feet closer to the hole. Is it better to hit two more fairways per round or take one fewer putt?

To answer these questions, we need to be able to compare different types of shots—drives, approach shots, sand shots, and putts—with each other. But it's not easy to compare driving distance measured in yards with putts measured by the number of strokes. The units just aren't comparable. What's needed is a consistent way to measure the quality of any type of shot.

The natural unit to use is strokes. If the quality of each golf shot can be measured in the unit of strokes, then we'll have a way to compare driving and putting. We can say that a drive is 0.2 strokes better than average and a putt is 0.1 strokes worse than average. We'll have a way to know if Luke Donald's incomparable putting is worth more than Bubba Watson's unparalleled driving, or the other way around. We'll be able to identify the strengths and weaknesses of any golfer's game. All of this, and much more, will be possible.

Strokes gained is the name for this new way to measure shot quality. It uses the same unit—strokes—to calculate the skill of the many kinds of shots taken throughout each round of golf. The origins of most new ideas can be traced to the earlier work of others, and strokes gained is no exception. The term owes its heritage to a brilliant applied mathematician of the mid 20th century, and a grand theory he called "dynamic programming," developed at the dawn of the computer era. Dynamic programming is a technique well known in finance and many other fields as a mathematical way to work through complicated, multistep problems involving risk and uncertainty. Using this technique, I developed a way to compare golf shots and quantify a golfer's skill.

Before explaining this new stat, and why it has been called revolutionary, revelatory, and a few other polysyllabic names, let's take a journey back a few decades in time.

Richard Bellman, who invented dynamic programming, in 1962

While in high school, Richard Bellman was interviewed for a prestigious college scholarship. At the time, he wanted to be a theoretical physicist and had read books on relativity and quantum mechanics. He knew the subjects were highly mathematical and were not easy to describe in words. When the interviewer asked what he knew of theoretical physics, he answered all too honestly that he knew nothing. That was the end of his scholarship chances. "I have always been cursed with this terrible objectivity," he wrote.

By 1952, Bellman had earned his PhD and become a professor of mathematics at Princeton. He then moved to Stanford as a tenured professor. At Stanford he received an offer to join the newly established RAND Corporation, a hotbed of applied mathematical research in Santa Monica, California (the acronym RAND comes from Research ANd Development). Bellman wrote that the choice was between being a "traditional intellectual, or a modern intellectual using the results of my research for the problems of contemporary society." He chose to go to RAND.

At RAND, Bellman applied his mathematical skills to solving multistage decision problems. In 1953, he wrote that applications of his research ranged from "the planning of industrial production lines to the scheduling of patients at a medical clinic; from the determination of long-term investment programs for universities to the determination of a replacement policy for machinery in factories; from the programming of training policies for skilled and unskilled labor to the choice of optimal purchasing and inventory policies for department stores and military establishments." Yet even Bellman couldn't have imagined how important and ubiquitous his multistage problem-solving techniques would become in modern life. In 1997, Bellman's research was used by IBM's Deep Blue computer to defeat chess champion Garry Kasparov. Indeed, part of the credit for landing a man on the moon and for the success of Walmart is due to the applications and extensions of Bellman's ideas.

You might be more familiar with his influence through navigation systems on cars and map apps on mobile devices. At the heart of many of these problems is a method for determining the shortest path from point A to point B, through a network of in-between points. (You can't blame Bellman for a poor implementation that occasionally leads you to a dead end or suggests driving off a cliff.) The *shortest path problem* is one example. An illustration of a simple shortest path problem is given in Figure 3.1.

Bellman chose "dynamic programming" as the name for these new problems in multistage decision making. He borrowed the word "programming" from the military term for planning and scheduling. The word "program" referred to a plan, policy, or set of instructions, as in the plan for getting from A to B. Computers had recently been invented, and a set of computer instructions was also called a program.

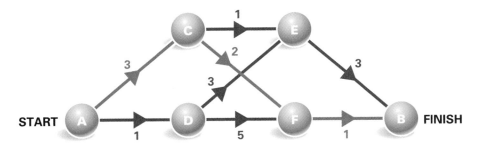

Figure 3.1. The shortest path problem: The shortest time to travel from A to B is six hours on the path A-C-F-B, while all other paths from A to B take 7 hours. Finding the shortest path through larger networks is more complicated, but can be solved using dynamic programming techniques. In this example, the shortest path takes the longer road from A to C, with a travel time of 3 hours, rather than the 1-hour trip on the road from A to D. In golf, it is sometimes better to take a longer route to the hole, for example, not cutting off distance on a dogleg hole or using a fairway wood off the tee rather than a driver.

The term "dynamic programming" also had the benefit of NOT being called "mathematical research." The main funding for the RAND Corporation came from the Air Force, which was, at the time, under the direction of Secretary of Defense Charles Wilson. According to Bellman, Wilson "had a pathological fear and hatred of the word 'research.' . . . His face would suffuse, he would turn red, and he would get violent if people used the term 'research' in his presence. You can imagine how he felt, then, about the term 'mathematical.'" Bellman wanted to shield RAND from Wilson, so he creatively renamed his work "dynamic programming" instead of mathematical research.

Bellman wrote, "It is impossible to use the word 'dynamic' in the pejorative sense. Try thinking of some combination which will possibly give it a pejorative meaning. It's impossible. Thus, I thought dynamic programming was a good name. It was something not even a Congressman could object to." Bellman, one of most eminent mathematicians of the past century, became known as the father of dynamic programming.

Golf as a dynamic programming problem

Dynamic programming helps to identify the best decisions through time, often in the presence of uncertainty. Financial planning—for example, choosing investments to plan for your retirement—is a topic often approached as a complex dynamic program. The goal in retirement planning is to have enough money to live comfortably in later years in spite of uncertain future asset returns, health care costs, and other factors. Dynamic programming helps to quantify these uncertainties and identify a plan for maximum return.

The same dynamic programming tools that are used to analyze financial planning, inventory management, or navigation problems can be applied to golf. In golf, the goal is to get the ball into the hole in the fewest strokes. As in financial planning, golf decisions are complicated because the outcomes are uncertain—no one knows exactly where a ball will finish because golf swings are human, and each one varies. Wind, uneven terrain, and other factors compound the uncertainty.

The game of golf can be seen as a multistage decision problem, and so can productively be approached using the principles of dynamic programming. Each shot is one stage. Decisions that must be made for each shot include choosing a club, an aimline, and a shot shape.

In golf strategy, as in chess, it pays to think ahead. In chess, you want to anticipate how your opponent will respond to your moves, and decide what moves and strategies you will make in response to his response. In golf, a good strategy depends not only on assessing what could happen on the first shot, but anticipating what could happen with the next shot and the one after that. The strategy on a putt should take into account where a miss might finish. The strategy on an approach shot should take into account good and bad places to miss the green. The strategy on a drive should take into account the width and contours of the fairway, and the hazards off the fairway, as well as the possible angles to the green for the next shot.

Golfers tend to make strategic decisions based on their stores of accumulated experience, otherwise known as hunches. To make golf decisions more objective and accurate, we can test conventional golf wisdom against the data now available thanks to ShotLink, using modern mathematical techniques. We can then apply principles from Richard Bellman's dynamic programming. Bellman's comment on the need to change old ways is certainly true for golf: "Progress is not due to those who roll up their sleeves and do things the way their fathers did."

Dynamic programming is useful because it formalizes the goal and the decisions to be made. The best plans and decisions made today take into account the wide range of possible future outcomes—all of the what-ifs. In the end, only one future unfolds. The objective in a dynamic program—whether the money in your bank account or the number of strokes on the scorecard—can be used as a performance measure. In fact, when golf is viewed as a dynamic program, with golfers attempting to minimize their scores, the strokes gained performance measure is the natural result. The quality of a golf shot is measured by progress to the goal of getting the ball in the hole in the fewest possible strokes.

A key insight provided by the dynamic programming viewpoint is that progress to the hole is measured in units of strokes rather than distance. Hitting a drive one yard farther is not worth the same as hitting a putt three feet closer to the hole, even though both strokes move the ball the same distance closer to the hole.

> A key insight provided by the dynamic programming viewpoint is that progress to the hole is measured in units of strokes rather than distance.

We will come back to dynamic programming in later chapters after considering the various shot types that make up the game of golf. The way to solve multistage decision problems is to start at the end and work backward. In this spirit, let's start at the green and work backward to the tee.

The main performance measure for shots on the green is strokes gained putting. This new measure is possible thanks to the PGA Tour's amazing ShotLink system, which records the starting and ending locations of every putt to one inch accuracy.

What is wrong with counting putts?

Before the strokes gained putting stat, people used to count putts as a way of judging golfers' skill. They'd say, "If you want to be a better putter, chip it closer." This is nonsensical, since starting closer to the hole does not, in fact, improve your putting skill. You might take fewer putts if you chip it closer, but you haven't become a better putter. Putts per round is a misleading statistic that distorts the way we talk about putting.

Counting putts was a reasonable way of tracking putting skill when all we had was pencil and paper. Now that we know more details from ShotLink data, such as how far from the hole putts start, we can measure putting performance in a more sophisticated manner.

In the opening round of the 2011 Frys.com Open, Tiger Woods carded a 73, taking 27 putts. To put this into perspective, PGA Tour pros average 29 putts per round. The 2011 leader in putts per round was Kevin Na, with an average of 27.8 putts per round. Tiger's 27 was nearly one less than the tour-leading average. Tiger had no three-putts on that day. He one-putted nine times and two-putted nine times. After the round, Tiger rated his putting performance in an interview. "That's probably one of the worst putting rounds I've ever had," he said. "I can't putt the ball any worse than I did today. I just had a hard time hitting my stroke, and then I started altering it. And my stroke got worse . . . and I started losing confidence in it because I wasn't hitting my line. So it was just a downward spiral."

Was Tiger a poor judge of his own putting skill? Or did the putts-per-round stat completely misrepresent his putting performance? Let's look at Tiger's point of view. On three holes, Tiger two-putted from three feet, he two-putted from four feet, and he two-putted from six feet. On holes where his first putt was longer than six feet he was one-for-seven. The longest putt Tiger sank in this round was a 12-footer. The average distance of his first putt was just over 11 feet, while the average for the tour is 17 feet. In other words, his skillful shots onto the green gave him such an advantage that he felt he should have been able to come in with even fewer putts. Hence his disappointment.

Counting putts is a deeply flawed way of measuring a golfer's skill, because it doesn't take into account distance, the most important factor in the difficulty of the putt. Distance matters. A two-putt from 60 feet is a good result. A two-putt from two feet is a poor result. A simple count of putts gives two in both cases, but the skill level involved in the two cases is clearly different.

Or, take a hypothetical example: One golfer holes a 30-foot putt. On the same hole another golfer misses the green, chips to one foot, and then sinks the one-footer. Both golfers took one putt on the hole, so their putt counts are the same. Sinking a 30-footer is harder than sinking a one-footer, but the simple count of putts doesn't distinguish between the two putting performances. The putts-per-round stat doesn't capture the difference between the two golfers' skills because it doesn't take into account the initial distance of putts.

Measuring against a benchmark

The key idea in strokes gained putting is to measure putt outcomes against a performance benchmark based on putt distance. The benchmark for pros is the PGA Tour average number of putts to hole out from a given distance. For example, the tour average from 33 feet is two putts. A one-putt from 33 feet gains one stroke compared to the tour average. A two-putt from 33 feet gains zero compared to the tour average. A three-putt from 33 feet loses one stroke compared to the tour average. Strokes gained putting for pros, then, is the tour average number of putts to hole out from a given distance minus the number of putts taken.

> Strokes gained putting is the tour average number of putts to hole out from a given distance minus the number of putts taken.

Figure 3.2. The tour average from 33 feet is two putts. A one-putt from 33 feet gains one stroke compared to the tour average. The tour average from eight feet is 1.5 putts. A one-putt from eight feet gains one-half a stroke compared to the tour average. Both golfers take one putt, so a simple count of putts suggests no difference in putting performance. The strokes gained stat properly reflects and quantifies the better outcome of sinking a 33-foot putt compared to an eight-foot putt.

From a distance of eight feet, PGA Tour pros one-putt half the time and two-putt half the time. They virtually never three-putt. The tour average putts to hole out from a distance of eight feet, then, is 1.5. A pro who one-putts from eight feet gains 0.5 strokes compared to the tour average. A pro who two-putts from eight feet loses 0.5 strokes compared to the tour average. Most people are not used to thinking in terms of fractional strokes, but the math is fairly simple: Suppose a pro has two eight-foot putts in a round. He one-putts once and he two-putts once. His overall strokes gained is zero, because he gained 0.5 strokes with the one-putt and lost 0.5 strokes with the two-putt. The average of one and two is 1.5, so the pro averaged 1.5 putts for the two eight-footers. The 1.5 strokes exactly matches the tour average from that distance, so the pro's overall strokes gained is zero.

Suppose a pro has four eight-foot putts in a round: He one-putts three times and he two-putts once. His overall gain is one stroke, because his one-putts gained 0.5 strokes each, for a total of 1.5 strokes gained. His single two-putt lost 0.5 strokes, compared to the tour average of 1.5. Overall, his strokes gained score for the round is 1.5 minus 0.5, or 1.0.

Here's another way to arrive at the same result: A pro took three one-putts and one two-putt, for a total of five putts. But we learned above that PGA Tour pros one-putt half the time and two-putt half the time on eight-foot putts, so the tour average for a round with four eight-foot putts is a total of six putts (two one-putts plus two two-putts). So the pro's five putts represent a gain of one putt compared with the tour average of six putts.

The same strokes gained calculation works from 33 feet, with the only difference being that the tour average number of putts is different from 33 feet than from eight feet. I wrote earlier that a two-putt from 60 feet is a good result while a two-putt from two feet is a poor result. From 60 feet the tour average is 2.2 putts to hole out. A two-putt is slightly better than tour average and gains 0.2 strokes. From two feet the tour average is slightly over 1.0 putts to hole out. A two-putt loses one stroke. It is comforting that the strokes gained calculation is consistent with our intuition that it takes more skill to sink a long putt than a very short one. But even better, it provides a quantitative measure of putting skill based on reliable data.

Table 3.1 shows the PGA Tour average number of putts for selected initial distances from the hole. It also gives one-putt and three-putt probabilities for various distances. The results in the table are based on millions of putts over years of tournament play in the ShotLink database. The PGA Tour average putts, calculated from all shots recorded at PGA tournaments from 2003 to 2012, is used as the benchmark in the strokes gained putting calculations in this book.

Table 3.1. One-putt probability, three-putt probability, and average number of putts to hole out for PGA Tour golfers by distance from the hole. The average putts column is the PGA Tour putting benchmark used in the strokes gained putting computations. The values in the table are based on an analysis of nearly four million putts on the PGA Tour from 2003 to 2012.

Distance (feet)	One-putt probability	Three-putt probability	Average putts
2	99%	0.0%	1.01
3	96%	0.1%	1.04
4	88%	0.3%	1.13
5	77%	0.4%	1.23
6	66%	0.4%	1.34
7	58%	0.5%	1.42
8	50%	0.6%	1.50
9	45%	0.7%	1.56
10	40%	0.7%	1.61
15	23%	1.3%	1.78
20	15%	2.2%	1.87
30	7%	5.0%	1.98
40	4%	10.0%	2.06
50	3%	17.0%	2.14
60	2%	23.0%	2.21
90	1%	41.0%	2.40

The benchmark is interesting in its own right as a way to calibrate expectations. PGA Tour pros, who represent a group of some of the best putters in the world, sink 50% of their eight-foot putts. A pro who misses an eight-footer may regret the lost opportunity, but he shouldn't beat himself up over something that happens as often as a coin coming up tails. Instead the golfer should look at the fraction of eight-footers (or putts in the seven- to nine-foot range) sunk over the course of several rounds and compare the result with the 50% benchmark. Does it make sense for a pro, or an amateur for that matter, to spend hours and hours of practice time trying to improve his putting skill to a level where he can sink 60% or 70% of his eight-foot putts? Luke Donald was ranked first in putting from 2009 through 2011, and during this period he sank 57% of his eight-foot putts. I leave it to you to decide how to spend your valuable time, but benchmarks such as this one provide a useful way to measure performance and to set reasonable goals.

On eight-foot putts, the difference between Luke's 57% conversion rate and the tour average of 50% might not sound like a lot, but it is. Let's rephrase in terms of baseball's familiar batting average convention. The tour batting average from eight feet is 0.500 and Luke's batting average is 0.570, or 70 points higher than the average. We'd certainly recognize 70 points as a big difference in batting averages, and it represents a big difference in putting performance as well. In the course of 10 eight-footers, the tour average putts-to-hole-out is 15 (five one-putts and five two-putts). Luke Donald's average is 14.3 putts, for a gain of 0.7 strokes against the tour average. Another way to see this is as a 7% advantage times 10 putts, to give a gain of 0.7 strokes. Gain a fraction of a stroke here and another fraction there and pretty soon you're the number one golfer in the world.

Strokes gained putting for a round is the sum of strokes gained for each hole in that round. Let's go back and use the strokes gained putting method to assess Tiger's round-one performance in the 2011 Frys.com Open, the one that he himself thought was so pathetic:

> On the first hole, Tiger sank a four-footer. The tour average from four feet is 1.1, so he gained 0.1 strokes there.

> On the second hole, he sank a three-footer, which gained zero strokes compared to the tour average (rounded to one decimal place for simplicity).

> On the third hole, he two-putted from three feet, which lost one stroke (tour average of one minus two putts taken).

Through three holes, Tiger lost 0.9 strokes compared to the tour average. Repeating the strokes gained procedure for Tiger's putting on each of the 18 holes in that round, and adding them together, we see that Tiger's total strokes gained putting for the round turned out to be -1.3. That is, he lost 1.3 strokes compared to the tour average from his putting. In fact, Tiger ranked 105th out of 132 golfers in strokes gained putting for this round.

Tiger was right about his poor putting performance, which is accurately reflected in the strokes gained putting stat. In contrast, looking at the number of putts alone, his 27 putts for the round ranked in the best 26 out of 132 golfers. Putts per round gives a completely misleading picture of his putting performance for this round. The main reason for the discrepancy is distance. Tiger's average initial putt distance was 11 feet. The field average for this round was almost 20 feet. Tiger took fewer putts because he started closer to the hole, not because he putted better.

Table 3.2. Putting results for Tiger Woods in round one of the 2011 Frys.com Open at CordeValle. Woods's overall strokes gained putting of -1.3 indicates a worse-than-average putting performance. Starting from Tiger's initial putt distances, the tour average number of putts is 25.7. Tiger took 27 putts, so his strokes gained putting is -1.3, or 1.3 putts worse than the tour average. The average initial distance of Tiger's putts was 11 feet, compared to the field average of 20 feet for this round. Tiger's 27 putts was less than the tour average of 29 because he started, on average, closer to the hole, not because he putted better. (The numbers in the table are rounded.)

Hole	1	2	3	4	5	6	7	8	9	Out
Distance (feet)	4	3	3	3	1	6	22	45	6	
Tour avg putts	1.1	1.0	1.0	1.0	1.0	1.3	1.9	2.1	1.3	11.9
Woods's putts	1	1	2	1	1	1	2	2	2	13.0
Strokes gained	0.1	0.0	-1.0	0.0	0.0	0.3	-0.1	0.1	-0.7	-1.1

Hole	10	11	12	13	14	15	16	17	18	In	Total
Distance (feet)	12	4	42	15	6	5	4	13	13		
Tour avg putts	1.7	1.1	2.1	1.8	1.3	1.2	1.1	1.7	1.7	13.8	25.7
Woods's putts	1	2	2	2	1	1	1	2	2	14.0	27
Strokes gained	0.7	-0.9	0.1	-0.2	0.3	0.2	0.1	-0.3	-0.3	-0.2	-1.3

How often have you heard that you'll be a better putter if you hit it closer to the hole? Standard putting statistics have warped our conversation and thinking. Putting is a separate skill from hitting onto the green. If you hit approach shots and chips closer to the hole, you are likely to take fewer putts, and score better. But this will be because of your approach shots and chips, not because of your putting. Strokes gained putting is a pure measure of putting ability that isn't corrupted by a golfer's relative skill, or lack of skill, in hitting onto the green.

A round with the great Bobby Jones

Bobby Jones

It is fun to compare golfers of different eras, but there is often little data available beyond scores. In the book *Down the Fairway*, the great Bobby Jones gives many details of his first qualifying round for the British Open in 1926 at Sunningdale. He described it as "the best round I ever played in important competition." At the time the book was written in 1926, Jones had already won five of his eventual 13 majors and came in second in five others.

Describing Jones's round at Sunningdale, Bernard Darwin wrote, "He was not quite satisfied with his game and was assiduously practising with different drivers before the round. Clearly he had found the secret, for at once he began to play such golf as has never been seen on the course. It was perfect." Jones shot a 66 that day, with only 3s and 4s on the card. Darwin continued, "The crowd dispersed, awe-stricken. They had watched the best round they ever had seen or would see." This was at a time when rounds in the 60s on championship courses were rare and top finishers in majors would often have rounds in the upper 70s and even the low 80s.

How was Bobby's putting in this "perfect" round? He had no three-putts and he had one-putts from 25 feet, seven feet, and six feet, for a total of 33 putts. Bobby Jones wrote parenthetically that the 25-footer was "the only long one of the round," which suggests it wasn't his best putting round by any stretch. Table 3.3 shows that he lost 0.7 strokes in his putting compared to the modern PGA Tour benchmark. The comments on his "perfect" round reflected his tee-to-green play and not his putting.

Table 3.3. Putting results for Bobby Jones in the first qualifying round for the British Open in 1926 at Sunningdale. His strokes gained putting was -0.7 relative to the PGA Tour benchmark from 2004 to 2012. Starting from his initial putt distances, the tour average number of putts is 32.3. His 33 putts represented at loss of 0.7 (32.3 minus 33) relative to the tour average. Exact putt distances are unknown for holes 1, 2, and 14 and are set to 35 feet.

Hole	1	2	3	4	5	6	7	8	9	Out
Distance (feet)	35	35	5	25	25	18	10	40	5	
Tour avg putts	2.0	2.0	1.2	1.9	1.9	1.8	1.6	2.1	1.2	15.9
Jones's putts	2	2	2	2	1	2	2	2	2	17.0
Strokes gained	0.0	0.0	-0.8	-0.1	0.9	-0.2	-0.4	0.1	-0.8	-1.1

Hole	10	11	12	13	14	15	16	17	18	In	Total
Distance (feet)	30	7	30	6	35	12	40	30	30		
Tour avg putts	2.0	1.4	2.0	1.3	2.0	1.7	2.1	2.0	2.0	16.4	32.3
Jones's putts	2	1	2	1	2	2	2	2	2	16.0	33
Strokes gained	0.0	0.4	0.0	0.3	0.0	-0.3	0.1	0.0	0.0	0.4	-0.7

A strokes gained view of exceptional putting performances

Paul Goydos shot a record-tying low score of 59 in the first round of the 2010 John Deere Classic. The round was also notable for being the second-best strokes gained putting round in the ShotLink era. Goydos gained 7.5 strokes with his putting relative to the tour average. He took just 22 putts. His round included a shot from the green fringe on the 16th hole, where he holed out from 14 feet. Since this shot was not a putt, neither strokes gained putting nor putts-per-round statistics include this exceptional shot. Table 3.4 contains the details. His 59 was 10.5 strokes better than the field average of 69.5 for that round. Putting contributed 71% (7.5/10.5) to his score versus the field. Unfortunately, his putting touch left him in the next three rounds, in which his total strokes gained putting was slightly worse than the field, at -0.3. Goydos finished the tournament in second place, losing by two strokes to Steve Stricker.

Table 3.4. Putting results for Paul Goydos in round one of the 2010 John Deere Classic at TPC Deere Run. His strokes gained putting of 7.5 was the second-best single-round putting performance in 2003–2012.

Hole	1	2	3	4	5	6	7	8	9	Out
Distance (feet)	10	6	45	18	54	18	12	36	22	
Tour avg putts	1.6	1.3	2.1	1.8	2.2	1.8	1.7	2.0	1.9	16.5
Goydos's putts	2	1	2	1	2	1	1	2	2	14.0
Strokes gained	-0.4	0.3	0.1	0.8	0.2	0.8	0.7	0.0	-0.1	2.5

Hole	10	11	12	13	14	15	16	17	18	In	Total
Distance (feet)	6	40	20	25	6	6	0	11	8		
Tour avg putts	1.3	2.1	1.9	1.9	1.3	1.3	0.0	1.6	1.5	13.0	29.5
Goydos's putts	1	1	1	1	1	1	0	1	1	8.0	22
Strokes gained	0.3	1.1	0.9	0.9	0.3	0.3	0.0	0.6	0.5	5.0	7.5

At the other extreme, even pro golfers' putting performances can be exceptionally bad. The single worst putting round, out of over 140,000 rounds on the PGA Tour in 2003–2012, belongs to Joe Durant in the second round of the 2008 Wachovia Championship at Quail Hollow. Joe Durant is a twenty-year veteran of the PGA Tour, with four tour victories to his credit. He is known for his solid ball striking and accurate drives, but not for his putting. In this round, he shot a 79 en route to missing the cut by nine strokes. Durant lost 9.8 strokes to the tour average on the greens. Details are given in Table 3.5. Durant had one four-putt, three three-putts, and only one one-putt in taking 40 putts for the round.

Table 3.5. Putting results for Joe Durant in round two of the 2008 Wachovia Championship at Quail Hollow. Durant lost 9.8 strokes to the tour average, the worst strokes gained putting round on the PGA Tour in 2003–2012.

Hole	1	2	3	4	5	6	7	8	9	Out
Distance (feet)	1	17	5	55	8	13	13	3	15	
Tour avg putts	1.0	1.8	1.2	2.2	1.5	1.7	1.7	1.0	1.8	14.0
Durant's putts	1	2	2	3	2	3	2	2	2	19.0
Strokes gained	0.0	-0.2	-0.8	-0.8	-0.5	-1.3	-0.3	-1.0	-0.2	-5.0

Hole	10	11	12	13	14	15	16	17	18	In	Total
Distance (feet)	20	49	14	14	20	60	8	20	5		
Tour avg putts	1.9	2.1	1.7	1.7	1.9	2.2	1.5	1.9	1.2	16.2	30.2
Durant's putts	2	2	2	2	2	4	2	3	2	21.0	40
Strokes gained	-0.1	0.1	-0.3	-0.3	-0.1	-1.8	-0.5	-1.1	-0.8	-4.8	-9.8

Measuring difficulty of the greens

What explains Joe Durant's abominable performance that day in 2008 at Quail Hollow? Any number of technical flaws could have contributed. At some point he might have "mailed it in" after realizing that he had no chance to make the cut. The tricky, hilly greens at Quail Hollow might have been a factor. To investigate this theory further, we can estimate the difficulty of the greens at Quail Hollow and other courses on the tour.

How challenging were the greens at Quail Hollow that day? The strokes gained approach gives us an easy way to measure the difficulty of greens by looking at the putting performance of the entire field.

Suppose in a single round of a regular tournament, the entire field putted better than average. It could be that the field consisted of better-than-average putters, but this isn't likely since a regular full-field tournament contains mostly the same pros that play in other tournaments. It could be that the entire field was sprinkled with putting magic from a bottle that round. This isn't likely, just as throwing snake eyes on a pair of dice 10 times in a row isn't likely. The most plausible explanation for the entire field putting better than average is that the greens were easier to putt than average. It could be that the greens were smoother, not lightning quick, or flatter than most. Perhaps the hole locations were far from any swales in the greens. The weather during that round probably was neither freezing cold nor particularly windy. The putting difficulty of a round can be measured by the average strokes gained putting of the field.

In the second round at Quail Hollow in 2008, Joe Durant lost 9.8 strokes to the PGA Tour benchmark, which represents the PGA Tour average putting performance over many courses. That day, the field lost an average of 0.6 strokes to the putting benchmark. The greens were more difficult to putt than average, but this explains very little of Durant's terrible putting round.

Another golfer's comment on Quail Hollow sheds light on its difficulty. It's extremely rare to see a professional golfer risk a two-stroke penalty by leaving the flagstick unattended while putting, but that's exactly what Phil Mickelson did on the 18th green of Quail Hollow in the third round in 2010. Standing 60 feet away from the hole with a large hump to traverse, he had no way to get his putt close to the hole. The best strategy, he felt, would be to aim 10 feet right of the hole and hope to sink the next one. Phil left the pin in the hole to help his depth perception. Nearly as planned, his putt finished eight feet right of the hole and he sank the next one. Interviewed after the round, and risking a fine for criticizing a course, Phil said, "For as beautifully designed as this golf course is tee to green, the greens are by far the worst designed greens we play on tour. Even though they're in immaculate shape, I would say that 18 would be the worst green that we have on tour, except that it's not even the worst on this golf course. Twelve is." Ouch.

Table 3.6 shows how courses on the PGA Tour rank in putting difficulty as measured by the average strokes gained of all golfers playing the course against the PGA Tour putting benchmark. The hardest greens to putt are often bumpy, hilly, or windy. The two hardest courses to putt are Pebble Beach and Westchester, both with Poa annua greens that tend to get bumpy as the grass grows throughout the day. The Plantation Course at Kapalua is known for its changes in elevation and high winds that can produce drives over 400 yards long on a regular basis. But high winds also have a pronounced effect on putting, as reflected in Kapalua's status as the third-hardest course to putt on tour.

Consistent with Phil Mickelson's comments, Quail Hollow's greens rank as the fourth-toughest to putt on the PGA Tour. Over years of tournaments on Quail Hollow's contoured greens, pros have lost an average

0.5 strokes to the PGA Tour putting benchmark. Easier putting conditions come from smooth bentgrass greens, calm weather, and relatively flat putting surfaces. The four easiest courses to putt are TPC Summerlin, TPC Deere Run (where Paul Goydos shot his exceptionally good 59), Doral's Blue Monster, and Colonial Country Club.

Table 3.6. Courses ranked by putting difficulty as measured by average strokes gained putting using ShotLink data from 2003 to 2011. Only courses with at least 12 rounds of ShotLink data are included. Pebble Beach was the hardest course to putt and Colonial was the easiest.

Rank	Course	Average SGP	Rank	Course	Average SGP
1	Pebble Beach	-0.77	24	En-Joie	-0.03
2	Westchester	-0.73	25	TPC Four Seasons	-0.02
3	Kapalua	-0.63	26	La Cantera	0.00
4	Quail Hollow	-0.52	27	Warwick Hills	0.01
5	TPC Sugarloaf	-0.43	28	Brown Deer Park	0.03
6	Riviera	-0.37	29	PGA West Palmer	0.04
7	Congressional	-0.35	30	TPC Southwind	0.05
8	Torrey Pines South	-0.31	31	Waialae	0.08
9	Montreux	-0.24	32	Cog Hill	0.08
10	Atunyote	-0.20	33	Firestone South	0.09
11	The Classic Club	-0.19	34	Magnolia	0.09
12	TPC Sawgrass	-0.19	35	Redstone: Tournament Course	0.09
13	Muirfield Village	-0.17	36	PGA National	0.10
14	Tucson National	-0.15	37	Forest Oaks	0.13
15	Bay Hill	-0.13	38	TPC Louisiana	0.15
16	Sedgefield	-0.13	39	East Lake	0.17
17	Innisbrook-Copperhead	-0.12	40	TPC Scottsdale	0.18
18	Glen Abbey	-0.10	41	TPC Boston	0.19
19	TPC River Highlands	-0.08	42	TPC Summerlin	0.21
20	Nemacolin–Mystic Rock	-0.08	43	TPC Deere Run	0.22
21	Harbour Town	-0.05	44	Doral Blue Monster	0.24
22	Redstone: Jacobsen/Hardy	-0.05	45	Colonial	0.26
23	Annandale	-0.03			

Sometimes the putting difficulty of a course isn't due to its geography, but to man-made factors. Unless there is a drastic change in the wind or weather, putting difficulty of a given course or hole usually doesn't vary very much from one round to the next. That wasn't the case at the Bethpage Black course in 2012. Between the second and third rounds, the greens were triple-rolled with a green rolling machine like a miniature steamroller to make them firmer, faster, and smoother. Tiger Woods said, "I've never seen greens change like this, from what they were yesterday to today. The grass even seems slippery." Pádraig Harrington said, "I don't think I've ever putted on greens faster. It doesn't look good from outside when you start on with a 64 and shoot 75-75." The 14th and 18th greens were "stimping about 20 around the hole," he said. From round one to round three, the average strokes gained putting of the field went from 0.4 strokes per round (very easy) to 0 (average difficulty) to -0.5 (very difficult).

To address golfers' concerns, the greens were drenched with water the night before the final round. The strokes gained putting of the field increased to 0.4 strokes. The greens became nearly a stroke easier per round compared to the previous day, an enormous man-made change in putting difficulty.

If the entire field putts better than the PGA Tour benchmark, that indicates the greens are easier to putt than the average greens on tour. The average of strokes gained putting for all golfers in the field gives a simple and reliable measure of the putting difficulty of greens.

Fine tuning a new stat: strokes gained putting to the field

Suppose one golfer plays a tournament at a difficult-to-putt course, such as Pebble Beach, while skipping a tournament at an easy-to-putt course, such as Colonial. Another golfer does the opposite, playing the easy-to-putt course and skipping the difficult-to-putt course. Comparing putting performances between the two golfers based on the same fixed benchmark isn't quite fair, because of the significant difference in putting difficulty between the two courses.

The same problem occurs when comparing scores of golfers competing at two different tournaments. In 2012, Mark Wilson won the Humana Challenge with a score of 24 under par, while Webb Simpson won the

U.S. Open with a score of one over par. Wilson's score was 25 strokes better than Simpson's relative to the par benchmark, but no serious follower of golf would argue that Wilson played better than Simpson, let alone 25 strokes better.

The Humana Challenge courses are set up to play easy, in part because of the pro-am format of the tournament. U.S. Open tournaments, in contrast, are known for their insufferably penal course setups. If the scoring average trophy was based on scores, Wilson would have a huge, and unfair, advantage over Simpson. Instead, when the PGA Tour presents the Byron Nelson trophy to the golfer who scored the best during the year, the award is based on the lowest adjusted scoring average, not the lowest scoring average. The adjustment takes into account the average score of the field for each round.

Similarly, a fair system for ranking putters should take into account the putting difficulty of each round. In the first round of Arnold Palmer's tournament at Bay Hill, European Ryder Cup star Edoardo Molinari gained 2.3 strokes against the PGA Tour putting benchmark. But the day was very windy, and strong winds make putting more challenging by affecting both the pace and line of putts. The difficulty in putting was reflected in the -0.8 strokes gained putting average for the field, ranking it harder than 19 out of 20 putting rounds on tour. Edoardo gained 2.3 strokes against the putting benchmark and the field as a whole lost 0.8 strokes against the putting benchmark, so we can say that Edoardo gained 3.1 strokes putting compared to the field. When I asked Edoardo how he did it, he said, "My experience putting in windy conditions in Europe helped me to putt well at Bay Hill that day."

The PGA Tour now uses *strokes gained putting to the field* as its primary putting stat. Strokes gained putting to the field is SGP compared to the putting benchmark, minus the tour average SGP for the round.

> Strokes gained putting to the field is SGP compared to the putting benchmark, minus the tour average SGP for the round.

Who was the best putter on the PGA Tour in the years 2004 through 2012? We're not looking for the putter on the back nine on Sunday, nor the best putter on testy six-footers, nor the one who went the longest without a three-putt, nor for the one whose putter has gotten the hottest for a few tournaments or even a few months. We're looking for the career best putter, the one who was the best over a number of years, considering every putt recorded in the ShotLink database. Strokes gained putting is the only stat that gives a reliable career measure of putting performance, unlike putts per round, putts per green in regulation, or length of holed putts. Strokes gained putting can be used to rank golfers purely on their putting ability, and identify who is the best.

Using the strokes gained putting stat, as shown in Table 3.7, the best putter on the planet is . . . Luke Donald. The top five career putters in the ShotLink era are Donald, Brad Faxon, Tiger Woods, Aaron Baddeley, and Greg Chalmers. Perhaps Brad Faxon would be ranked higher if the data included more of his prime putting years. Perhaps Tiger would rank higher if putting at the majors was included, but unfortunately those tournaments aren't included in the ShotLink data. Still, most golf observers would agree that these five are some of the finest putters in the game.

Luke Donald played college golf at Northwestern University from 1997 to 2001, where he graduated with a degree in art theory and practice. Pat Goss was, and still is, Luke's coach. At 27 years old in 1997, Goss was named *Golfweek*'s National Coach of the Year and was the youngest head golf coach in the country. "We knew he'd be our best player," Goss said. In 1999, Luke won the NCAA individual title and he broke the record Tiger Woods held for the lowest scoring average. Luke won the Southern Farm Bureau Classic in 2002, his rookie season on the PGA Tour. Luke continued to improve, winning tournaments on the PGA and European tours, and rose to number one in the world in May 2011. The secret to his putting success? "It's just a process of keep working on it, try to get it better every time, every year." Even though he's the best putter in the world, Luke says he spends about twice as much time practicing the short game and putting compared to hitting balls on the range. His talent plus hard work has paid off.

Through many rounds and tournaments over the years, Luke's putting gained him an average of 0.7 strokes per round compared to a typical PGA Tour field. That's almost three strokes every tournament. For Luke Donald, putting is quantifiably a huge factor in his success as a golfer.

Table 3.7. Top 50 putters on the PGA Tour from 2004 through August 2012. Only golfers with at least 120 rounds are included in the ranking. Strokes gained putting (SGP) results are per round and relative to the average PGA Tour field (as discussed in the appendix).

Rank	Golfer	SGP	Rank	Golfer	SGP
1	Luke Donald	0.70	26	Parker McLachlin	0.40
2	Brad Faxon	0.64	27	Nathan Green	0.39
3	Tiger Woods	0.64	28	Webb Simpson	0.39
4	Aaron Baddeley	0.64	29	Jeff Quinney	0.38
5	Greg Chalmers	0.63	30	Scott McCarron	0.38
6	Jesper Parnevik	0.62	31	Jason Day	0.38
7	Brian Gay	0.62	32	Brent Geiberger	0.38
8	Loren Roberts	0.62	33	Matt Gogel	0.38
9	Bryce Molder	0.58	34	Shigeki Maruyama	0.38
10	Ben Crane	0.56	35	Richard S. Johnson	0.36
11	Brandt Snedeker	0.54	36	Geoff Ogilvy	0.35
12	Dean Wilson	0.52	37	Eric Axley	0.35
13	Steve Stricker	0.50	38	Blake Adams	0.35
14	Stewart Cink	0.49	39	Stephen Ames	0.34
15	José María Olazábal	0.48	40	Marc Turnesa	0.34
16	Fredrik Jacobson	0.47	41	Daniel Chopra	0.34
17	Michael Thompson	0.46	42	Bob Tway	0.34
18	Charlie Wi	0.45	43	Gavin Coles	0.32
19	Chad Collins	0.45	44	Ryan Moore	0.32
20	Zach Johnson	0.44	45	Jeff Klauk	0.31
21	Corey Pavin	0.44	46	Matt Kuchar	0.31
22	Carl Pettersson	0.43	47	David Mathis	0.30
23	Jim Furyk	0.41	48	Darren Clarke	0.30
24	Len Mattiace	0.40	49	Bob Heintz	0.29
25	Mark O'Meara	0.40	50	Kevin Na	0.29

Diagnosing strength and weakness in putting

Strokes gained putting can be used to determine whether a pro golfer is a good or a poor putter, relative to the tour average. Without data on a putter's grip, stance, or stroke, though, it is difficult to answer why. But we can use the strokes gained approach to tease more information out of the data, and to determine whether a golfer's strength or weakness lies with testy short putts, makeable medium-distance putts, or longer lag putts. We can also use this information to identify the best short-, medium-, and long-distance putters.

Suppose a pro golfer two-putts from 33 feet. We already know that the tour average is two putts, so this is an average performance that neither gains nor loses strokes. But suppose that the 33-foot putt stopped eight feet from the hole. Not a good first putt, right? This intuition can be quantified using the PGA Tour putting benchmark from Table 3.1. From eight feet, the tour average is 1.5 putts to hole out, so a holed putt from eight feet gains 0.5 strokes against the tour average. In this example, the first putt from 33 feet to eight feet lost 0.5 strokes, the second putt gained 0.5 strokes, and both putts together gained zero strokes compared to the tour average.

If the pro putted this way again and again, we could say that he was an overall average putter who happened to be a poor putter from 33 feet and a great putter from eight feet. In this way, strokes gained analysis can be used to diagnose a golfer's strengths and weaknesses on putts of different distances.

Here's another way to analyze the quality of the first putt: It started 33 feet from the hole and ended eight feet from the hole. The tour average putts to hole out decreased from 2.0 to 1.5, so the putt brought the pro an average of 0.5 strokes closer to the hole. That's not very good, because the golfer took one putt to reduce the average putts to hole out by 0.5. In strokes gained lingo, the first putt lost 0.5 strokes to the tour average.

For an individual putt, strokes gained is the decrease in the average putts to hole out from the starting to the ending distance, minus one to account for the putt itself.

> The strokes gained of an individual putt is the decrease in the average putts to hole out minus one to account for the stroke taken.

A key idea is that *progress to the hole* is measured in terms of average putts to hole out. That first putt moved the ball closer to the hole; we are used to thinking in terms of distance because it's visible and tangible. Strokes gained uses Table 3.1, which shows average putts to hole out by distance from the hole, to translate distance into strokes. Once the quality of all putts is measured in a common unit of strokes, we can compare, for example, a 60-foot putt that stops eight feet from the hole with a missed six-footer. We can figure out whether a three-putt is due to a poor first or a poor second putt. And we can break down putting prowess into skill on short, medium, and long putts.

How good is a 60-foot putt that stops eight feet from the hole? We know that not all 60-foot putts are created equal, but distance is the most important factor in the difficulty of a putt. According to Table 3.1, the tour average from 60 feet is 2.2 putts. The tour average from eight feet is 1.5 putts. The decrease in average putts to hole out is 0.7. Accounting for the putt itself, the strokes gained of the putt is -0.3. In other words, the putt lost 0.3 strokes to the tour average.

How about a 60-foot putt that stops four feet from the hole? According to Table 3.1, the tour average from four feet in the ShotLink era is 1.13 putts. The decrease in average putts to hole out is 1.07 (2.20 minus 1.13). Accounting for the putt itself, the strokes gained of the putt is 0.07. The closer a 60-foot putt finishes to the hole the better; the strokes gained measure increases accordingly to reflect the improved outcome.

Suppose a pro golfer three-putts from 33 feet. The first putt stops eight feet from the hole and the second putt just lips out and finishes two inches from the hole. For the first putt, the tour average from 33 feet is 2.0 and the tour average from eight feet is 1.5. The decrease in average putts to hole out is 0.5. So accounting for the putt itself, the strokes gained of the first putt is -0.5. For the second putt, the tour average from eight feet is 1.5 and the tour average from two inches is 1.0, so the strokes gained of the second putt is also -0.5. The three-putt from 33 feet lost one stroke to the tour average, with equal blame going to a poor first putt and a poor second putt.

Now that strokes gained can be measured for individual putts, the results can be combined for putts falling into any set of distance categories. The three distance categories that I use are short putts (zero to six feet), medium putts (seven to 21 feet) and long putts (22 feet and over). Table 3.8 shows that golfers have roughly the same number of putts in each of the three categories, once gimmes from zero to two feet are ignored.

Only three distances are used because too many distance categories can lead to nonsensical results. For example, you can't be the best putter on tour from five feet and seven feet but horrible at six-footers. Brad Faxon related to me this story about Justin Leonard. Justin was leading the third round of the Honda Classic in 2003 when a reporter asked him why he thought he was in the top 10 in putting from five feet and in the top 10 from seven feet, but ranked worse than 100th in putting from six feet. He hadn't realized he was ranked so poorly in six-footers! Imagine what was going through his mind on the 8th hole of the final round, when he stood over his first six-foot putt of the day. Fortunately for Justin, he did sink the putt, and he sank another six-footer on the 10th hole on the way to a final-round 67 and a one-stroke victory over Chad Campbell.

Table 3.8. Number of putts by putt distance for PGA Tour golfers.

	Total	0–2 feet	3–6 feet	7–21 feet	22 feet and over
Number of putts	29.2	8.9	7.0	8.0	5.3
Fraction of putts	100%	30%	24%	27%	18%

Table 3.9 shows strokes gained putting results for 2011 broken down into these three categories. Luke Donald led in putting in 2011, gaining 0.95 strokes against an average tour field. He did this primarily by gains in the short- and medium-distance putt categories, where he ranked second and fourth, respectively. As a group, the top 10 putters in 2011 gained a total of 0.73 strokes due to putting, with 0.63 strokes gained from putts 21 feet and under and only 0.08 strokes gained from putts 22 feet and over. None of the top five lag putters, that is, in the 22+ feet category, are ranked in the top 30 in putting overall. Short- and medium-distance putts contribute more to great putting than long putts. Few putts are made outside 21 feet, so it is very hard for pros to distinguish themselves by superior lag putting.

What is the best annual putting performance that is reasonably possible? If in 2011 Luke Donald had been in the top five in long putts with a gain of 0.3 strokes, then his total strokes gained putting would have been almost 1.2 strokes per round. It is hard to imagine an annual putting performance much better than that.

Table 3.9. Strokes gained putting per round in 2011, broken down into three distance categories: short putts (0–6 feet), medium-length putts (7–21 feet), and long putts (22 feet and over). Ranks are out of the 204 golfers with at least 30 rounds in 2011.

Golfer	Rank				Strokes gained putting per round			
	All	0–6 ft	7–21 ft	22+ ft	Total	0–6 ft	7–21 ft	22+ ft
Luke Donald	1	2	4	41	0.95	0.40	0.46	0.09
Steve Stricker	2	12	2	36	0.87	0.27	0.49	0.10
Charlie Wi	3	11	5	34	0.82	0.27	0.44	0.11
Bryce Molder	4	29	1	76	0.76	0.21	0.51	0.04
Kevin Na	5	8	23	26	0.68	0.30	0.25	0.13
Fredrik Jacobson	6	3	22	68	0.68	0.37	0.25	0.05
Jason Day	7	40	16	19	0.65	0.19	0.31	0.15
Brandt Snedeker	8	25	24	12	0.64	0.23	0.24	0.18
Greg Chalmers	9	10	20	38	0.64	0.28	0.26	0.10
Zach Johnson	10	16	3	167	0.63	0.26	0.47	-0.10
Average					0.73	0.28	0.37	0.08
Top five 0–6 feet								
Jeff Quinney	15	1	34	192	0.58	0.56	0.20	-0.18
Luke Donald	1	2	4	41	0.95	0.40	0.46	0.09
Fredrik Jacobson	6	3	22	68	0.68	0.37	0.25	0.05
Geoff Ogilvy	14	4	12	163	0.59	0.36	0.32	-0.09
Will Strickler	62	5	134	134	0.22	0.33	-0.07	-0.04
Top five 7–21 feet								
Bryce Molder	4	29	1	76	0.76	0.21	0.51	0.04
Steve Stricker	2	12	2	36	0.87	0.27	0.49	0.10
Zach Johnson	10	16	3	167	0.63	0.26	0.47	-0.10
Luke Donald	1	2	4	41	0.95	0.40	0.46	0.09
Charlie Wi	3	11	5	34	0.82	0.27	0.44	0.11
Top five 22+ feet								
Matt McQuillan	33	113	65	1	0.39	-0.02	0.11	0.30
Tim Petrovic	77	58	183	2	0.15	0.12	-0.27	0.30
Paul Casey	32	92	80	3	0.39	0.04	0.08	0.28
Graeme McDowell	60	105	126	4	0.23	0.00	-0.04	0.26
Hunter Haas	38	148	31	5	0.34	-0.11	0.20	0.25
Notable golfers								
Vijay Singh	131	141	143	43	-0.08	-0.09	-0.08	0.09
Bubba Watson	139	134	145	79	-0.11	-0.07	-0.09	0.04
Phil Mickelson	140	18	188	148	-0.11	0.25	-0.31	-0.06
Adam Scott	149	165	101	113	-0.16	-0.16	0.02	-0.02
Dustin Johnson	180	195	138	115	-0.47	-0.38	-0.07	-0.02
Ernie Els	194	200	195	15	-0.66	-0.49	-0.34	0.16

Looking at the breakdown of strokes gained putting results by distance in Table 3.9, we see that Ernie Els, Dustin Johnson, and Adam Scott all had trouble with short putts. Ernie Els was great from 22 feet and over, ranking 15th in this category. Phil Mickelson had trouble with medium-length putts. Strengths and weaknesses in different types of putts can be determined by breaking down strokes gained putting in this way.

How well do amateur golfers putt?

Many amateurs count every shot with a putter as a putt, whether or not it is a stroke on the green. This skews the strokes gained statistic. A friend of mine once complained about being a poor putter. He offered as evidence the 34 putts he took in our round together. I pointed out that this total included the three times he used his putter from off the green, once putting through 10 yards of fairway.

When counted according to the standard convention—in which putts are strokes taken on the green, not including the fringe—my friend took only 31 putts in his round. His strokes gained putting was a respectable minus two relative to the PGA Tour benchmark. If amateurs want to compare their own stats to the professionals', it is important to use the same conventions that they do.

How well do amateurs putt? Using Golfmetrics amateur data, we can quantify the difference between pro and amateur putting. Pros score better than amateurs, playing every type of shot and every type of putt better, but perhaps surprisingly, it turns out that many amateurs are pretty good putters.

Table 3.10 compares one-putts, three-putts, and average putts for a typical tour pro, scratch golfer, and 90-golfer (a golfer whose average score is 90). As the table shows, a typical 90-golfer one-putts 27% of the time from eight feet, while a scratch golfer one-putts 41% of the time, and a pro one-putts 50% of the time from the same distance. The 90-golfer averages 1.75 putts to hole out compared to 1.5 for a pro. That's a loss of a quarter stroke versus a pro for every eight-foot putt the amateur faces. Without a doubt, that's a significant difference. Pros are better putters than amateurs, from eight feet and from all other distances.

How much do the per-putt differences between pros and amateurs add up over the course of an 18-hole round? Pros average 29 putts for 18

Table 3.10. One-putt probability, three-putt probability, and average number of putts to hole out for PGA Tour golfers, scratch golfers, and 90-golfers.

Distance (feet)	One-putt probability			Three-putt probability		
	Tour pro	Scratch golfer	90-golfer	Tour pro	Scratch golfer	90-golfer
2	99%	99%	95%	0%	< 1%	< 1%
3	96%	93%	84%	0%	< 1%	< 1%
4	88%	80%	65%	0%	< 1%	< 1%
5	77%	66%	50%	0%	< 1%	< 1%
6	66%	55%	39%	0%	< 1%	1%
7	58%	47%	32%	1%	1%	1%
8	50%	41%	27%	1%	1%	2%
9	45%	36%	23%	1%	1%	2%
10	40%	33%	20%	1%	1%	2%
15	23%	21%	11%	1%	2%	5%
20	15%	14%	6%	2%	4%	8%
30	7%	6%	2%	5%	9%	18%
40	4%	2%	< 1%	10%	15%	30%
50	3%	1%	< 1%	17%	23%	41%
60	2%	< 1%	< 1%	23%	30%	51%

Distance (feet)	Average number of putts		
	Tour pro	Scratch golfer	90-golfer
2	1.01	1.01	1.06
3	1.04	1.07	1.17
4	1.13	1.20	1.36
5	1.23	1.34	1.51
6	1.34	1.45	1.62
7	1.42	1.54	1.69
8	1.50	1.60	1.75
9	1.56	1.65	1.79
10	1.61	1.68	1.82
15	1.78	1.81	1.94
20	1.87	1.89	2.02
30	1.98	2.03	2.16
40	2.06	2.14	2.30
50	2.14	2.22	2.41
60	2.21	2.30	2.51

holes. A typical 90-golfer averages 33.4 putts per round. But that overstates the skill difference, because amateur putts start a little farther from the hole than pros', on average. If you gave a 90-golfer the putting skill of a pro, his or her average score would drop by about four strokes.

We all have good days on the course. How often does a 90-golfer putt better than a tour pro? Strokes gained putting to the PGA Tour benchmark provides a good estimate of the answer: A 90-golfer will beat a pro in almost 10% of rounds. An 80-golfer's SGP will beat a pro's almost 20% of the time. And a scratch golfer will putt better than a pro more than 30% of the time. Amateur golfers aren't bad putters!

You could argue that the playing field is not level, with pros putting on fast, smooth, tour-quality greens and amateurs on slow, bumpy greens. But we're not asking how many times an amateur would putt off the green at Augusta National during Masters week. Faster greens are harder to putt, but so are bumpier ones. When pros putt on greens that are slower and less well manicured, they putt worse than they do on a tournament course. It is hard to know just how much worse, since most of our amateur benchmark data come from courses with very good greens that are only a foot or so slower than tour greens.

Even though the pro and amateur data come from different courses, it is still interesting for amateurs to compare their SGPs to those of the pros. They might find out where their strengths and weaknesses are, what parts of their game are most worth working on, and other useful facts.

Old habits die hard, but using putts per round these days instead of strokes gained putting is like driving a horse and buggy when a car is parked out front. For decades, even though counting putts could be misleading and give wrong answers, counting putts was the best we could do to measure putting skill. We did not have more detailed information. With the advent of the PGA Tour's ShotLink system for pros and the Golfmetrics system for amateurs, though, putt counting became passé. Starting locations, ending locations, and other shot information could be easily stored and analyzed. Putting performance can now be measured much more accurately using strokes gained putting, and there is little reason to rely on counting putts.

I implemented the strokes gained database for putts and off-green shots in the Golfmetrics system in 2005. In 2008, I published the first strokes gained results, comparing professional and amateur play across a variety of shots. I used the term "shot value" at the time. The same basic concept was used by researchers from MIT to rank putters on the PGA Tour, and they coined the term "strokes gained." Together with the group from MIT, we worked with the PGA Tour on the design and details. The PGA Tour rolled out strokes gained putting (to the field) in May 2011, their first new core stat in 15 years, and it quickly became accepted and used as their primary stat for measuring putting.

The basic idea of strokes gained has been rediscovered a number of times, with perhaps the earliest mention of a similar idea appearing in a *Golf* magazine article from the 1970s. But the intellectual foundation of strokes gained goes back to the dynamic programming ideas of Richard Bellman. The connection arises because choosing how to play a golf hole can be viewed as a multistage decision problem. In later chapters, we'll apply the strokes gained idea to shots off the green, and eventually see what we can learn by looking at the entire game as one dynamic program.

19th Hole Summary

- Putts per round is a flawed measure of putting skill because it doesn't take putt distances into account.

- Strokes gained putting is a better measure of putting skill because it takes into account putt distance, the most important factor in the difficulty of a putt.

- The definition of strokes gained putting is the tour average number of putts to hole out *from a given distance,* minus the number of putts taken.

- The best golfers in the world in terms of strokes gained putting gain about one stroke per round compared to an average field.

- For an individual putt, strokes gained measures progress to the hole in terms of average putts to hole out rather than distance to the hole.

- The strokes gained of an individual putt is the decrease in the average putts to hole out minus one, to account for the stroke taken.

- The strokes gained putting measure uses a dynamic programming approach, analyzing putting as a multistage problem.

CHAPTER 4

SCRAMBLE AND SWITCHEROO:
What Simulation Can Tell Us about Golf

Who's more likely to win: an amateur playing a best-ball scramble, or a pro playing a worst-ball scramble? Our scramble works this way: An amateur playing best-ball scramble hits two balls from the tee. He chooses the best of the two shots and that counts as his first shot. He then hits two balls from that spot and the best of the two counts as his second shot. The process is repeated until a ball goes in the hole. The amateur is in mulligan heaven. His opponent, a pro playing worst-ball scramble, hits two balls from the tee. The amateur chooses the worst of the pro's two tee shots, and that counts as the pro's first shot. Then the pro hits two balls from that spot, and the worst counts as the pro's second shot. The process is repeated until both balls are holed out. The pro is going through golf's version of waterboarding. The best-ball scramble format gives an indication of a golfer's potential to shoot lower scores. The worst-ball scramble format shows the cost of inconsistency. If the amateur doesn't receive any handicap strokes, does the worst-ball-professional versus the best-ball-amateur scramble favor the professional or the amateur?

How can we answer this question? The outcome depends on the skill of both the amateur and the pro, the course that the two play, and how each shot is played. Let's suppose that our amateur is a typical 90-golfer, the pro is a typical PGA Tour pro, and the course is a challenging 6,500-yard course. How much would the 90-golfer's score decrease in the best-of-two scramble format? How would the pro score in the worst-of-two scramble?

It doesn't appear that there have been any pro-am scramble matches that we can learn from. We could get a bunch of pros and amateurs together and run an experiment, but that could be quite costly. Perhaps we could ask a TV network to create a golf reality special, like they did with the *Golf Digest* U.S. Open Challenge. We could poll knowledgeable golfers, but even if there were a consensus, we couldn't be sure that they were right.

In the absence of actual results to inform us, the best we can do is to run a simulation. The technique of simulation, developed at the dawn of the computer and atomic eras, models the behavior of real-world systems inside a computer. Running scenarios many times illuminates the probability of reaching various outcomes. Simulation is now so common that my kids played simulated pinball on a computer before they ever saw a pinball machine in real life. ("Daddy, they made this pinball machine just like the computer game!")

Simulation allows us to have pros and amateurs play thousands of scramble matches in a computer, observe the outcomes, and answer the who-would-win question. If I just told you the result, you might not believe me. Even if you did, it's still interesting to go back and revisit the origins of simulation, a technique that is used today in a wide variety of applications, including weather and climate forecasting, medicine, the design of traffic light systems, flight simulators for pilot training, and video games. One of the first computer programs calculated the trajectories of missiles to make artillery more accurate for the military, a challenge that is a lot like simulating the flight of a golf ball.

Computers, simulation, and golf

In 1943, work started on a machine that would profoundly affect U.S.-Soviet relations, change the course of applied mathematics and science, and affect the everyday life of millions throughout the world. Finished just after World War II ended in 1945, the machine contained 17,000 vacuum tubes, 70,000 resistors, 10,000 capacitors, and 500,000 hand-soldered connections. It weighed 30 tons, filled 1,800 square feet, and cost a fortune in electricity to run. The Electronic Numerical Integrator And Computer, commonly known as the ENIAC, is widely regarded as the world's first electronic computer.

By late 1942, over 100 "computers"—mostly female math and science students—worked two shifts, six days a week, using desktop calculators to create firing tables. Yes, before there were electronic computers, the term "computers" referred to humans whose job was to calculate.

As military historian William Atwater wrote, "These computers, these ladies that computed these firing tables—it was absolutely vital work. And without their contributions to the war effort, we would have lost World War II." But in 1942, the backlog of work kept increasing because of the time-consuming computations involved: It would take a skilled human computer about two days to complete one trajectory calculation. Plans were initiated to build an electronic computer and work began in July 1943, even though many thought a machine with so many unreliable vacuum tubes would never work. After an intense effort, the ENIAC was completed in the fall of 1945 at a cost estimated at $500,000 (about six million in today's dollars), including research and development. The ENIAC, without a single moving part, could perform 5,000 additions, 400 multiplications, 40 divisions, or three square-root operations per second. What took two or more days of manual effort could be done in 30 seconds on the ENIAC.

The ENIAC computer

The war ended before the ENIAC was completed, but from late 1945 through its retirement in 1955, the ENIAC was the primary workhorse for the U.S. Army and Air Force for the computation of firing tables, and it was used in many other scientific and engineering applications. Though still a secret, the ENIAC was first put to use in December 1945 to compute the potential feasibility of thermonuclear reactions. The first ENIAC program is still classified. The War Department unveiled the top-secret ENIAC to the public in February of 1946.

At its core, the ENIAC could do arithmetic very fast. The artillery firing problems it solved, which showed, for example, what angle to set a 105mm howitzer to hit a target at a range of 700 yards, were quite similar to the calculations of golf ball trajectories that are used in the design of new golf balls, in the testing of golf balls by the United States Golf Association (USGA), and in golf simulators found in retail golf stores. Golf ball trajectory calculations form the basis for the slope-adjusted distance information provided by golf laser range finders. One number in the range finder gives the usual straight-line distance to the hole, and a second number gives the effective distance taking into account the difference in elevation between the current position and the hole. The artillery firing tables of the 1940s, brought into the computer age with the ENIAC, contained similar adjustments for elevation, wind speed, temperature, atmospheric pressure, and other factors, and were indispensable for military operations.

In the April 1946 issue of *Popular Science* magazine, writer Allen Rose observed that "nothing that man has ever built has been possible without the use of numbers. . . . [The ENIAC] promises cheaper air travel, better radios, wider use of micro-waves, and more efficient motors, for example. With the help of lightning-fast computers to do most of the drudgery on problems that have baffled men for many years, today's equation may be tomorrow's rocket ship." No one foresaw that ENIAC's 30 tons of electronics would be reduced to a chip the size of a fingernail that could do calculations thousands of times faster than the original machine, though a female computer who saw an early demonstration of the ENIAC did remark, "I was astounded that it took all this equipment to multiply 5 by 1,000."

At a meeting at Los Alamos labs in the spring of 1946, the first test results of the ENIAC were presented. Among those in attendance was the mathematician Stan Ulam, who had rejoined the lab after a stint on the mathematics faculty at the University of Southern California. Stan enjoyed playing Canfield solitaire and in his spare time he tried to determine the chances of winning. He attempted to answer the question using combinatorial analysis, but the equations were too complex for him to have any hope of solving them, and he wondered if a practical solution was possible. At the meeting, he realized that this miraculous new computing machine could be programmed to "play" hundreds of solitaire hands and count the number of wins.

Eventually, simulation would show that the chances of winning at solitaire were about one in 30.

From left: John von Neumann, Richard Feynman, and Stan Ulam around 1949

Ulam described his idea to the mathematician John von Neumann, mentioning that the same method could be used to solve important questions in mathematical physics that involved a succession of random events. Together they started to plan the calculations for a problem involving neutron diffusion, a necessary step in the development of the hydrogen bomb. Ulam's uncle often gambled at the Monte Carlo Casino; because of the connection between random processes and games of chance, the simulation approach was called the Monte Carlo method.

Programs were input to the ENIAC with IBM paper card readers, a familiar product long used in business accounting machines. IBM commissioned a study in 1947 to determine whether it should develop this new invention into one of its standard products. The study concluded no, since "six electronic digital computers would be sufficient to satisfy the computing needs of the entire United States." Of course, IBM came around and in 1952 produced the IBM 701, the first electronic computer manufactured in quantity. The RAND Corporation installed an IBM 701 computer the next year, which was one of the reasons Richard Bellman was attracted to RAND.

THE INSTITUTE FOR ADVANCED STUDY
Founded by Mr. Louis Bamberger and Mrs. Felix Fuld
PRINCETON, NEW JERSEY
School of Mathematics

March 11, 1947

VIA AIRMAIL: REGISTERED

Mr. R. Richtmyer
Post Office Box 1665
Santa Fe, New Mexico

Dear Bob:

This is the letter I promised you in the course of our telephone conversation on Friday, March 7th.

I have been thinking a good deal about the possibility of using statistical methods to solve neutron diffusion and multiplication problems, in accordance with the principle suggested by Stan Ulam. The more I think about this, the more I become convinced that the idea has great merit. My present conclusions and expectations can be summarized as follows:

(1) The statistical approach is very well suited to a digital treatment. I

I cannot assert this with certainty yet, but it seems to me very likely that the instructions given on this "computing sheet" do not exceed the 'logical' capacity of the ENIAC. I doubt that the processing of 100 'neutrons' will take much longer than the reading, punching and (once) sorting time of 100 cards; i.e., about 3 minutes. Hence, taking 100 'neutrons' through 100 of these stages should take about 300 minutes; i.e., 5 hours.

Please let me know what you and Stan think of these things. Does the approach and the formulation and generality of the criticality problem seem reasonable to you, or would you prefer some other variant?

Would you consider coming East some time to discuss matters further? When could this be?

With best regards;

Very truly yours,

John von Neumann

First and last portions of an eleven-page letter from John von Neumann in March 1947 outlining the use of "statistical methods," now called Monte Carlo simulation, for a problem in neutron diffusion. This outline led to the first use of simulation on an electronic computer.

The scramble simulation

Solitaire, neutron diffusion, and golf shots have one thing in common: variability. There's almost no chance of playing the same two hands of solitaire, just as no two golf shots follow the exact same trajectory. When we hit a golf shot, differences in clubhead speed, path, and angle of attack all lead to differences in the ball's trajectory. The Monte Carlo method allows us to simulate the variability in golf shots that leads to different scores on a golf hole. The speed of modern computers, together with the Monte Carlo method initiated by Ulam and von Neumann, allows us to simulate thousands of golf shots to answer the question of who's more likely to win the scramble match: the worst-ball professional or the best-ball amateur.

Have you made your prediction? Most golfers that I polled believed the pro was more likely to win. Before giving the results, let's follow our two golfers, whom I'll call Pro and Am, for two holes of a computer-simulated scramble match, using a simulation program that I designed with a graduate student, Soonmin Ko. Though anything can happen in two holes, this will help clarify how the scramble match works and provide some intuition for the result.

Pro and Am are playing their match on a 6,500-yard course with narrow tree-lined fairways and demanding green complexes. The first hole is a short par-five, and Pro launches a 300-yard drive into the narrow fairway. Pro's second tee shot travels 310 yards but trickles into the left rough, where he might have tree trouble on the next shot. Playing from the same set of tees, Am nervously steps up and hits a booming, for him, 210-yard drive in the fairway. Am hits again, his next drive strikes a tree on the right, just 150 yards from the tee. Am makes the easy choice to play from the fairway. He hits a hybrid, which clears an area of fescue, leaving him 90 yards from the hole. With one shot safely in play, he tries a fairway wood, but hits a worm burner into the fescue.

Am's second shot is now beyond Pro's tee shots, so Am inspects both and makes him play from the rough. Pro only has 165 yards to the hole, but a tree forces a draw in order to hit the green. Pro hits a great shot onto the green, 20 feet from the hole for eagle. Playing again from the same position, this time Pro overcooks his shot, missing the green to the left.

Now it's Am's turn to play. His first pitching wedge is hit a touch fat. It clears a greenside bunker but finishes in the rough short of the green. On the second try, Am's wedge reaches the front of the green, 45 feet from the hole.

Pro uses his lob wedge from the gnarly rough for his third, stopping it nine feet from the hole. Playing again, he puts it three feet from the hole, so this shot becomes meaningless. Am powers his first putt seven feet by the hole. Overcompensating, Am leaves his next try four feet short.

Pro's nine-foot birdie putt slides by the hole. His second try misses as well, but both are within one foot. Twice Pro taps in for his par. Am sinks his first four-footer, rendering the second irrelevant, and both golfers walk off the hole with pars.

The second hole is a 220-yard downhill par-three. Pro puts both tee shots on the green, but the worst one leaves him 50 feet from the hole. Am hits two drivers, one into the rough and the other into the fairway, both around 30 yards short of the hole. Am chooses to play from the fairway, and he puts both of his next shots on the green, one 40 feet from the hole and the other 15 feet from the hole.

Pro is away and he putts the first one six feet by the hole and the second one to two feet. Pro just misses his six-footer for par, and then he sinks the next six-footer. Twice he sinks the one-footer to walk about with a three-putt bogey. Am misses both 15-footers, but sinks the next one for his two-putt bogey. After two holes, Pro and Am are tied at one over par. The scramble match remains close, and both players finish with the same score, 78.

If it's easy to imagine different outcomes on the first two holes, the number of possible combinations of shots in 18 holes is mind-boggling. The beauty of simulation is that it allows us to work through myriad possibilities to see which outcomes are more likely than others. In hundreds of matches played on our computer simulation program, *Pro and Am each won about half of the matches that didn't end in ties.* Both averaged about 78 strokes for a round.

The *top* pros in the world, we found, would win more than half the time. We didn't (and couldn't) build in the nerves an amateur might feel if he was playing against a pro in a real match. But our simulation showed that an average tour pro and a typical 90-golfer would be nearly evenly matched in our hypothetical scramble match.

Surprised? Think how hard it is for a pro at each step of the way in worst-ball scramble. Two quality shots are needed from every position. The average tour pro hits 63% of fairways, so with two chances he'll be in the fairway only 40% of the time. Hitting a green with an approach shot requires two successful shots, which is made harder with more shots starting from the rough. Tour pros get up and down from the sand about half the time, so in worst-ball scramble it would have to happen less than one time in four. (In fact, because two shots are involved, a sand save happens less than one time in five for a pro in this format.) Sinking a 10-footer for par doesn't count unless the next one is sunk as well.

The pro will take about four extra putts per round as a result. From ShotLink data, we know that pros birdie about one in five holes. Taking the worst score of each hole means, roughly, that they'll birdie only one in 25 holes. Taking the worst of each shot is even tougher than the worst score of each hole. All of these factors lead to an average score of 78 for the pro in worst-ball scramble.

We see pros hitting beautiful shots with such consistency; it is easy to imagine that a worst-ball scramble wouldn't hurt their score by much. Amateurs hit so many poor shots—often several in a row—that a best-ball scramble might not appear to help very much. But both are illusions. Table 4.1 shows how golfers would be likely to fare playing several variations of the scramble format. An 80-golfer playing a best-ball scramble on all shots would average 70 strokes for a round, and would likely destroy a pro playing worst-ball scramble on all shots. A more competitive match would have the pro play the worst of two tee shots and then one ball from there.

Table 4.1 shows that scores go up in worst-shot scrambles more than they go down in best-shot scrambles. Bad shots hurt scores far more than good shots help.

Table 4.1. Average scores of golfers playing a challenging 6,500-yard course under several scramble formats. Column "All" is the format described in the chapter in which the best or worst of two balls is played for every shot. Column "Off green" means that two balls are played until the best or worst of two balls finishes on the green. From there the golfer putts one ball into the hole. Column "Tee only" means that two balls are played on the tee shot of each hole. After choosing the best or worst of the two tee shots, the golfer plays one ball into the hole. The worst-of-two scramble results for the 100-golfer aren't given because of the torture it would be for the group playing behind.

Golfer	One ball	Worst-of-two scramble			Best-of-two scramble		
		All	Off green	Tee only	Tee only	Off green	All
PGA Tour pro	68	78	76	71	66	63	60
80-golfer	80	97	93	83	77	73	70
90-golfer	90	112	107	93	86	82	78
100-golfer	100	-	-	-	95	90	85

Better-ball simulation

It might help to compare the scramble results with the best scores on a hole-by-hole basis. Many golfers are familiar with the latter format, called "better ball," in which two players form a team and the team score on a hole is the lower of the two individual scores. When there is a better-ball competition between two teams of two golfers, it is more formally called "fourball."

Table 4.2 shows average scores in better-ball and worst-ball formats. If a team of two 90-golfers took the best of their two scores on each hole, their team would average a score of 81. If they took the worst of their two scores on each hole, their team would average a score of 99.

A scramble that takes the best of two shots leads to a lower score than taking the best of two hole scores. Consistent with this observation, Tables 4.1 and 4.2 show that a team of two 90-golfers shoots an average 78 in a "best of each shot" scramble but only 81 in the "best of each hole" better-ball format. Likewise, a scramble that takes the worst of two shots leads to a higher score than taking the worst of two hole scores. Tables 4.1 and 4.2 show that a team of two 90-golfers shoots an average 112 in a "worst of each shot" scramble but only 99 in the "worst of each hole" better-ball format.

Table 4.2. Average scores of teams of two golfers playing in better-ball and worst-ball formats. In better ball, the best of two scores on each hole is counted. In worst ball, the worst of two scores on each hole is counted.

Golfer	One ball	Teams of two	
		Better ball	Worst ball
70-golfer	70	64	76
80-golfer	80	73	87
90-golfer	90	81	99
100-golfer	100	89	111

Why trust simulation results?

How can the results of a computer simulation be trusted? History is rife with examples of fiascos caused by bugs in computer programs, which are ultimately caused by human error. The $300 million Mars Climate Orbiter, launched by NASA in December 1998, crashed because a programmer forgot to convert numbers from English into metric units. Computer programming errors have caused power blackouts, helicopter crashes, and overdoses of radiation given to cancer patients. Fortunately, even though software errors abound, those that cause catastrophes are rare.

A simulation model that lives inside a computer is necessarily a simplification of reality, so we need ways to validate the results. We check our golf simulation results against the scores, standard statistics (number of putts, number of fairways hit, driving distance, and so forth), and shot patterns from actual ShotLink data. We check that the average distance to the hole after a shot from 150 yards from the rough in the simulation matches the data. We check that scores on 180-yard par-three holes match, we check that the fraction of sand saves from 30 yards match, and we check that the fraction of three-putts from 40 feet match, to give just a few examples. Knowing that simulation results match the data for regular rounds of golf gives us confidence that the results in Table 4.1 reflect what would happen in real scramble matches. Figure 4.1 illustrates a small simulation of a 90-golfer's play on a par-four hole.

Of course, your actual mileage may vary, depending on many factors. For example, if our amateur is a 90-golfer (on the 6,500-yard course) but plays the PGA Tour pro on a 7,100-yard championship course, the advantage in the scramble match would go to the professional: The 90-golfer would average 82 and the pro would average 80, according to simulation results.

Additional factors that affect the results include the number and type of hazards on the course, width of fairways, weather conditions, and course setup. Golfers come in all shapes and sizes, and different 90-golfers would have slightly different scramble results. Some 90-golfers are long drivers with poor short games. Other 90-golfers aren't as long but they play steady golf and are good putters. Some golfers might relish the pressure of the scramble format; others not. While many factors influence scramble scores, the simulation results give a good idea what can be expected.

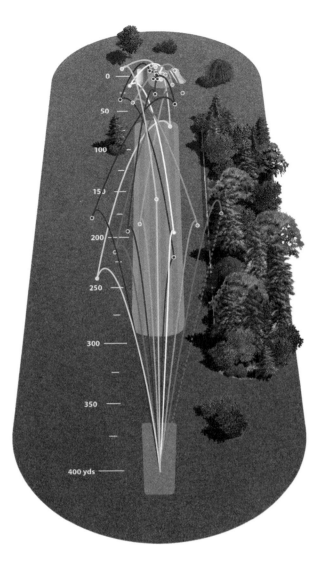

Figure 4.1. Simulation of plays of a par-four hole by a 90-golfer. In a real experiment, hundreds or thousands of plays of a hole would be simulated to determine the fraction of fairways hit, fraction of shots hit out of bounds, average hole score, fraction of birdies, pars, bogeys, and other quantities of interest. The simulation model is built from real data, but can be used to analyze a golfer's play on a new hole, say a longer or shorter hole, or a hole with a different-width fairway.

Table 4.1 serves as a useful benchmark for different types of games and practice. Worst-ball and best-ball scramble can be a fun alternative to playing a match with handicap strokes. Scramble can also be combined with best-ball or worst-ball by hole. For example, consider a foursome with two 80-golfers and two 100-golfers. The two 100-golfers could play best-ball scramble, with an average score of 85. The two 80-golfers could play worst-ball by hole, with an average score of 87 (so they'd be at a slight disadvantage).

Worst-ball and best-ball scramble formats are valuable for practice, and they provide an interesting change of pace. Luke Donald often uses a variation of worst-ball scramble when he practices. Worst-ball scramble is great practice because it provides a real test of concentration, patience, and consistency. It can help change the habits of a golfer who has a tendency to take too many risks on the course. It adds pressure and forces the golfer to focus on every shot and putt. If it's too hard playing all the way into the hole, you can make it easier by playing one ball once you reach the green, or even easier by playing the worst of two tee shots only. Practice using the best-ball scramble format is not only a lot of fun; it is fantastic for building confidence. It shows a golfer's scoring potential when the number of poor shots is reduced.

Legendary golfer Ben Hogan is said to have prepared for majors by playing worst-ball scramble. At the peak of his career, Greg Norman practiced using worst-ball scramble. "I'd play two golf balls, and you always had to hit the worst shot. So if you hit a great drive, you had to hit the next drive great, too," Norman said. "The best score I remember playing was 72. So, it really makes you concentrate." According to our simulation, a typical tour pro would average about 80 playing worst-ball scramble on a championship course. A golfer's best worst-ball score is lower than his average by about eight strokes, so Norman's best worst-ball score of 72 is perfectly consistent with our simulation results.

Hall of Fame golfer Lanny Wadkins won 21 tournaments on the PGA Tour, including the PGA Championship in 1977. He was ranked in the top 10 golfers in the world for 86 weeks between 1986, when the Official World Golf Rankings started, and 1988. In 1989, Wadkins was challenged to a worst-ball-pro/best-ball-amateur scramble match by businessman Jim Leake. The match is described in Leake's book *Reflections of a Society Gambler*. Leake was an eight-handicap golfer, so his average score was about 85 on a 6,500-yard course. According to our simulation results, Leake should have had an advantage in this format, even over one of the best golfers in the world. The match was held at Preston Trail Golf Club in Dallas. More than 100 people turned out to follow the two golfers, and there were reports of $30,000 or more wagered on the match.

The outcome of a single match can't prove or disprove anything, but it can add or subtract credence to the simulation results. What happened? Leake won on the 17th hole, two holes up. He wrote of best-ball/worst-ball, "This format heavily favors the eight-handicap golfer over the world's best golfers." Leake said he would be willing to wager a "*very, very* large amount" on the outcome. I wouldn't bet against him.

Switcheroo: the long game versus the short game

Would you score better if you had a PGA Tour pro hit all of your shots outside 100 yards from the hole, or if the pro hit all of your shots within 100 yards of the hole? This format, with partners switching the ball they hit at 100 yards, is sometimes called "switcheroo." What fun to be partnered with a pro in this format. Pros are better than amateurs at every type of shot. Pros drive it longer and straighter, hit approach shots closer to the hole, get up and down more often, and sink more putts.

But is the scoring difference between pros and amateurs due more to long shots or to short shots? A switcheroo format, in real time or played in a computer simulation, is a good way to explore the importance of the long game. Which would you pick, the team of the pro hitting the long shots and amateur hitting the short shots (team Pro-long/Am-short) or the team in which the amateur hits the long shots and the pro hits the short shots (team Am-long/Pro-short)?

It's pretty clear which team sports psychologist Bob Rotella would pick. Rotella coaches the mental side of the golf game, and his clients include golf luminaries Tom Kite, Ernie Els, Davis Love III, Pádraig Harrington, and Keegan Bradley. In his book *Golf Is Not a Game of Perfect,* he describes a contest similar to switcheroo between Tom Kite and an amateur "duffer." Rotella says, "I am prepared to bet that the score of the ball Tom takes over from the duffer will be lower than the score of the ball the duffer takes over from Tom." If you gave most 20-handicappers the short game of Nick Price, says Rotella, "they'd be shooting in the 70s instead of the 90s."

It's interesting to speculate on which team would win, but for me, it's more fun to investigate objectively, using real data and unbiased analysis. An obvious way to answer the switcheroo question is to get a group of pros and amateurs together playing switcheroo and see what happens. To get definitive results would require a large

Gene Sarazen, winner of the 1923 PGA at Pelham Country Club

number of golfers, but Connell Barrett of *Golf* magazine tried just such an experiment.

Connell and I arranged a switcheroo match between two PGA club professionals and two amateur golfers at Pelham Country Club, best known for hosting the 1923 PGA Championship. The 36-hole match play final of that 1923 tournament, contested by two of the best golfers of the era, Walter Hagen and Gene Sarazen, is considered by many to be the most dramatic in the history of the PGA. The two golfers were tied after the morning 18. Hagen came back from two down with three holes to play to send the match into sudden death. On the 38th hole, Sarazen hit a niblick, roughly equivalent to a 9-iron, from heavy rough to two feet to set up the winning birdie. Asked later about playing Hagen in match play, Sarazen said, "I knew that Hagen could play magnificent recovery shots, and I knew how good he was on the greens, but I figured I was a better shotmaker than he was. I felt I could beat him by outplaying him from tee to green."

Our match was contested by Pelham Country Club's head professional Mike Diffley and assistant pro Dennis Hillman. Diffley won the Met Open in 1991, the same tournament won by Gene Sarazen in 1925 when it was considered to be a major. Hillman defeated a 14-year-old named Tiger Woods in the semifinals of the 1990 U.S. Junior Amateur.

In golf, your "Tiger Woods number" is the smallest number of games connecting you to Tiger Woods. Thanks to my having played a match against Dennis Hillman, and Dennis having played against Tiger Woods, my "Tiger number" is just two. The transitive property doesn't apply in golf, however. Even though I beat Dennis once, and Dennis beat Tiger once, my chances of beating Tiger are infinitesimally small. Tiger numbers are explored in a small book by Fran Scheid, who played an instrumental part in the development of the USGA's handicap system.

Back to our switcheroo match. The two amateur competitors were Lou Aronne, physician, author, and 16-handicapper, and Ken Chow, graduate student and 17-handicapper. A coin toss selected Mike Diffley and Lou Aronne as the Pro-long/Am-short team. Ken Chow and Dennis Hillman formed the Am-long/Pro-short team. For Mike and Dennis, this match wasn't about any long-game versus short-game theory; their pride was on the line. Mike said confidently, "I will hit every green in regulation and hit it close because it's my home course." Dennis countered that he'd get up and down from anywhere.

I'll describe a few holes to illustrate the "switch at 100 yards" format and show how the nine-hole match developed. On a sunny summer afternoon at Pelham, the two teams started on the short downhill par-three 10th hole. Mike opened with a crisp short iron, stopping it on the hard green 18 feet from the hole. Ken's tee shot landed on the green, but without enough spin it rolled off, leaving Dennis a difficult 10-yard bunker shot. At this point, the Pro-long/Am-short team had the advantage. It was more likely that Dennis would not get a sand save than Lou would three-putt. Dennis swung hard, splashing his ball onto the green with enough spin to stop it on the slick green six feet from the hole. Lou's tentative putt came up two feet short, but he tapped in for par. Dennis calmly sank the six-footer to tie the hole.

On the 16th hole, Mike chose a 3-wood to stay short of a fairway bunker. Hitting driver, Ken managed to avoid the bunker and landed in the right side of the fairway. Mike continued his strong iron play, hitting onto the green 10 feet from the hole. Ken faced a 135-yard shot with a small pond between his ball and the hole, and he had to worry about a tree just to the right of his intended line. Ken chunked his shot into the pond. "Just a horrible, fat, ugly swing," Ken said. After the penalty stroke, Dennis still had 95 yards to the hole from the rough. His short-game magic deserted him this time, and after Lou's low-stress two-putt par, team Pro-long/Am-short picked up three shots on the hole.

Team Pro-long/Am-short led by two shots going into the final hole. On the par-three 18th, Mike hit a gorgeous 175-yard iron to nine feet. Faced with another shot over water, this time Ken delivered, landing his shot on the green, 27 feet from the hole. At this point on the hole, the odds again favored the Pro-long/Am-short team, but Dennis confidently sank the 27-footer for birdie. Lou put a nice stroke on his birdie putt, but the nine-footer hit the edge and didn't drop. Team Pro-long/Am-short gave one shot back on the hole, but they won the nine-hole match by one stroke.

This one match provides just an inkling of the truth about the switch-eroo question. It would take many matches to give a definitive answer to which team is more likely to win in this test of the long game versus the short game. Rather than recruiting many pros and amateurs to play real matches, we did the next-best thing. We used a database of real golf shots actually hit by pros and amateurs to simulate many matches. We took thousands of long shots of pros and then paired them with thousands of short shots of amateurs to generate computer-simulated Pro-long/Am-short golf rounds. Similarly, we used thousands of long shots taken by actual amateurs, and thousands of short shots taken by pros, and simulated Am-long/Pro-short golf rounds.

The results of hundreds of simulated rounds clearly show that the long game (shots starting outside of 100 yards from the hole) explains more of the scoring difference between pros and amateurs than the short game. The bottom line is given in Table 4.3. Amateur golfers would score better by having PGA Tour pros hit the long shots, outside of 100 yards from the hole, rather than the short-game shots and putts inside of 100 yards. For an amateur with an average score of 90 on a 6,500-yard course, the Pro-long/Am-short team would score an average of seven strokes better than the Am-long/Pro-short team. The Pro-long/Am-short advantage increases to nine strokes on a 7,200-yard course. The Pro's long game advantage is even greater when paired with a 100-golfer.

Table 4.3. Average scores for teams of amateur and PGA Tour golfers. Pro-long/Am-short means the PGA Tour pro golfer plays long shots that start outside of 100 yards from the hole and the amateur golfer plays all shots and putts starting within 100 yards of the hole. If the PGA Tour golfer plays the long shots and the 90-golfer plays the short shots on the 6,500-yard course, their average score will be 74. However, if the 90-golfer plays the long shots and the PGA Tour golfer plays the short shots on the same course, their average score will be 81, or seven strokes higher. In all cases, the average score of the Pro-long/Am-short team is lower than that of the Am-long/Pro-short team. The difference is larger for less-skilled amateur golfers. The Pro-long/Am-short teams do relatively better on the longer 7,200-yard course.

Am golfer	6,500-yard course			7,200-yard course		
	Pro-long / Am-short	Am-long / Pro-short	Difference	Pro-long / Am-short	Am-long / Pro-short	Difference
80-golfer	70	74	4	73	78	5
90-golfer	74	81	7	77	86	9
100-golfer	77	87	10	80	93	13

The long game (shots outside of 100 yards) explains more of the scoring differences between pros and amateurs than the short game and putting.

If you still aren't convinced after all of the simulation analysis, here are some intuitive reasons to support the results, starting with a general comparison of long-game prowess for pros and amateurs.

- On many par-five holes, a PGA Tour pro is close to the green in two shots, and sometimes even on the green. Pros are usually scrambling for birdies and occasionally putting for eagles. Most amateurs need three good shots just to get within 100 yards of the hole. Often it takes four or more shots. Many times amateurs are scrambling to make par, bogey, or worse.
- A PGA Tour pro can hit a driver 280–350 yards. Their average drive is more than 290 yards. The average drive of a 90-golfer is closer to 210 yards. Pros gain 50 to 100 or more yards *on every drive* compared to the vast majority of amateurs.
- Even when the pros are hitting their drives so much farther than amateurs, they are hitting a larger fraction of fairways. Pro drives are not only longer, they're also straighter.
- Pros hit approach shots about half as far from the hole as amateurs.

These skill differences on long-game shots add up to a ton of strokes. But what about skill differences in putting?

- Pros and amateurs both make most of their very short putts.
- Both pros and amateurs miss most of their long putts, so the overall gain from putting is modest.
- Even for an amateur, it is hard to hit a putt out of bounds!

Sure, pros putt better than amateurs, but it is rare for an amateur to lose two strokes on a single green compared to a pro. It is easy for an amateur to lose two strokes to a pro in the long game by hitting a shot out of bounds or losing a ball. Pros are better than amateurs in every phase of the game, but the long game accounts for more of the separation between pros and amateurs than the short game and putting combined. Notice what I didn't claim. I didn't claim that these results are true for every individual golfer. I'm sure in the world there are amateur golfers with pro-quality long games and short games that keep them from playing on tour. But these aren't your typical 80-golfers or 90-golfers. I didn't say that your score would be better when your long game is "on" compared to when your short game is "on." You might have a pretty consistent long game and score best when you get a hot putter. Our simulation compared many pros and amateurs, not the long game and short game of a single amateur.

You still might not be convinced by my simulation results, or swayed by the analysis. If you are still skeptical, then you may be surprised that Dave Pelz, a well-known expert on the short game, and coach to Phil Mickelson and other tour pros, agrees with me. John Paul Newport wrote a *Wall Street Journal* article titled "The Short Game's the Thing? Nope" in which he presented some of my evidence for the importance of the long game. In researching the article, he interviewed Dave Pelz, who said, "If you could improve any one aspect of your game to pro level, what would you choose? It would be the long game, absolutely." In the comments section of the *Journal*'s website, John Paul Newport continued, "Pelz and Broadie agree that for almost everyone, the best and surest way to lower your score is to work on the short game, because rapid improvement is possible there, quickly. Making substantial improvements in the long game takes months and years of hard work. But that's a different issue than where players actually lose the most strokes to par or to the field."

Effect of a larger golf hole

Who would benefit more from a larger hole: good putters or poor putters? Some would argue that good putters suffer from more lip outs and putts that burn the edge without dropping, while poor putters tend to miss badly. A slightly larger hole would lead to more putts dropping by good putters than poor putters, so the good putters would benefit more, or so this argument goes. Others feel that poor putters would gain: Luke Donald told me that his distance control was a big advantage, and he felt that a larger hole would negate this effect. He argued that a larger hole would reduce his putting advantage.

To get more people to play golf, and for golf to be more fun and faster to play, Jack Nicklaus hosted a tournament in September 2011 at Muirfield Village with an eight-inch-diameter hole instead of the traditional four and a quarter inches. Inspired by a suggestion of TaylorMade CEO Mark King, a massive 15-inch-diameter hole was used at *Golf Digest*'s W I D E Open Championship in March 2011.

These were not the first times a larger hole was suggested. Golfer Gene Sarazen believed that putting was too important in golf, so he proposed an eight-inch-diameter hole back in 1933. Harry Vardon, holder of a record six British Open championships from 1896 to 1914, said, "Truly the putting has too great an effect on the results." Ben Hogan expressed a similar view. Sarazen and Hogan felt a larger hole would make putting less important by narrowing the gap between the best and worst putters. In a May 2005 article in *Golf Digest*, Johnny Miller argued the opposite in writing, "If they widened the hole tomorrow the best putters, Loren Roberts, Tiger Woods and Phil Mickelson, would run the tables every week."

Who decided on the current 4.25-inch-diameter hole? In 1829, a golf superintendent at the Musselburgh Golf Club invented a hole cutter from some excess pipe that was lying around. The pipe just happened to be 4.25 inches in diameter. Hole sizes weren't very uniform before then. The rule makers at the Royal and Ancient officially adopted the size in their rules for 1891.

My son Christopher putting to an eight-inch-diameter hole

Which side is right on the effect of the larger hole? There's only very limited amateur data and no data from professionals playing tournaments with a larger hole. Collecting pro data under tournament conditions would be incredibly expensive. Simulation is ideally suited to answer the question. Simulation can fully take into account that gravity will have a larger effect with a larger hole size, and it can also account for changes in putting strategies that respond to the larger hole size.

Our simulation of thousands of pro and amateur putts to a hypothetical larger hole shows that Luke Donald and Gene Sarazen were right: Poor putters would benefit from a larger hole more than good putters. Simulation results with an eight-inch-diameter hole show that a typical pro putter would gain five strokes from a larger hole; a 90-golfer would gain 6.5 strokes.[1] The gap between good and poor putters narrows with a larger hole. Here's the intuition: Poor putters have more room for improvement, so the larger hole will benefit them more. Pro putters rarely three-putt and they average about seven one-putts and 11 two-putts in 18 holes. The only room for improvement is turning some two-putts into one-putts. With a larger hole, a 90-golfer will eliminate most three-putts and will have a bigger increase in one-putt holes.

---

[1] Details are given in Bansal and Broadie, 2008, "A Simulation Model to Analyze the Impact of Hole Size on Putting in Golf," in *Proceedings of the 2008 Winter Simulation Conference*.

A larger hole narrows the difference between good and poor putters, making putting less important. At the extreme, every golfer could add one stroke onto his or her score every time the ball reached the green. Then putting would have no importance, just as in Putter-Fairyland.

> A larger hole favors poor putters more than good putters; this means putting becomes less important as the hole size increases.

19th Hole Summary

- Computer simulation is a tool that allows real systems to be analyzed in a computer to gain insights that would be difficult, expensive, or simply impossible to obtain by collecting data in real time.

- Simulation of golf shots allows us to predict the outcome of various golf decisions by golfers of different skill levels.

- Simulation can help us to obtain insights into what separates pros from amateurs.

- A 90-golfer playing a best-ball scramble against the worst-ball scramble of a pro is a nearly even match.

- Worst-ball scramble is a challenging way to practice concentration, patience, consistency, and course strategy.

- Best-ball scramble builds confidence and is a fun way to shoot lower scores.

- Simulation reveals that the long game explains far more of the scoring difference between pros and amateurs than the short game and putting combined.

- The gap between good and poor putters narrows with a larger hole size.

CHAPTER 5

STROKES GAINED OFF THE GREEN: A Better Measure of Tee-to-Green Golf Performance

Rory McIlroy was voted PGA Tour player of the year in 2012. He won one major and three other tournaments, had 10 top-10 finishes (tied for the most top-10 finishes that year), had the lowest scoring average on the tour, and topped the money list. Yet a look at the stats makes it hard to figure out how he did it. For the year, he did not even make the top 50 in three of the main golf statistics: total driving, greens in regulation, and strokes gained putting. How could Rory have had such a remarkable year and yet have been mediocre in all the classic areas covered by statistics: getting off the tee, getting to the green, and getting the ball in the hole? Something is rotten in the land of standard golf stats.

Standard golf stats are deficient in several ways when it comes to linking golf skill to golf scores. One deficiency is the loss of information. Recording only that a fairway was missed loses information about whether the shot finished in the sand, rough, water, or out of bounds. Recording only that a green was hit loses information about how close the shot finished to the hole. A more subtle loss of information happens because many standard stats are averages, and the averaging process loses information. Two golfers can average the same distance from the hole, but their shots can have very different impacts on scores. For example, an inconsistent golfer hits one shot to two feet and another to 28 feet; a consistent golfer hits two shots to 15 feet. Both average 15 feet from the hole, but the inconsistent golfer has a distinct scoring advantage since he is likely to sink the two-footer.

Another deficiency in standard stats is incommensurability. This is a fancy way of saying that it's hard to compare stats measured in different units, such as driving distance (measured in yards) and putts (counted by number). The "total driving" stat attempts to measure driving skill by adding a golfer's driving distance rank to his driving accuracy rank, but this creates more problems than it solves. Treating distance and accuracy ranks equally is questionable. Adding two ranks is simply mathematical nonsense. Golfers ranked 50 and 70 are 20 apart, as are golfers ranked one and 21. But the latter pairing typically reflects a much bigger difference in skill than the former. Rory McIlroy's driving distance rank was five, but he was crushed in the total driving stat because his driving accuracy rank in 2012 was 156.

The strokes gained stat solves all of these problems by tracking the quality of individual shots, and by measuring shot quality in a common unit: strokes. We've seen how strokes gained works for putting. In this chapter, we'll extend the strokes gained idea to golf shots from the tee to the green. When Rory's year is viewed through the strokes gained lens, we'll see that he was first in total strokes gained (consistent with the lowest scoring average), second in strokes gained driving, second in strokes gained approach shots, 35th in strokes gained short game, and 73rd in strokes gained putting. Strokes gained paints a clear picture: Rory's long game contributed the most to his stellar season. This chapter explains the simple concept behind strokes gained and shows how it matches our golf intuition and how easy it is to compute.

What makes for a good golf stat?

The answer to that question depends on what you are trying to measure. In baseball, batting average was long the main stat used to measure proficiency at the plate. Then came Bill James, the pioneer of the sabermetrics revolution in baseball stats that was popularized in the book and movie *Moneyball*. James showed that another stat, the on-base plus slugging percentage (OPS), is a better predictor of a batter's contribution to runs scored. Even though batting average is still the hitting stat that you see on TV and in newspapers, OPS has been widely accepted as much better at measuring a batter's value to his team.

In golf, if you want to know who's the longest driver, then driving distance is a good place to start.[2] But golf tournaments aren't long-driving contests. While it's fun to know who drives the longest, driving distance is only one component of scoring, and an indirect one at that. A more useful measure would be a driving stat that tells how much driving contributes to scoring. I'd like to know who's the *best* driver on tour, not who's the *longest* driver on tour. Strokes gained driving, the new stat described in this chapter, does just that.

Other stats in the strokes gained family can answer similar questions relating golf skill to golf scores. Where do the 10 strokes that separate 90-golfers from 80-golfers come from? What separates the best pros from average pros? Who has the best sand game on tour? The promise of strokes gained is to answer these questions by measuring the quality of all types of golf shots, not just putts. And you don't need an advanced degree from Columbia to understand it. I hope to convince you that strokes gained is a simple, intuitive, and powerful statistic. It's simple because the math only involves subtraction. It's intuitive because the answers make good golf sense. And it's powerful because it can be used to accurately measure performance of all types of golf shots.

No stat is perfect, and strokes gained is limited by what is contained in the data. There is no information about whether an approach shot started from a divot, whether a shot hit a rock in a pond and bounced onto the green, or whether a sand shot started in a footprint. In defense of strokes gained, this information isn't factored into greens in regulation, sand saves, or any of the other standard golf stats either. There's no stat for putts per round adjusted for spike marks, or fairways hit adjusted for bounces off trees. If it's not in the data, it can't be in the stat. But the ShotLink professional data and Golfmetrics amateur data capture the most important information about golf shots: where they start and where they finish. As more information becomes available, strokes gained can be refined and improved, but the current data are good enough for calculating driving's contribution to scores.

---

[2] Even this simple stat has issues. When PGA Tour pros play at the Plantation course in Kapalua, Hawaii, elevation changes and wind lead to more 400-yard drives than on any other course on tour. The average driving distance stat can be improved to take into account varying course and weather conditions that significantly affect driving distance.

How strokes gained works

With apologies to my friend Jason Day for baring one of his rare flubs, let's analyze how he played the par-four 13th hole at Kapalua in the Hyundai Tournament of Champions in 2011. By rating his four shots on this hole, we'll get a sense of how strokes gained works. Jason played in the tournament thanks to his victory at the HP Byron Nelson Championship the previous year. Later in 2011, he was ranked as high as number seven in the world, at age 23, after finishing second in the Masters and U.S. Open. Jason's incredible talent has been guided by his longtime coach, Colin Swatton, who watched this round from the sidelines.

Top: Jason Day after his tee shot. Bottom, left to right: Colin Swatton (Jason's coach), the author, and Jason Day

The 13th hole at Kapalua is just under 400 yards long, and the PGA Tour average score on this hole is four strokes. On that day in 2011, on that hole, Jason hit a remarkable tee shot for a pro. His driver hit the turf a couple of inches behind the ball, and the result was a drop-kick shot that traveled a grand total of 106 yards, but finished in the fairway. Many amateurs would turn red with a combination of anger, frustration, disappointment, and embarrassment at such a shot. Nick Faldo described Jason's reaction on live TV: "He's laughing his head off."

The shot was funny because it was so unusual. From the fairway, starting at 278 yards from the hole, Jason's second shot landed in a bunker 62 yards from the hole. With the pin on the back of the green, he exploded from the sand onto the green 17 feet from the hole. He then sank the putt for par. The recovery from a difficult situation says a lot about Jason's mental game, and his ability to forget about one shot and focus on the next, traits that surely affected his skill at golf. His shots on the 13th hole are illustrated in Figure 5.1.

Figure 5.1. Jason Day's play on the par-four 13th hole at Kapalua.

Table 5.1. For each of the four shots, rate the shot as better or worse than an average pro shot. Then estimate the strokes gained for each shot.

Shot	Distance to hole (start)	End location	Distance to hole (end)	Shot quality (better or worse than average?)	Strokes gained
1	394 (yards)	Fairway	278 (yards)		
2	278 (yards)	Sand	62 (yards)		
3	62 (yards)	Green	17 (feet)		
4	17 (feet)	Hole	0		

To rate each of Jason's shots qualitatively, we can ask if each seemed better or worse than an average pro shot. To check your golf intuition, write your answers in Table 5.1 before proceeding. In one column, note whether you think each shot is better or worse than an average pro shot. In the right-hand column, estimate the strokes gained for each shot. The latter is harder, but just give your best guess.

Was Jason's tee shot better or worse than an average pro tee shot? Clearly it was worse. That means the strokes gained of his tee shot was negative: He lost strokes relative to an average pro tee shot. How many strokes do you think he lost? A whiff—a complete miss—would lose one stroke. But since he advanced the ball 106 yards into the fairway, it wasn't as bad as that. (It wasn't one of those shots that don't travel beyond the ladies' tees, where tradition used to dictate that if you hit the shot that poorly you were supposed to whip it out and finish the hole in that condition to show your lack of manliness.) He lost between zero and one stroke on the shot, and closer to the latter, so let's estimate that he lost 0.7 strokes on his tee shot.

His second shot traveled 216 yards and finished in a bunker 62 yards from the hole. Was it better or worse than an average pro shot? It's rare that pros hit the green from that far, but it wasn't a good "leave." I'd say this shot was below average. How many strokes do you think it lost? Let's estimate that Jason lost 0.5 strokes on his second shot.

His third shot from the bunker finished on the green 17 feet from the hole. Better or worse than average? Some say a long bunker shot is the hardest shot in golf. Even for a pro, finishing on the green is a good outcome; finishing within 20 feet of the hole is even better. This shot is clearly better than average. How many shots do you think it gained? Let's estimate that he gained 0.4 strokes on his sand shot.

His fourth shot was a putt from 17 feet that he holed. Clearly better than average. We know that a one-putt from 30 feet gains one stroke, and a one-putt from eight feet gains a half stroke. So a one-putt from 17 feet gains between 0.5 and 1 stroke. In fact, he gained 0.8 strokes with his putt.

In order, we've rated Jason's four shots as below average, below average, above average, and above average, with corresponding strokes gained -0.7, -0.5, 0.4, and 0.8. His score on the hole, four, matched the tour average, so his total strokes gained on the hole must be zero, and it is. Though none of his shots was average, the sum total of his play on the hole was average for a pro. Assigning exact strokes gained numbers is hard—that's where the millions of shots in the ShotLink database come into play. You might have guessed individual numbers that differed somewhat, but you'd probably agree that he started the hole with two poor shots and then came back with two good shots to salvage a par. Strokes gained allows us to quantify our golf intuition.

If Jason played all holes like this one, strokes gained analysis would show that his long game was very poor and his short game was superb. He'd be ranked as the worst driver on tour and the greatest putter of all time. While one hole of play isn't enough to allow us to draw any meaningful conclusions, the same analysis can be done over many holes and rounds to identify a golfer's strengths and weaknesses.

Calculating strokes gained values

Golf is about getting the ball in the hole in the fewest possible strokes. One shot is better than another if it moves the ball closer to the ultimate goal of a hole out. The important twist is that strokes gained defines closer in terms of number of strokes remaining to hole out, not in terms of distance. Why? Because three feet on a drive isn't worth the same as three feet on a putt. A drive that travels one yard longer isn't much "closer" to the ultimate goal. But a putt that finishes three feet closer—say, two feet from the hole instead of five—is considerably closer to a hole out. Strokes gained measures progress to the hole in terms of the average number of strokes to hole out, not by the distance to the hole. For any golf shot, strokes gained is the decrease in the average number of strokes to hole out minus one to account for the stroke taken.

> The strokes gained of a golf shot is the decrease in the average number of strokes to hole out minus one to account for the stroke taken.

Let's apply it to Jason's tee shot. The shot started 394 yards from the hole. According to Table 5.2, the PGA Tour average strokes to hole out is 4.0 from this distance. The shot finished in the fairway 278 yards from the hole, where the average strokes to hole out is 3.7. He progressed 0.3 strokes "closer" to the hole with his tee shot. But he took one stroke, giving a strokes gained value of -0.7 (a decrease of 0.3 in the average strokes to hole out minus one to account for the stroke). His below-average tee shot lost 0.7 strokes to the PGA Tour average.

Once you have access to a database showing average strokes to hole out from any given distance, there's no rocket science involved in calculating strokes gained, just subtraction. Okay, I confess that I use a computer to do subtraction these days, but I could do it myself if I had to.

The same procedure can be used for each of his shots. His second shot started in the fairway 278 yards from the hole. As we just saw, the tour average strokes to hole out is 3.7 from this position. The shot finished in the sand 62 yards from the hole, where, according to Table 5.2, the average strokes to hole out is 3.2. He progressed 0.5 strokes closer to the hole (3.7 minus 3.2), but he took a full stroke to do it, so the strokes gained for the shot is -0.5 (a decrease of 0.5 in the average strokes to hole out minus one to account for the stroke). His below-average fairway shot lost 0.5 strokes to the PGA Tour average.

Jason's third shot started in the sand 62 yards from the hole, where the tour average strokes to hole out is 3.2. The tour average on this 62-yard bunker shot is larger than the tour average from 200 yards from the tee. Long bunker shots are hard! Yet his bunker shot finished on the green 17 feet from the hole, where the tour average to hole out is 1.8. He progressed 1.4 strokes closer to the hole (3.2 minus 1.8), so the strokes gained for the shot is 0.4 (a decrease of 1.4 in the average strokes to hole out minus one to account for the stroke). His above-average bunker shot gained 0.4 strokes against the PGA Tour average.

Table 5.2. Pro baseline: average strokes to hole out by distance. For example, starting from the tee 400 yards from the hole, PGA Tour pros average 3.99 strokes to hole out. Starting on the green eight feet from the hole, the PGA Tour average strokes to hole out is 1.50. Note that the "fairway" category also includes the "fairway fringe" or "first cut." A *recovery* is an obstructed shot to the hole, e.g., a shot from behind a tree that forces a pitch back to the fairway. For more information on the treatment of recovery shots, penalty shots, and out of bounds shots in strokes gained computations, see Broadie, M., 2012, "Assessing Golfer Performance on the PGA TOUR," *Interfaces*, Vol. 42, No. 2, 146–65.

Distance (yards)	Tee	Fairway	Rough	Sand	Recovery	Distance (feet)	Green
20		2.40	2.59	2.53		3	1.04
40		2.60	2.78	2.82		4	1.13
60		2.70	2.91	3.15		5	1.23
80		2.75	2.96	3.24		6	1.34
100	2.92	2.80	3.02	3.23	3.80	7	1.42
120	2.99	2.85	3.08	3.21	3.78	8	1.50
140	2.97	2.91	3.15	3.22	3.80	9	1.56
160	2.99	2.98	3.23	3.28	3.81	10	1.61
180	3.05	3.08	3.31	3.40	3.82	15	1.78
200	3.12	3.19	3.42	3.55	3.87	20	1.87
220	3.17	3.32	3.53	3.70	3.92	30	1.98
240	3.25	3.45	3.64	3.84	3.97	40	2.06
260	3.45	3.58	3.74	3.93	4.03	50	2.14
280	3.65	3.69	3.83	4.00	4.10	60	2.21
300	3.71	3.78	3.90	4.04	4.20	90	2.40
320	3.79	3.84	3.95	4.12	4.31		
340	3.86	3.88	4.02	4.26	4.44		
360	3.92	3.95	4.11	4.41	4.56		
380	3.96	4.03	4.21	4.55	4.66		
400	3.99	4.11	4.30	4.69	4.75		
420	4.02	4.15	4.34	4.73	4.79		
440	4.08	4.20	4.39	4.78	4.84		
460	4.17	4.29	4.48	4.87	4.93		
480	4.28	4.40	4.59	4.98	5.04		
500	4.41	4.53	4.72	5.11	5.17		
520	4.54	4.66	4.85	5.24	5.30		
540	4.65	4.78	4.97	5.36	5.42		
560	4.74	4.86	5.05	5.44	5.50		
580	4.79	4.91	5.10	5.49	5.55		
600	4.82	4.94	5.13	5.52	5.58		

If Jason had put his bunker shot to one foot from the hole, he would have gained 1.2 strokes. A hole out from the bunker would have gained 2.2 strokes. A shot that lands closer to the hole is usually better and has a larger strokes gained. But closer is not always better. A shot that ends closer to the hole in the rough is not better than one that ends a little farther from the hole but on the green. Strokes gained measures closeness to the hole by the average strokes to complete the hole, not by distance. Jason's putt started 17 feet from the hole, where the tour average strokes to hole out is 1.8. He sank the putt. The decrease in the average strokes to hole out is 1.8, so the strokes gained of the putt is 0.8.

That's all there is to it! Jason's strokes gained for his four shots was -0.7, -0.5, 0.4, and 0.8. His above-average shots had positive strokes gained. His below-average shots had negative strokes gained. After two below-average shots, Jason had lost a total of 1.2 strokes, but then he gained 1.2 strokes with his final two shots. Overall, he had a total strokes gained of zero. The results are summarized in Table 5.3.

Table 5.3. Strokes gained example: Jason Day at Kapalua. The decrease in the average number of strokes to hole out is the "average strokes to hole out at the start of the shot" minus the "average strokes to hole out at the end of the shot." This decrease minus one (to account for the shot itself) is the strokes gained of the shot. The example shows Jason Day's play on the 13th hole of the second round at the 2011 Hyundai Tournament of Champions.

Shot	Distance to hole (start)	End location	Distance to hole (end)	Average strokes to hole out (start)	Average strokes to hole out (end)	Strokes gained
1	394 (yards)	Fairway	278 (yards)	4.0	3.7	-0.7
2	278 (yards)	Sand	62 (yards)	3.7	3.2	-0.5
3	62 (yards)	Green	17 (feet)	3.2	1.8	0.4
4	17 (feet)	Hole	0	1.8	0.0	0.8
					Total	0.0

A strokes gained analysis of Tiger Woods's play at the 18th hole at Bay Hill

In chapter 2 we revisited Tiger Woods's dramatic win at the 2008 Arnold Palmer Invitational at Bay Hill. He birdied the difficult final hole of the tournament to win. His 290-yard drive in the fairway, 165-yard second shot, and his winning putt are illustrated in Figure 5.2. How does strokes gained rate the quality of each of the three shots? Was the birdie due to the fractional accumulation of gains on each shot, or was it mainly due to one shot?

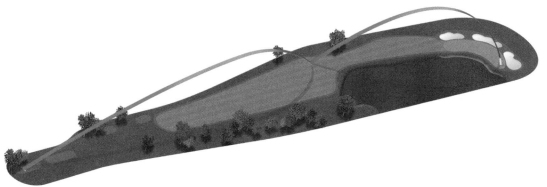

Figure 5.2. Tiger Woods's play on the par-four 18th hole at Bay Hill.

The strokes gained calculation for each of Tiger's shots is given in Table 5.4. His tee shot gained 0.1 strokes, and his approach shot gained another 0.1 strokes. Finally, his tournament-winning putt gained another 0.9 strokes. Strokes gained supports our intuition: a good drive, a good approach, and a great putt. His total gain on the hole was 1.1 strokes, with the majority of the gain coming from his putt.

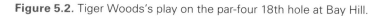

Table 5.4. Strokes gained example: Tiger Woods at Bay Hill. The decrease in the average number of strokes to hole out is the "average strokes to hole out at the start of the shot" minus the "average strokes to hole out at the end of the shot." This decrease minus one (to account for the shot itself) is the strokes gained of the shot. The example shows Tiger Woods's play on the 18th hole of the fourth round of the 2008 Arnold Palmer Bay Hill Invitational.

Shot	Distance to hole (start)	End location	Distance to hole (end)	Average strokes to hole out (start)	Average strokes to hole out (end)	Strokes gained
1	452 (yards)	Fairway	164 (yards)	4.1	3.0	0.1
2	164 (yards)	Green	24 (yards)	3.0	1.9	0.1
3	24 (yards)	Hole	0	1.9	0.0	0.9
					Total	1.1

Tiger gained 3.4 strokes per round during the tournament, with a gain of one stroke per round coming from his putting. Tiger missed 20 putts over 20 feet before sinking his final putt. So how did he gain one stroke per round with his putting? He sank five of fifteen putts between 10 and 15 feet, so his make percentage was 33% against the field average of 28%. He sank three of eight putts between 15 and 20 feet, so his make percentage was 38% against the field average of 21%. Together with additional gains on putts inside of 10 feet, the cumulative effect was a gain of 1.0 stroke per round. It is really difficult to judge a putting round based on limited information about a three-putt here or there or putting performance outside of 20 feet. Strokes gained easily summarizes and conveys the important information: Tiger gained one stroke per round with his putting, and was ranked 18th out of 120 golfers in SGP.

The total strokes gained on a hole is the sum of the strokes gained on each shot. This "additive" property extends to adding strokes gained for a round or an entire season. If a golfer gains five strokes in a round, it is possible to examine each shot to see where the gains came from. Just as we added strokes gained for all putts in computing strokes gained putting, we can add strokes gained for all drives to measure a golfer's performance on tee shots on par-four and par-five holes.

Long or steady: accuracy, distance, and strokes gained driving

Who was the best driver on the PGA Tour in the ShotLink era, from 2004 to 2012? We're not looking for the longest driver or the straightest driver, but the golfer whose tee shots on par-four and par-five holes contributed the most to his low scores. Joe Durant, a 20-year PGA Tour veteran with four victories, is one of the most accurate drivers on tour. Measuring tee shots on all par-four and par-five holes from 2004 to 2012, he hit 80% of fairways and first cuts. His average drive traveled 278 yards, compared to the tour average of 281 yards. Lee Westwood played on eight Ryder Cup teams for Europe and was ranked number one in the world in late 2010. Based on the PGA Tour ShotLink data, he hit 66% of fairways and first cuts and his drives averaged 290 yards. Durant's driving is shorter and straighter than Westwood's. Who is the better driver, Joe Durant or Lee Westwood? We'll come back to this question after comparing standard driving statistics with the strokes gained in a hypothetical match between Mr. Longdrive and Mr. Steadypro.

Mr. Longdrive and Mr. Steadypro play a 340-yard par-four hole on two consecutive days. The first day, Mr. Longdrive plays it safe, hitting an iron 220 yards in the fairway. The second day, he hits a driver 320 yards onto the green, leaving a 60-foot putt for eagle. Mr. Steadypro, meanwhile, plays the same strategy each day, both times hitting it 270 yards in the fairway. Were Mr. L's two tee shots better than Mr. S's?

Strokes gained analysis using the data from Table 5.2 shows that Mr. Longdrive gained an average of 0.34 strokes on his two tee shots, while Mr. Steadypro gained an average of 0.14 strokes.

Mr. Longdrive strokes gained tee shot 1: 3.86 - 2.85 - 1 = 0.01
Mr. Longdrive strokes gained tee shot 2: 3.86 - 2.20 - 1 = 0.66
Mr. Longdrive average strokes gained: **0.34**
Mr. Steadypro average strokes gained: 3.86 - 2.73 - 1 = **0.14**

I would much rather be in Mr. Longdrive's shoes. I hope you agree. Strokes gained results agree with our intuition. Both golfers averaged 270 yards off the tee. The average driving distance stat does not distinguish between the two sets of drives. Mr. Longdrive hit one tee shot 50 yards longer than the average, and another 50 yards shorter, but his long tee shot gained more than his short tee shot lost. Mr. Longdrive's long tee shot was better by 0.52 strokes, and this more than offset his short tee shot, which was worse by 0.13 strokes.[3]

When a long tee shot gains more than a short tee shot loses, the effect is called "nonlinear." Nonlinearities abound in real life. Ten dollars to a hungry person is worth more than 10 dollars to Bill Gates. A one-foot rise in the water level at low tide may not be noticeable, but a one-foot rise that breaches a levee could cause great damage. In golf, hitting an approach shot one foot closer to the hole hardly matters at 40 feet, but it matters a lot at five feet. Strokes gained captures this nonlinear effect by measuring the effect of each shot on a golfer's score relative to the field.

[3] Mr. Longdrive's long tee shot's strokes gained of 0.66 was an increase of 0.52 over Mr. Steadypro's strokes gained of 0.14; his short tee shot strokes gained was 0.01, a decrease of 0.13 relative to Mr. Steadypro's tee shot.

Johan Jensen, 1859–1925

Johan Jensen was a Danish engineer who worked for the Copenhagen Telephone Company. He did mathematics in his spare time and proved a fundamental result in 1906 that bears his name: Jensen's inequality. His result shows the importance of nonlinearity. A joke shows the gist of Jensen's inequality: If you put your feet in the oven and head in the refrigerator, on average you should be comfortably warm.

The real meaning of Jensen's result is that *averages are flawed when effects are nonlinear*. Applying Jensen's result to golf, we can see that average driving distance alone is doomed to failure as a measure of driving performance. It cannot capture the nonlinear effect of distance on scoring.

Put another way, the average strokes gained of a set of drives is not the same as the strokes gained of the average drive. The right way to measure driving performance is to measure the effect of each drive on score, which is exactly how strokes gained driving works.

Similarly, we can see that if you hit a drive one yard out of bounds, the effect is much greater than if you go one yard into the rough, though both count as a missed fairway under the statistic "fairways hit," a standard golf statistic that measures driving accuracy by counting the fraction of tee shots that end in the fairway. Fairways hit doesn't distinguish between a big miss (out of bounds) and a small miss (in the rough). When a drive goes out of bounds, the golfer has to retee and hit shot three because of the stroke and distance penalty. The strokes gained of the out-of-bounds drive is minus two, representing the loss of two strokes. A drive that misses the fairway by one yard in the rough, by contrast, loses only a fraction of a stroke. That the big miss and the small miss both count as a missed fairway is another example of nonlinearity.

As these examples illustrate, the average driving distance and fairways hit statistics alone aren't enough to accurately rank golfers based on their driving skill. Two golfers can have the same average driving distance and the same driving accuracy, but their driving performances can be different. It's even harder to compare the performance of golfers with different driving distance and accuracy stats, as in the case of Joe Durant and Lee Westwood.

Using the shot location information available in the PGA Tour ShotLink data and the Golfmetrics amateur data, it is possible to overcome these problems of nonlinearity. The solution is to measure the quality of each individual tee shot, taking into account both shot distance and circumstances, such as whether the ball finished in the fairway, rough, sand, trees, or worse. Strokes gained driving (SGD) is the average of the strokes gained of tee shots on par-four and par-five holes throughout a round. SGD is then used to rank golfers based on their driving performance. Note that ShotLink data do not include club information, and golfers do not use their drivers on every par-four and par-five hole. In the case that a golfer chooses another club, say, a 3-wood, long iron, or hybrid, there is an implied judgment that the shot outcome and strokes gained would be better than when hitting the driver. Strokes gained driving measures the shot outcome without regard to the actual club used.

Strokes gained per round allows for better comparisons

Table 5.5 shows the top 40 PGA Tour golfers from 2004 through 2012 ranked by strokes gained driving per round.[4] One choice in compiling the results is whether to rank golfers based on strokes gained driving per round or strokes gained driving per shot. As a pure measure of driving skill, strokes gained per shot makes more sense. Golfers, however, hit an almost equal number of par-four and par-five tee shots per round, so strokes gained per round and strokes gained per shot give virtually identical results. The per-round stat makes it easier to compare results across shot categories. For example, if we want to compare whether driving or putting explains more of the difference in round scores, we must look at per-round results, not per-shot results. For baseball fans, strokes gained per round is similar to counting hits, while strokes gained per shot is similar to batting average.

Leading the pack in strokes gained driving are Bubba Watson and Rory McIlroy. (McIlroy is included in the table with an asterisk, because he has only 120 ShotLink rounds, compared to the cutoff of 200 rounds used for other golfers.) Bubba gained 0.91 strokes per round relative to an average tour field. After winning the 2012 Masters, Bubba said, "My favorite club is the driver." Table 5.5 shows that Bubba's average drive is 20 yards longer than the tour average, though he sacrifices some accuracy. In 2008, he said, "Every man in the world wants to hit it long. They want

---

[4] Strokes gained results in Table 5.5, and elsewhere in the book, measure performance relative to an average PGA Tour field. After computing strokes gained using the baseline in Table 5.2, minor adjustments are made that account for the difficulty of each round and the strength of the field. For more of these adjustments, see page 224 in the appendix.

Table 5.5. Strokes gained driving (SGD) per round: top 40 drivers on the PGA Tour from 2004 through 2012. Ranks are out of 240 golfers with at least 200 rounds during 2004–2012, with the exception of Rory McIlroy, who has only 120 rounds of ShotLink data (and so has an asterisk by his name). The 75% driving distance measures the length of good drives: One out of four drives travels longer than the 75% distance. The penalty column reports the fraction of tee shots hit into a penalty situation.

Rank	Golfer	SGD	Average distance	75% distance	Accuracy in degrees	Fairway and first cut	Penalty
1	Rory McIlroy*	0.98	295	312	3.01	63%	1.8%
1	Bubba Watson	0.91	301	324	3.53	61%	1.7%
2	J. B. Holmes	0.84	302	323	3.78	56%	2.2%
3	Boo Weekley	0.82	287	302	2.83	72%	0.8%
4	Dustin Johnson	0.81	300	320	3.56	61%	3.1%
5	Charles Warren	0.70	290	307	3.07	68%	1.2%
6	Kenny Perry	0.64	287	303	3.04	72%	0.7%
7	Robert Garrigus	0.64	297	317	3.54	61%	1.9%
8	Brett Wetterich	0.64	294	313	3.34	63%	2.2%
9	Vijay Singh	0.64	291	306	3.24	67%	1.1%
10	Lee Westwood	0.62	290	303	3.09	66%	1.0%
11	Joe Durant	0.62	278	292	2.69	80%	0.5%
12	Josh Teater	0.61	292	308	3.23	68%	0.9%
13	Tiger Woods	0.58	289	309	3.49	64%	0.7%
14	Adam Scott	0.56	290	307	3.37	66%	1.1%
15	Angel Cabrera	0.54	294	313	3.68	59%	1.6%
16	Lucas Glover	0.54	287	305	3.17	69%	1.2%
17	Rickie Fowler	0.54	287	303	3.16	66%	1.2%
18	Martin Laird	0.53	291	309	3.26	66%	1.3%
19	Sergio Garcia	0.52	287	304	3.31	66%	1.1%
20	Charley Hoffman	0.50	290	306	3.45	64%	1.4%
21	John Rollins	0.49	286	302	3.06	72%	1.2%
22	Nick Watney	0.48	289	307	3.41	68%	1.3%
23	D. J. Trahan	0.47	285	301	3.31	71%	1.5%
24	Nicholas Thompson	0.46	287	302	3.45	71%	1.3%
25	Sean O'Hair	0.45	287	304	3.31	68%	1.3%
26	Hunter Mahan	0.45	286	301	3.01	72%	1.0%
27	Bo Van Pelt	0.45	285	302	3.12	70%	0.9%
28	John Senden	0.44	284	301	3.17	71%	0.8%
29	Robert Allenby	0.44	284	300	3.08	71%	0.8%
30	Kevin Streelman	0.44	284	301	3.45	72%	1.0%
31	Davis Love III	0.43	288	307	3.30	66%	1.1%
32	Ernie Els	0.43	285	301	3.36	66%	0.9%
33	Mathew Goggin	0.43	286	301	3.24	67%	1.5%
34	Chris Smith	0.43	287	304	3.29	69%	0.9%
35	Bill Haas	0.42	288	305	3.32	68%	1.0%
36	Greg Owen	0.42	281	296	3.24	70%	1.0%
37	Steve Marino	0.40	288	303	3.46	64%	1.0%
38	Fred Couples	0.39	289	303	3.54	63%	1.8%
39	Chris Couch	0.39	289	306	3.33	66%	1.4%
40	Phil Mickelson	0.39	292	308	3.58	62%	1.8%
	Top 40 average	0.54	289	306	3.30	67%	1.3%
	PGA Tour average	0.00	281	296	3.40	69%	1.2%

to be able to say, I hit that past you. . . . It's just one of those things that I've been lucky enough to be able to do that, so that's what everybody knows me as. I always thought it was my pretty face, but I guess not." His length off the tee led to the phrase "Bubba long." Strokes gained driving takes into account both length and accuracy, but Bubba's length more than makes up for his driving accuracy.

Now back to our earlier question of who's the better driver, Joe Durant (rank 11) or Lee Westwood (rank 10). Remember that Durant hit 80% of fairways and first cuts, and his average drive traveled 278 yards, compared to the tour average of 281 yards. Westwood hit only 66% of fairways and first cuts, but his drives averaged 290 yards. As it turns out, strokes gained analysis reveals that Durant and Westwood were tied as drivers. Each gained 0.62 strokes per round with their driving, compared to the tour average of zero. Interestingly, Durant is the only golfer in the top 40 whose driving distance is less than the tour average. Table 5.5 includes new measures of distance and accuracy. These new measures are explained in chapter 6 and are then used to show how distance and accuracy affect driving performance.

Tiger Woods was ranked 2, 4, and 4 in strokes gained driving from 2005 through 2007, yet he was ranked 86, 28, and 45 for the same three years in the total driving stat. Tiger didn't have enough rounds to be included in the official stats in 2008, the year he won four times in six starts, but he would have ranked 8 in SGD and 124 in total driving. Total driving gives a distorted view, in part because it places far too much emphasis on accuracy through the driving accuracy rank. Sean Foley, Tiger Woods's instructor, told me that Tiger would have thought very differently about his driving had strokes gained driving been available back then.

In chapter 2 we saw that putting contributes about 15% to scores. Now, using strokes gained driving, we can see the contribution of driving and putting to scores. Table 5.6 shows the top 40 golfers ranked by their total strokes gained to the field, with strokes gained broken down into three shot categories: drives, putts, and all other shots. Driving contributed an average of 28% to the scoring advantage of the top 40 golfers, putting contributed 15%, and all other shots contributed the remaining 57%.

Table 5.6 shows that there is considerable variation from one golfer to another. Driving contributed far more to Vijay Singh's scoring advantage over the field than Steve Stricker's. Yet averaged across the top 40 golfers, *driving was nearly twice as important to scoring as putting.*

In 2004–2012, driving contributed 28% to the top 40 golfers' scoring advantage, putting contributed 15%, and all other shots accounted for 57%.

Table 5.6. Total strokes gained per round broken down by shot category: top 40 golfers in total strokes gained on the PGA Tour from 2004 through 2012. Ranks are out of 240 golfers with at least 200 rounds during 2004–2012 (also included is Rory McIlroy with only 120 rounds). "Appr & short" refers to approach shots and short-game shots, that is, shots that are neither drives nor putts.

	Rank				Strokes gained per round			
Golfer	Total SG	Drive	Appr & short	Putt	Total SG	Drive	Appr & short	Putt
Tiger Woods	1	13	1	3	2.79	0.58	1.58	0.63
Jim Furyk	2	9	4	19	1.84	0.27	1.17	0.40
Luke Donald	3	29	2	1	1.82	-0.09	1.21	0.71
Phil Mickelson	4	14	3	86	1.70	0.39	1.18	0.14
Rory McIlroy*	5	1	6	153	1.66	0.98	0.75	-0.07
Vijay Singh	5	19	5	193	1.58	0.64	1.12	-0.18
Ernie Els	6	6	6	164	1.43	0.43	1.09	-0.08
Sergio Garcia	7	3	8	156	1.43	0.52	0.98	-0.07
Steve Stricker	8	32	7	13	1.34	-0.23	1.08	0.49
Adam Scott	9	10	9	178	1.33	0.56	0.89	-0.12
Zach Johnson	10	40	34	16	1.24	0.29	0.50	0.45
Pádraig Harrington	11	1	11	50	1.17	0.09	0.85	0.23
David Toms	12	59	18	62	1.15	0.22	0.73	0.20
Justin Rose	13	11	10	140	1.15	0.30	0.88	-0.03
Retief Goosen	14	4	21	45	1.13	0.20	0.68	0.26
Stewart Cink	15	28	26	12	1.09	-0.02	0.61	0.50
Geoff Ogilvy	16	7	48	34	1.05	0.27	0.44	0.34
K. J. Choi	17	31	22	64	1.02	0.15	0.67	0.20
Rickie Fowler	18	41	74	77	1.02	0.54	0.32	0.17
Robert Allenby	19	23	16	191	1.00	0.44	0.73	-0.18
Tim Clark	20	48	15	60	0.99	0.05	0.74	0.21
Kenny Perry	21	5	41	180	0.98	0.64	0.47	-0.12
Bo Van Pelt	22	15	69	79	0.95	0.45	0.34	0.17
Scott Verplank	23	16	12	130	0.94	0.13	0.82	0.00
Lee Westwood	24	72	60	160	0.92	0.62	0.38	-0.08
Dustin Johnson	25	27	97	165	0.92	0.81	0.20	-0.09
Webb Simpson	26	17	49	22	0.90	0.08	0.43	0.39
Paul Casey	27	25	53	42	0.88	0.17	0.42	0.29
Bubba Watson	28	8	122	176	0.88	0.91	0.09	-0.12
Jason Day	29	89	100	24	0.87	0.30	0.19	0.39
Brandt Snedeker	30	2	47	10	0.87	-0.13	0.44	0.56
Rory Sabbatini	31	97	25	146	0.85	0.28	0.61	-0.04
Matt Kuchar	32	116	35	38	0.85	0.02	0.50	0.33
John Senden	33	26	46	152	0.83	0.44	0.45	-0.07
Charles Howell III	34	83	38	78	0.81	0.16	0.48	0.17
Ben Crane	35	22	111	9	0.80	0.10	0.14	0.56
Anthony Kim	36	51	66	58	0.80	0.24	0.35	0.21
Nick Watney	37	37	98	91	0.79	0.48	0.20	0.11
Davis Love III	38	101	52	159	0.78	0.43	0.43	-0.07
Arron Oberholser	39	38	31	88	0.78	0.13	0.53	0.12
Ian Poulter	40	36	54	59	0.78	0.15	0.42	0.21
Top 40 average	20	32	38	87	1.13	0.32	0.64	0.17
Top 40 average, fraction of total					100%	28%	57%	15%

19th Hole Summary

- The strokes gained of a golf shot is the decrease in the average number of strokes to hole out minus one to account for the stroke taken.

- Shots that are better than average have a positive strokes gained; shots that are worse than average have a negative strokes gained.

- Strokes gained can be used to compare driving, approach shots, short-game shots, and putting because all shots are measured in a common unit of strokes.

- Across the top 40 golfers from 2004 to 2012, driving contributed 28% to their scoring advantage, putting contributed 15%, and all other shots contributed the remaining 57%.

DISTANCE, ACCURACY, AND THE SECRET OF TIGER WOODS: Measuring the Performance of Pros and Amateurs

How much would your score change if you could hit your drives 20 yards farther? Unless you're still playing with balata balls and a driver made of wood, adding that many yards in the short term is not very realistic. But understanding the trade-off between distance and accuracy is important for on-course strategy, for example, in deciding whether to hit a driver or a 4-metal off the tee. In this chapter, we'll see how driving performance, measured by strokes gained driving, depends on a combination of distance and accuracy.

In chapter 5 we saw that driving explained 28% of the best pros' scoring advantage and putting explained 15%. In this chapter, we'll find out how much of the remaining 57% is due to approach shots and how much is due to the short game. In the end we'll be able to put it all together to answer the age-old question: What's the most important part of golf?

New measures of distance and accuracy in driving

In spite of the flaws of *average driving distance* and *fairways hit* as performance measures, it is true that longer drives in the fairway are better than shorter drives in the fairway, and straighter drives are usually better than wilder drives. But the fairways hit stat doesn't distinguish between big misses and small misses. Instead of counting whether a fairway is hit or not, I measure *accuracy in degrees* offline (see Figure 6.1). Shot location information in the ShotLink and Golfmetrics data allows us to do this.

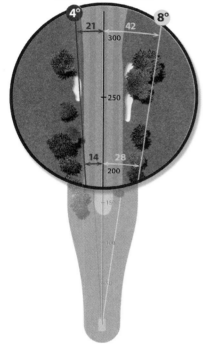

All measurements in yards unless indicated otherwise

A 300-yard drive that is four degrees offline represents a 21-yard miss from the target line. Think of the target line as a seam running down the center of the fairway. In practice, I measure the target line using the middle of the shot pattern of tee shots that land in the fairway. (This method accounts for fairways that are sloped at the landing area, causing most shots to finish near the edge of the fairway.) A 200-yard drive that is four degrees offline misses the target by 14 yards. Accuracy in degrees is independent of the shot distance and makes it easier to compare the accuracy of short hitters against long hitters. Accuracy in degrees distinguishes between small and large misses.[5]

The straightest drivers on tour have accuracies between 2.7 and 3.1 degrees; the wildest drivers have accuracies between 3.7 and 4.4 degrees. The average accuracy on the PGA Tour is 3.4 degrees. A typical 90-golfer has an accuracy of about 6.5 degrees, meaning his drives are about twice as far offline compared to a typical tour pro. Fairways hit doesn't reflect the difference in accuracy between pros and amateurs nearly as well. Most important, accuracy measured in degrees is more highly correlated with driving performance (measured by SGD) than fairways hit.[6]

Figure 6.1. Measuring offline shots in degrees. A 300-yard drive that is eight degrees offline finishes twice as far from the target line as one that is four degrees offline.

As the main measure of driving distance, I prefer to use the 75th percentile, rather than the average driving distance. For amateurs, average driving distance is often not representative of a golfer's typical distance. If a golfer hits drives of 255, 250, 245, 240, and 60 yards, the last because of hitting a tree, the average distance is 210 yards. The occasional very short drive can have an undue influence on the average-distance metric. The 75th percentile

---

[5] More precisely, accuracy is computed as the standard deviation of directional error, measured in degrees.

[6] For PGA Tour pros, the correlation of fairways hit with SGD is -12%. The correlation of accuracy in degrees with SGD is -44%. That is a huge difference.

measure is the distance such that one out of four drives travels longer and three out of four travel shorter. In this example, the 75th percentile distance is 250 yards (the 255-yard drive travels longer, and the 245-, 240-, and 60-yard drives travel shorter). On many short holes, and holes with narrow landing areas, pros often choose a club other than a driver to increase accuracy at the expense of distance. For pros, the 75th percentile measure is more reflective of their typical distance using a driver.

What is the value of 20 extra yards of driving distance?

If a pro could magically add 20 yards to his drives, by how much would his score drop? With these new measures of distance and accuracy, we can see how each contributes to scoring. Perhaps the pro could now reach that par-five in two shots and save a stroke. On another hole, a longer drive might allow him to hit a wedge onto the green instead of an 8-iron into a bunker. Savings like this on many holes might drop his score by four or five strokes per round.

On the other hand, imagine the pro picking up each drive, walking 20 yards farther in the same direction from the tee, and playing from the new location. Though all drives would be closer to the hole, some that would have finished in the fairway would now be in the rough. Some that finished in the rough might now find the trees or water. All things considered, maybe 20 extra yards would only shave off a fraction of a stroke per round. Those extra yards might even hurt rather than help.

Which reasoning is closer to the truth? We can get an inkling by looking at pairs of actual pro golfers with similar accuracies but different driving distances. Tiger Woods's average driving distance is about 23 yards longer than Dudley Hart's, and their accuracy in degrees is almost identical. Our calculations show that Tiger's SGD is 0.58 strokes per round; Dudley's is -0.40 strokes per round. For these two golfers, a 20-yard driving distance difference is worth about 0.85 strokes per round.

Bubba Watson drives it farther than Notah Begay, but their accuracies are almost identical. For this pair, a 20-yard driving distance difference is worth about 0.76 strokes per round.[7]

---

[7] Bubba Watson's average driving distance is 32 yards longer than Notah Begay's. Bubba's SGD is 0.91 strokes per round; Notah's is -0.31 strokes per round. Since they have comparable driving accuracies, 20 yards is worth 0.76 strokes per round, where 0.76 = (1.22/32) x 20.

The relative importance of driving distance can't be summarized by two distance and accuracy comparisons alone, so these examples merely serve as motivation to get us in the right ballpark. I continued this analysis with all of the available pro data, not just a few pairs of golfers, using a statistical technique called regression. This analysis showed that an extra 20 yards of driving distance is worth about three-quarters of a stroke per round.

Here's another way to understand this. On a 460-yard hole, about average for par-four and par-five holes on tour, a drive that travels 300 yards and finishes in the fairway leaves 160 yards to go. The PGA Tour average strokes to hole out from 160 yards is 2.98 strokes, according to Table 5.2. A drive that travels 20 yards farther and finishes in the fairway leaves 140 yards to go, where the PGA Tour average strokes to hole out is 2.91 strokes, a gain of 0.07 strokes. If the longer drive finishes in the rough, the PGA Tour average strokes to hole out is 3.15, representing a loss of 0.17 strokes (3.15 strokes compared with 2.98 strokes). Suppose, in a round with 14 par-four and par-five holes, one longer drive finishes in the rough. The total gain for the round is 13(0.07) - 1(0.17) = 0.74 strokes.

In reality, the gains from longer drives differ substantially by the hole length, and some of the longer drives finish in worse situations than the rough. On shorter holes it might not pay to use the 20 extra yards, even if they are available. But this simple calculation illustrates why a gain of 0.75 strokes for 20 extra yards of driving distance for a pro is about right.

> For pros, an extra 20 yards of driving distance is worth about three-quarters of a stroke per round.

Three-quarters of a stroke per round might not sound like a lot, but for a pro it could mean hundreds of thousands of dollars in increased prize money. In 2012, Keegan Bradley was 10th on the money list with nearly $4 million in prize money and a scoring average of 70. Jonathan Byrd's scoring average was 70.75, and he earned $1.6 million in prize money. Erik Compton, golf pro and two-time heart transplant recipient, had a 2012 scoring average of 71.5 and he earned $360,000 in prize money. Matt Bettencourt had a 2012 scoring average of 72.2 and he earned $335,000 in prize money. In another example of nonlinearity, we see that three-quarters of a stroke per round is worth a lot more in prize money for pros with lower scoring averages.

I used a 20-yard distance increment because it's easy to remember. To get back to the question of whether distance or accuracy is more important, we need to use increments that represent comparable changes for a pro. The top third of pro golfers in distance hit drive eight yards longer than average-distance pros and score 0.3 strokes per round better. The top third of pro golfers in accuracy are 0.3 degrees straighter than average-accuracy pros and score 0.2 strokes per round better.[8]

All else equal, longer-than-average pros score better than straighter-than-average pros. For pros, driving distance is more important than driving accuracy.

As shown in Table 5.5, the top 40 ranked golfers in driving drive the ball 10 yards longer than the tour average, but only 0.1 degree more accurately. There are only two golfers in the top 40, Joe Durant and Greg Owen, who have driving distances that are tour average or shorter. There are 13 golfers who are less accurate than the tour average when accuracy is measured in degrees, and 27 who are less accurate when measured by fairways hit. To be ranked among the top drivers on tour, distance matters more than accuracy.

Figure 6.2 combines driving distance, accuracy, and strokes gained in a single chart, which shows how longer and straighter drives lead to lower scores. It's a myth that all tour pros drive it long and straight; there is quite a lot of variation even among pros. The longest drivers on tour are more than 40 yards longer than the shortest drivers. The wildest drivers on tour have 60% more directional dispersion than the straightest drivers. Sure, they all drive it long and straight compared to amateurs, but compared to each other, there are huge differences in both distance and accuracy.

---

[8] For statistically minded readers, eight yards represents a change of one standard deviation in driving distance among tour pros. This change in distance, eight yards, leads to a 0.3 strokes reduction per round. A one standard deviation improvement in accuracy, 0.3 degrees, leads to a 0.2 strokes reduction per round. This calculation shows that distance is indeed more important for scoring than accuracy.

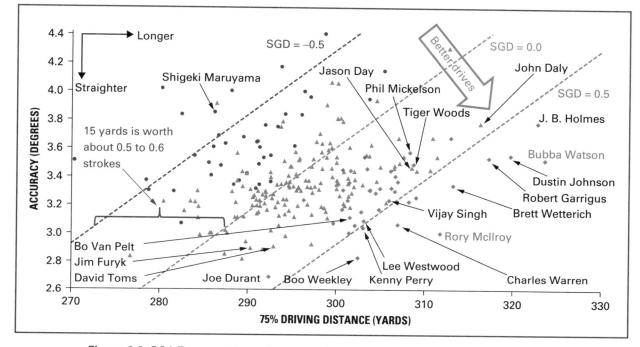

Figure 6.2. PGA Tour pro driving distance and accuracy: results for approximately 240 PGA Tour golfers with at least 200 ShotLink rounds from 2004 through 2012 (also included is Rory McIlroy with only 120 rounds). Red diamond markers represent golfers in the top 40 of strokes gained driving (SGD). Their average SGD is 0.5 strokes per round. Blue circular markers represent golfers in the bottom 40 of SGD. Their average SGD is -0.5 strokes per round. Green triangular markers represent the remaining golfers in the middle of SGD, with an average SGD of zero. The 75% driving distance measures the length of good drives: One out of four drives travels longer than the 75% distance. Accuracy is measured in degrees. Dashed lines show distance-accuracy combinations with approximately equal SGD. The best drivers, both long and straight, are found near the bottom right of the chart. The top-ranked golfers in SGD are Rory McIlroy and Bubba Watson.

The value of extra driving distance for amateurs differs from that for pros. Table 6.1 shows that 20 extra yards of driving distance will reduce the scores of high-scoring golfers far more than those of low-scoring golfers. Twenty yards is worth only three-quarters of a stroke per round to pros, but it's worth almost three strokes to a short-hitting 115-golfer. Short-hitting golfers often can't reach greens in the regulation number of strokes (one stroke for par-threes, two strokes for par-fours, and three strokes for par-fives), so extra driving distance has even more impact on scores for these golfers. If a golfer hits a 190-yard drive seven degrees offline, it's only 23 yards off the target line. Wild drives don't hurt short hitters as much as long hitters, and improvements in accuracy aren't a tremendous help either. A one-degree improvement in accuracy helps pros by 0.8 strokes per round and helps a typical 115-golfer by only 1.1 strokes per round. For amateur golfers, driving distance is even more important for scoring than driving accuracy.

> For pros, driving distance is more important than driving accuracy. For amateur golfers, driving distance is even more important for scoring than driving accuracy.

It's worth emphasizing that these are average results across many golfers and courses, not specific results that hold for every golfer and every course. For pros playing on a course with narrow tree-lined fairways and heavy rough, the importance of accuracy increases. Extra driving distance matters less, or not at all, on a hole where a nasty cross-bunker forces golfers to use an iron off the tee. For a 90-golfer who hits wild 300-yard drives, accuracy is the weakness that needs to be addressed. Except for qualifications like these, the results show that it's hard to overstate the importance of distance.

Junior golfers who hit it long can often learn to hit it straight later. Golfers who never develop into long hitters will always have limited scoring potential. Arnold Palmer's father, Deacon, was the golf pro and greenskeeper at Latrobe Country Club. His swing advice to a young Arnie was simple and direct: "Hit it *hard* boy. Go find it and hit it hard again." That was good advice then and it's still good advice today.

Table 6.1. The impact of driving distance and accuracy on scores: For a 20-yard increase in driving distance, a typical 100-golfer's score will decrease by an average of 2.3 strokes per round. For a one-degree improvement in accuracy, a typical 100-golfer's score will decrease by an average of one stroke per round. Extra driving distance is worth more to high-scoring golfers than low-scoring golfers. Results are based on simulation analysis in a 2013 Columbia Business School working paper by Broadie and Ko.

	PGA Tour	80-golfer	90-golfer	100-golfer	115-golfer
Strokes per 20 yards	0.8	1.3	1.6	2.3	2.7
Strokes per degree	0.8	0.9	0.9	1.0	1.1

For years many people in the golf community have debated the wisdom of "rolling the ball back," changing the rules so the ball doesn't fly as far. Strokes gained and simulation can be used to analyze the impact of a reduced-distance ball on golf scores. While the effect on scoring would depend on the characteristics of such a ball, the results strongly suggest that shorter hitters would feel a bigger impact than longer hitters.

Longer hitters and the quest for accuracy

Across a wide range of golfers, from 115-golfers to tour professionals, do longer or shorter drivers of the ball hit it straighter? From Figure 6.2 we see that John Daly's average distance is 20 yards longer than Jim Furyk's. Compared with Jim Furyk, John Daly hits fewer fairways and his directional error is almost one degree larger, a huge difference in accuracy. Intuition might suggest that long and wild go together. But let's compare Boo Weekley to Shigeki Maruyama. Weekley's average distance is 15 yards longer than Maruyama's, he hits more fairways, and his directional error is one degree smaller. Weekley is longer and straighter than Maruyama. For every long-wild and short-straight pair of pro golfers, there's another long-straight and short-wild pair. For tour pros, there's little relation between distance and direction. Looking across a range of golfers from amateurs to pros, a clear pattern emerges: Longer hitters tend to be straighter hitters.

> Longer hitters tend to be straighter hitters.

Figure 6.3 shows the longer-straighter pattern across golfers. The reason long hitters tend to be straighter hitters is simple: Golfers with better skills score lower because they hit better golf shots, and better drives are both long and straight. Tour pros are the longest and straightest of all.

The baseline curve in Figure 6.3 can be used to gauge whether an individual golfer is distance-challenged or accuracy-challenged compared with the average trend among amateur golfers. A golfer whose driving game is substantially above the baseline should focus on improving ac-

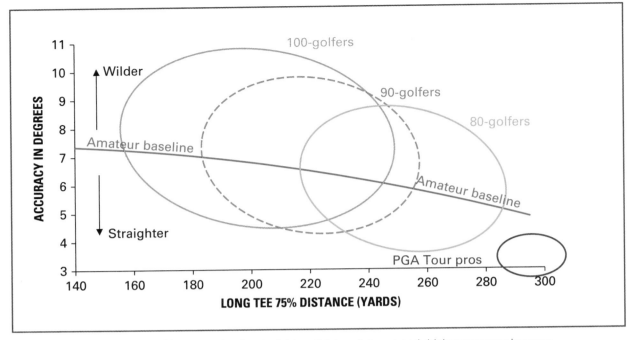

Figure 6.3. Longer hitters tend to be straighter: Driving distance and driving accuracy improve with golfer skill. The red line shows the average trend across golfers. The 75% driving distance measures the length of good drives: One out of four drives travels longer than the 75% distance. Accuracy is measured in degrees.

curacy; a golfer who is substantially below the baseline should focus on increasing distance.

Golfers who can't hit it long and straight never even make it to the tour. You need to drive the ball longer than 280 yards to have any chance of competing on the PGA Tour. It's nearly impossible for an amateur golfer whose good drives travel less than 220 yards to have an average score close to 80 on a 6,500-yard or longer course.

The longest drivers on tour hit their good drives about 320 yards while the shortest are about 40 yards shorter. The shortest tour drivers are about 40 yards longer than some good amateur golfers (240 yards), who in turn are 40 yards longer than average amateurs (200 yards), who in turn are 40 yards longer than some of the shortest amateurs (160 yards). The longest pros hit their drives twice as far as the shortest amateurs. With these huge differences in driving distance, is it any wonder that driving is such a big factor in explaining the score differences between pros and amateurs?

The importance of driving distance on scores is one reason that the Tee it Forward initiative of the PGA of America and the USGA, which allows you to set your tees at distances that match your skill level, makes so much sense. Rounds are faster, you get to play many shots from new positions on the course, and it is really a lot of fun to make a boatload of pars and birdies.

Measuring iron play using strokes gained approach (SGA)

The "approach shot" category includes all shots over 100 yards from the hole, except for tee shots on par-four and par-five holes.[9] Pros hit an average of 18 of these shots per round. That compares to just under 14 tee shots on par-four and par-five holes, 10 short-game shots, and 29 putts per round. Let's rank pros based on their approach shot performance.

To begin, let's consider the play of Mr. Steadypro and Mr. Wildpro on a 190-yard par-three hole on two tournament days. Mr. Steadypro hit the green both days, and his average distance to the hole was 30 feet. Mr. Wildpro hit the green one out of two days, and his average distance to the hole was 40 feet. Whose shots were better?

Hitting a green is better than missing. Hitting it closer to the hole is usually better than hitting it farther from the hole. It would appear that Mr. Steadypro's tee shots were better than Mr. Wildpro's. But wait! Mr. Steadypro had two 30-foot putts. Pros take an average of four strokes to finish both holes from there. Mr. Wildpro hit one tee shot to two feet and another into the sand 26 yards from the hole. From two feet on the green, the average for pros to finish is one. From 26 yards in the sand, the average for pros to finish is 2.6 strokes (they get up and down about 40% of the time). Pros take an average of 3.6 strokes to finish out the two holes from Mr. Wildpro's shot locations. According to my strokes gained calculations, Mr. Wildpro gained 0.4 strokes on his tee shots against Mr. Steadypro, even though he hit fewer greens and his proximity to the hole was worse.

---

[9] I created the "approach shot" category label for convenience and simplicity. This category also includes layup shots when the green can't be reached after a tee shot, as well as recovery or escape shots from trouble.

How can it be that Mr. Wildpro's performance was better, when he hit fewer greens and his shots were farther from the hole? It's another example of the importance of nonlinearity that we learned from Johan Jensen and his Jensen's inequality. In this case, the math reveals that one great shot and one poor shot are better than two middling shots.

Ranking the approach shot performance of golfers based on greens hit or proximity to the hole is problematic because of the nonlinearity problem. It's hard to combine greens hit, expressed in percent, with proximity to the hole, expressed in feet. It's hard to understand true performance when a golfer ranks high on greens hit and low on proximity to the hole or vice versa. The strokes gained method overcomes these problems by measuring the quality of each approach shot in the same unit of strokes and then averaging the results. Strokes gained for each approach shot takes into account how far the shot finished from the hole and whether it finished in the fairway, rough, or sand, or on the green.

Table 6.2 shows the top 40 PGA Tour golfers from 2004 through 2012 ranked by strokes gained approach (SGA) per round. The leader in SGA is Tiger Woods, who gained 1.3 strokes per round against an average tour field. This gain is remarkable because the second-ranked golfer, Robert Allenby, is a full 0.4 strokes behind Tiger, and the average gain for the top 40 is 0.55 strokes per round. Tiger Woods is the best golfer in the ShotLink era, if not the best golfer in history. He excels in every aspect of the game, but the part of his game that stands out the most, that makes him the very best, is his approach game. Rounding out the top 10 are some of the best ball-strikers in the game: Furyk, Els, Garcia, McIlroy, Mickelson, Scott, Singh, Donald, and Campbell.

Table 6.2. Strokes gained approach (SGA) per round: top 40 golfers in SGA on the PGA Tour from 2004 through 2012. Approach shots are all shots over 100 yards from the hole, except for tee shots on par-four and par-five holes. Ranks are out of 240 golfers with at least 200 rounds from 2004 to 2012, with the exception of Rory McIlroy, who has only 120 rounds of ShotLink data (and so has an asterisk by his name). The median leave is the value such that half of shots finish closer to the hole.

Rank	Golfer	SGA	100–150 Median leave	150–200 Median leave	200–250 Median leave	100–150 Green and fringe	150–200 Green and fringe
1	Tiger Woods	1.28	4.9%	5.2%	6.2%	80%	75%
2	Robert Allenby	0.88	5.2%	5.5%	6.4%	83%	72%
3	Jim Furyk	0.78	5.1%	5.4%	6.6%	84%	73%
4	Ernie Els	0.77	5.6%	5.5%	6.5%	80%	69%
5	Sergio Garcia	0.75	5.5%	5.7%	6.6%	80%	70%
6	Rory McIlroy*	0.73	5.5%	5.7%	6.5%	79%	68%
6	Phil Mickelson	0.72	5.3%	5.7%	6.8%	80%	68%
7	Adam Scott	0.72	5.4%	5.5%	6.9%	82%	69%
8	Vijay Singh	0.71	5.2%	5.5%	6.7%	80%	70%
9	Luke Donald	0.70	5.1%	5.7%	7.3%	81%	69%
10	Chad Campbell	0.65	5.2%	5.4%	6.8%	81%	72%
11	Tom Lehman	0.61	5.3%	5.4%	7.1%	84%	73%
12	Scott Verplank	0.60	4.6%	5.3%	7.1%	83%	69%
13	Joey Sindelar	0.58	5.7%	5.4%	7.2%	82%	70%
14	Kenny Perry	0.57	5.4%	5.4%	6.5%	82%	71%
15	Lee Westwood	0.57	5.5%	5.8%	6.4%	79%	70%
16	Kris Blanks	0.56	5.3%	5.5%	6.5%	82%	70%
17	David Toms	0.56	5.0%	5.5%	6.7%	84%	70%
18	Paul Casey	0.55	5.7%	5.6%	6.9%	79%	70%
19	Tim Clark	0.53	4.9%	5.3%	6.6%	82%	70%
20	Justin Rose	0.52	5.4%	5.5%	6.7%	81%	69%
21	John Senden	0.51	5.5%	5.7%	6.9%	82%	73%
22	Alex Cejka	0.49	5.0%	5.2%	6.9%	82%	69%
23	Camilo Villegas	0.47	5.2%	5.8%	7.0%	83%	69%
24	Brendon de Jonge	0.47	5.0%	5.5%	7.0%	83%	69%
25	Davis Love III	0.46	5.7%	5.8%	6.7%	80%	68%
26	Steve Stricker	0.46	5.0%	5.8%	7.0%	82%	68%
27	Stewart Cink	0.45	5.5%	5.8%	7.0%	81%	69%
28	Ricky Barnes	0.43	5.4%	5.4%	8.0%	78%	66%
29	Joe Durant	0.42	5.1%	5.3%	6.9%	83%	72%
30	Zach Johnson	0.42	5.1%	5.6%	6.9%	82%	70%
31	Heath Slocum	0.41	5.2%	5.4%	6.7%	82%	71%
32	Trevor Immelman	0.40	5.4%	5.8%	7.2%	81%	69%
33	Retief Goosen	0.40	5.7%	5.7%	6.6%	80%	67%
34	Boo Weekley	0.39	5.3%	5.7%	6.5%	81%	69%
35	Jeff Sluman	0.38	5.0%	5.5%	7.1%	86%	70%
36	Briny Baird	0.38	5.4%	5.9%	7.2%	83%	71%
37	Jason Bohn	0.38	5.2%	5.7%	6.8%	81%	69%
38	Stephen Ames	0.37	5.4%	5.6%	7.3%	82%	70%
39	K. J. Choi	0.37	5.3%	5.7%	7.0%	81%	70%
40	Dudley Hart	0.36	5.3%	6.1%	7.9%	77%	65%
	Top 40 average	0.55	5.3%	5.6%	6.9%	82%	70%
	PGA Tour average	0.00	5.5%	5.9%	7.3%	80%	67%

What is the value of hitting approach shots closer to the hole?

As we've seen, greens hit and proximity to the hole are flawed measures of approach shot performance. Nevertheless, hitting the ball on the green closer to the hole is almost always better than missing the green farther away.

In order to connect SGA to a more tangible performance measure, I use "median leave" as a measure of approach shot accuracy. A shot from 100 yards that finishes five yards from the hole represents a leave of 5% (final distance to the hole relative to the initial distance). A shot from 200 yards that finishes 10 yards from the hole also represents a leave of 5%. If a golfer hits five approach shots with leaves of 2%, 3%, 6%, 7%, and 25%, the middle value, 6% in this case, is the median leave. The median leave is the value such that half of shots finish closer to the hole and half finish farther from the hole, where distance is measured as the final distance to the hole relative to the initial distance to the hole.

I use median leave because it is more highly correlated with scores than greens hit or proximity to the hole. The median, or middle, value works better than the average because it is unaffected by the occasional foozled shot. For most golfers, shots that start 150 yards from the hole will finish about 50% farther from the hole than shots starting from 100 yards. Computing the median leave as a fraction of the initial distance makes it easy to compare shots with different initial distances. If you are looking for one single number, other than a golfer's average score, that reveals a golfer's ability, median leave is a great candidate. For amateurs, the median leave for shots starting between 100 and 150 yards from the hole is a telling stat. For pros, the median leave between 150 and 200 yards is more informative, because that is the range most highly correlated with pros' scores.

Camilo Villegas, born in Medellin, Colombia, has won three times on the PGA Tour since he joined in 2006. Until 2012, Camilo hit half of his shots starting between 150 and 200 yards from the hole to within 5.8% of the initial distance to the hole. That's 30 feet from the hole on shots starting from 175 yards. Camilo ranks 120th in this stat. Another golfer hit half of his shots starting 175 yards from the hole to within 27 feet of the hole, three feet closer. What rank do you estimate for this other golfer?

You might be surprised that this other golfer is Tiger Woods, who ranks first in the category. On the putting green, the PGA Tour average to hole out from 27 feet is only 0.025 strokes lower than from 30 feet. The three-foot difference in proximity to the hole hardly seems significant, but in reality it's crucial. First, a fractional gain for each approach shot adds up over an average of 18 approach shots per round. On top of that, the three-foot difference matters because of shots that finish on the green instead of in the rough or sand. Because of that, Tiger hits the green 75% of the time versus the tour average of 67% on shots starting 150 to 200 yards from the hole. More important, the three-foot difference matters for five-foot putts that become two-footers and for eight-foot putts that become five-footers. Those differences really add up. Tiger's three-foot advantage from 175 yards, when applied to all approach shots in a round, accumulates to a 1.3-stroke advantage per round or five strokes every tournament. That's an enormous advantage!

SGA reveals more about approach shot performance than greens hit, proximity to the hole, and median leave. In spite of the flaws of the latter stats, it is true that hitting more greens is better than hitting fewer and hitting shots closer to the hole is better than hitting them farther from the hole. Next, I will show you how median leave is connected to strokes gained and how closer approach shots lead to lower scores.

Tiger's median leave from 150 to 200 yards is 5.2%, compared to the tour average of 5.9%.[10] His closer approach shots translate to a 1.3-stroke gain against an average tour field. Figure 6.4 combines median leaves from 150 to 200 yards, median leaves from 200 to 250 yards, and strokes gained in a single chart to show how closer approach shots lead to lower scores for PGA Tour pros. Tiger Woods stands apart from the pack. His gain from approach shots is one of the biggest factors in explaining his remarkable performances.

PGA Tour pros hit half of their shots from 100 to 150 yards to within 5.5% of the initial distance to the hole.[11] Many people are surprised that pros aren't better from this distance. But the pro results are compiled

[10] The 5.9% value includes shots from the rough, fairway, and tee, but excludes sand and recovery shots. From the fairway from 150 to 200 yards, the median leave for PGA Tour pros is 5.6%; from the rough it's 8.9%.

[11] The 5.5% value includes shots from the rough, fairway, and tee, but excludes sand and recovery shots. From the fairway from 100 to 150 yards, the median leave for PGA Tour pros is 5.0%; from the rough it's 8.2%.

DISTANCE, ACCURACY, AND THE SECRET OF TIGER WOODS • 109

from play on difficult courses with firm and fast greens, tight fairways, and difficult rough. From 100 to 150 yards, a typical 90-golfer hits half to within 12%, more than double the distance to the hole of pros. Expressed slightly differently, from 125 yards, PGA Tour pros hit half of their shots to within 21 feet of the hole; a typical 90-golfer hits half to within 45 feet. The gap between pro and amateur performance is huge.

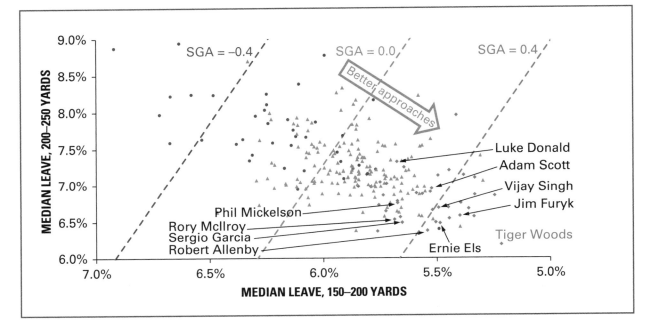

Figure 6.4. PGA Tour approach shots, 150 to 250 yards: results for approximately 240 PGA Tour golfers with at least 200 ShotLink rounds from 2004 through 2012 (also included is Rory McIlroy with only 120 rounds). Red diamond markers represent golfers in the top 40 of strokes gained approach (SGA). Their average SGA is 0.55 strokes per round. Blue circular markers represent golfers in the bottom 40 of SGA, with an average SGA of -0.4 strokes per round. Green triangular markers represent the remaining golfers in the middle of SGA. A shot from 100 yards that finishes five yards from the hole represents a leave of 5%, i.e., the final distance to the hole relative to the initial distance. The median leave is the value such that half of shots finish closer to the hole. Dashed lines show median leave combinations with approximately equal SGA. The golfers with the best approach shots between 150 and 250 yards are found near the bottom right of the chart. Tiger Woods leads in SGA with a gain of 1.3 strokes per round. Half of Tiger Woods's shots from 150 to 200 yards finish within 5.2% of the initial distance (e.g., nine yards on a 175-yard shot). Half of his shots from 200 to 250 yards finish within 6.2% of the initial distance (e.g., 14 yards on a 225-yard shot).

PGA Tour pros hit the green or fringe 80% of the time starting from 100 to 150 yards from the hole; a typical 90-golfer hits the green or fringe only 46% of the time. This result hints at the application of performance stats to golf strategy: Most 90-golfers would be better off aiming for the middle of the green on shots starting between 100 and 150 yards from the hole. (Additional amateur results are given in the appendix.)

Measuring wedge play using strokes gained short game (SGS)

Short-game stats, like other standard golf statistics, often miss important aspects of play. Short-game shots are shots that start within 100 yards of the hole, including sand shots but excluding putts on the green. Pros hit an average of 10 of these shots per round. One standard short-game golf statistic is sand saves, which measures the fraction of time a golfer gets up and down (takes one or two shots to hole out) starting from a greenside sand bunker. A problem with this stat is that it mixes sand skill and putting skill. If a golfer has a low sand save percentage, you can't tell whether it is caused by poor sand play or poor putting.

Another short-game stat is scrambling. The scrambling stat measures the fraction of time a golfer makes par after missing the green in the regulation number of strokes. This stat mixes short-game skill and putting in a similar way. Neither sand saves nor the scrambling stat shows exactly how much short-game skill contributes to scoring.

Strokes gained short game (SGS) uses the strokes gained method to compute the number of strokes per round a pro golfer gains against the field on short-game shots. Table 6.3 shows the top 40 PGA Tour golfers from 2004 through 2012 ranked by strokes gained short game per round. The leader in SGS is Steve Stricker, who gained 0.6 strokes per round against an average tour field. Steve Stricker puts half of his zero- to 100-yard off-green shots to within 7.8% of their initial distance, against the tour average of 10.2%. Also in the top ten are Luke Donald and Phil Mickelson, who are well known for their short-game prowess. It might come as a surprise that Vijay Singh, who is in the top 10 in driving and approach shots, is also in the short-game top 10.

Table 6.3. Strokes gained short game (SGS) per round: top 40 golfers in SGS on the PGA Tour from 2004 through 2012. Short-game shots are all shots starting within 100 yards from the hole, except for putts on the green. Ranks are out of 240 golfers with at least 200 rounds from 2004 to 2012. The median leave is the value such that half of shots finish closer to the hole. The 0–100, 0–20, 20–60, and 60–100 shot groups exclude sand shots and putts. Greenside sand shots start from the sand within 50 yards of the hole.

Rank	Golfer	SGS	0–100 Median leave	0–20 Median leave	20–60 Median leave	60–100 Median leave	Greenside sand median leave
1	Steve Stricker	0.63	7.8%	11.7%	8.2%	4.8%	14.3%
2	Corey Pavin	0.54	8.4%	11.5%	9.1%	5.4%	13.2%
3	Chris Riley	0.52	9.1%	11.7%	9.5%	5.8%	12.4%
4	Luke Donald	0.51	9.4%	12.6%	9.9%	5.7%	12.6%
5	Mike Weir	0.50	9.3%	12.9%	9.5%	5.8%	11.8%
6	Pádraig Harrington	0.50	9.1%	11.6%	9.6%	5.3%	13.9%
7	Phil Mickelson	0.46	9.2%	12.5%	9.0%	6.2%	13.9%
8	Vijay Singh	0.42	9.5%	12.9%	9.7%	6.4%	13.6%
9	Justin Leonard	0.41	8.6%	11.8%	9.1%	5.4%	15.3%
10	Brian Gay	0.39	8.6%	12.1%	9.9%	5.3%	14.3%
11	Ryuji Imada	0.39	9.3%	12.1%	9.7%	5.8%	13.0%
12	Jim Furyk	0.39	8.5%	11.4%	9.3%	5.5%	14.8%
13	Nick O'Hern	0.38	9.0%	12.2%	9.9%	5.7%	13.5%
14	Kevin Na	0.38	9.7%	12.7%	9.4%	6.0%	14.2%
15	Shigeki Maruyama	0.37	10.2%	12.9%	10.3%	6.8%	12.6%
16	Justin Rose	0.36	9.5%	13.1%	9.7%	5.7%	13.2%
17	Stuart Appleby	0.36	9.3%	12.6%	9.3%	5.8%	14.4%
18	Todd Fischer	0.35	9.1%	11.5%	9.6%	6.6%	18.4%
19	Rory Sabbatini	0.34	9.5%	13.1%	9.7%	5.9%	13.1%
20	Ian Poulter	0.33	10.2%	12.7%	11.0%	6.3%	14.5%
21	Ernie Els	0.32	9.6%	12.8%	9.9%	5.5%	15.3%
22	Aaron Baddeley	0.30	10.2%	13.0%	10.4%	6.9%	14.4%
23	K. J. Choi	0.30	9.8%	13.2%	10.8%	6.1%	13.3%
24	Tiger Woods	0.30	9.8%	13.5%	9.7%	6.2%	14.9%
25	Rod Pampling	0.30	9.9%	12.5%	11.1%	6.3%	13.4%
26	Kirk Triplett	0.29	8.3%	11.0%	10.6%	5.6%	16.9%
27	Arron Oberholser	0.28	9.5%	11.9%	9.5%	6.5%	14.2%
28	Retief Goosen	0.28	9.8%	12.7%	10.5%	6.2%	14.7%
29	Kevin Sutherland	0.28	9.9%	12.1%	10.8%	6.4%	13.9%
30	Matt Kuchar	0.28	9.4%	12.7%	9.5%	5.9%	14.6%
31	Bob Heintz	0.27	8.9%	12.6%	10.0%	5.6%	17.5%
32	Brandt Snedeker	0.27	9.6%	13.2%	10.3%	6.1%	15.1%
33	Bryce Molder	0.27	9.2%	12.7%	10.6%	5.7%	16.4%
34	Jonathan Byrd	0.27	9.5%	12.3%	9.7%	5.9%	14.3%
35	Webb Simpson	0.27	10.2%	14.4%	10.5%	6.7%	13.5%
36	Geoff Ogilvy	0.26	10.0%	13.5%	11.1%	6.2%	13.4%
37	Omar Uresti	0.26	9.1%	12.7%	9.8%	6.0%	19.3%
38	Glen Day	0.26	8.8%	12.7%	9.3%	5.4%	15.6%
39	Tom Pernice Jr.	0.26	9.8%	12.8%	10.3%	5.9%	15.0%
40	Tim Petrovic	0.25	9.6%	12.2%	10.2%	6.2%	16.8%
	Top 40 average	0.35	9.4%	12.5%	9.9%	5.9%	14.5%
	PGA Tour average	0.00	10.2%	13.6%	10.9%	6.3%	16.1%

Not surprisingly, golfers with great short games tend to hit their short-game shots closer to the hole than others. Figure 6.5 combines median leaves from zero to 100 yards, median leaves from greenside sand, and strokes gained in a single chart to show how closer short-game shots lead to lower scores for PGA Tour pros. (Amateur short-game results are given in the appendix.)

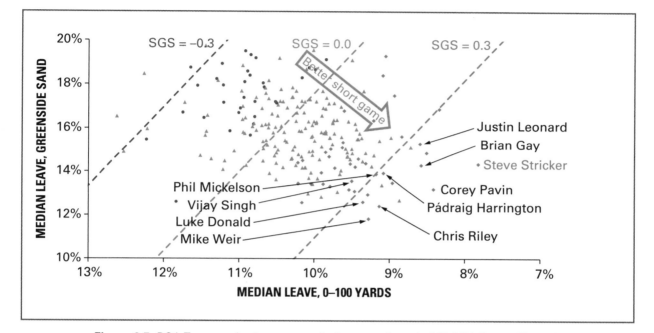

Figure 6.5. PGA Tour pro short game: results for approximately 240 PGA Tour golfers with at least 200 ShotLink rounds from 2004 through 2012. Red diamond markers represent golfers in the top 40 of strokes gained short game (SGS). Their average SGS is 0.35 strokes per round. Blue circular markers represent golfers in the bottom 40 of SGS, with an average SGS of -0.3 strokes per round. Green triangular markers represent the remaining golfers in the middle of SGS. Dashed lines show median leave combinations with approximately equal SGS. The golfers with the best short games are found near the bottom right of the chart. Steve Stricker leads in SGS with a gain of 0.6 strokes per round. Half of Stricker's shots from zero to 100 yards (excluding shots from the sand and putts on the green) finish within 7.8% of the initial distance. Half of his greenside sand shots from zero to 50 yards finish within 14% of the initial distance.

The biggest factor in scoring and Tiger's secret weapon

In chapter 2 we put to bed the idea that putting is the key to scoring. When golfing legend Ben Hogan was asked which are the three most important scoring clubs in order, he responded, "The driver, the putter, and the wedge." Debating this point might be fun, but my preference is to look to the data for objective answers. Detailed golf shot data don't go back to Hogan's time, but we can use the strokes gained method and data from today's era to provide insights into which shots contribute most to a current golfer's performance. Then from this we can infer the importance of each type of club.

Total strokes gained per round tells how many shots a pro golfer gains or loses to the field.[12] The real merit of the strokes gained method is using it to break down the total into the gain from each part of the game. In the Jason Day example in chapter 5, his total strokes gained for the hole was zero, but some shots were better than average and some were worse than average. Repeating this process for all of a golfer's shots shows how each shot category contributes to total strokes gained. In short, we can break down total strokes gained to see how much of the gain comes from driving, approach shots, short-game shots, and putting.

Table 6.4 shows the top 40 golfers in total strokes gained on the PGA Tour from 2004 through 2012. The top 40 is a who's who of modern golf. Topping the list is Tiger Woods, who gained 2.8 strokes per round against an average PGA Tour field. That's more than an 11-shot advantage every four-round tournament against an average PGA Tour field, which represents many of the best golfers in the world. Second and third on the list are Jim Furyk and Luke Donald, each gaining an incredibly impressive 1.8 strokes per round, but nearly one stroke less than Tiger. The next golfers on the list are all household names, if you live in a household of golf fans, known by their first names: Phil, Rory, Vijay, Ernie, and Sergio.

Ranking golfers by total strokes gained gives results that make perfect sense. But the full power of strokes gained is showing where the gains come from. What is Tiger's secret weapon? Approach shots. The biggest portion of Tiger's gain, 46% (1.3 strokes out of 2.8), comes from

---

[12] Total strokes gained per round is simply the sum of strokes gained per shot over all shots in the round. Total strokes gained gives results very similar to adjusted scoring average, which is a golfer's average score modified to take into account the scoring of the field in each round.

Table 6.4. Total strokes gained per round broken down by shot category: top 40 golfers in total strokes gained on the PGA Tour from 2004 through 2012. Ranks are out of 240 golfers with at least 200 rounds from 2004 to 2012 (also included is Rory McIlroy with only 120 rounds).

Golfer	Rank					Strokes gained per round				
	Total	Drive	Appr	Short	Putt	Total	Drive	Appr	Short	Putt
Tiger Woods	1	13	1	24	3	2.79	0.58	1.28	0.30	0.63
Jim Furyk	2	9	3	12	19	1.84	0.27	0.78	0.39	0.40
Luke Donald	3	29	10	4	1	1.82	-0.09	0.70	0.51	0.71
Phil Mickelson	4	14	7	7	86	1.70	0.39	0.72	0.46	0.14
Rory McIlroy*	5	1	6	124	153	1.66	0.98	0.73	0.02	-0.07
Vijay Singh	5	19	9	8	193	1.58	0.64	0.71	0.42	-0.18
Ernie Els	6	6	4	21	164	1.43	0.43	0.77	0.32	-0.08
Sergio Garcia	7	3	5	47	156	1.43	0.52	0.75	0.23	-0.07
Steve Stricker	8	32	27	1	13	1.34	-0.23	0.46	0.63	0.49
Adam Scott	9	10	8	68	178	1.33	0.56	0.72	0.17	-0.12
Zach Johnson	10	40	32	101	16	1.24	0.29	0.42	0.08	0.45
Pádraig Harrington	11	1	44	6	50	1.17	0.09	0.35	0.50	0.23
David Toms	12	59	18	67	62	1.15	0.22	0.56	0.17	0.20
Justin Rose	13	11	21	16	140	1.15	0.30	0.52	0.36	-0.03
Retief Goosen	14	4	35	28	45	1.13	0.20	0.40	0.28	0.26
Stewart Cink	15	28	28	71	12	1.09	-0.02	0.45	0.16	0.50
Geoff Ogilvy	16	7	96	36	34	1.05	0.27	0.17	0.26	0.34
K. J. Choi	17	31	42	23	64	1.02	0.15	0.37	0.30	0.20
Rickie Fowler	18	41	71	102	77	1.02	0.54	0.24	0.08	0.17
Robert Allenby	19	23	2	189	191	1.00	0.44	0.88	-0.15	-0.18
Tim Clark	20	48	20	56	60	0.99	0.05	0.53	0.21	0.21
Kenny Perry	21	5	15	173	180	0.98	0.64	0.57	-0.10	-0.12
Bo Van Pelt	22	15	49	125	79	0.95	0.45	0.33	0.01	0.17
Scott Verplank	23	16	13	54	130	0.94	0.13	0.60	0.21	0.00
Lee Westwood	24	72	16	202	160	0.92	0.62	0.57	-0.19	-0.08
Dustin Johnson	25	27	76	137	165	0.92	0.81	0.22	-0.02	-0.09
Webb Simpson	26	17	99	35	22	0.90	0.08	0.16	0.27	0.39
Paul Casey	27	25	19	181	42	0.88	0.17	0.55	-0.12	0.29
Bubba Watson	28	8	92	169	176	0.88	0.91	0.18	-0.09	-0.12
Jason Day	29	89	132	90	24	0.87	0.30	0.07	0.12	0.39
Brandt Snedeker	30	2	98	32	10	0.87	-0.13	0.17	0.27	0.56
Rory Sabbatini	31	97	60	19	146	0.85	0.28	0.28	0.34	-0.04
Matt Kuchar	32	116	78	30	38	0.85	0.02	0.22	0.28	0.33
John Senden	33	26	22	151	152	0.83	0.44	0.51	-0.06	-0.07
Charles Howell III	34	83	73	44	78	0.81	0.16	0.23	0.24	0.17
Ben Crane	35	22	159	66	9	0.80	0.10	-0.04	0.17	0.56
Anthony Kim	36	51	85	74	58	0.80	0.24	0.19	0.16	0.21
Nick Watney	37	37	70	144	91	0.79	0.48	0.24	-0.04	0.11
Davis Love III	38	101	26	143	159	0.78	0.43	0.46	-0.04	-0.07
Arron Oberholser	39	38	67	27	88	0.78	0.13	0.25	0.28	0.12
Ian Poulter	40	36	127	20	59	0.78	0.15	0.09	0.33	0.21
Top 40 average	20	32	44	71	87	1.13	0.32	0.45	0.19	0.17
Top 40 average, fraction of total						100%	28%	40%	17%	15%

his approach shots. He ranks high in all four categories, and that's the reason for his dominance in total strokes gained, but a strokes gained calculation reveals that approach shots are the key to his success.

> Tiger's secret weapon is approach shots. These shots account for the biggest portion, 46%, of his scoring advantage.

The best golfers in the world excel in different ways. In the top 10 in total strokes gained, Tiger is ranked first in approach shots, Luke Donald is ranked first in putting, Rory McIlroy is ranked first in driving, and Steve Stricker is ranked first in the short game. All four areas of the game are important.

In order to be one of the world's top 10 golfers, you have to be as good as or better than number 10, who in Table 6.4 is shown to be Zach Johnson. Johnson's total strokes gained is 1.2, so to be in the top 10 you must have an overall strokes gained of 1.2 or higher. That 1.2 can be put together in a variety of ways, from drives, approach shots, the short game, or putting. Sergio Garcia could get into the top 10 with only his drives and approach shot strokes gained: His putting is actually worse than the field. Tiger Woods gains the critical advantage that puts him in the top 10 from approach shots alone: His strokes gained on approach shots, as shown in Table 6.4, is 1.28.

Table 6.4 shows that it is possible to be relatively weak, by tour pro standards, in one area and still be in the top 10 (or 11, including Rory McIlroy) in total strokes gained. Out of the top 11 golfers in total strokes gained, two are ranked outside the top 100 in driving, two are outside in the short game, and five are outside in putting. On the other hand, none of the top 11 golfers in total strokes gained is outside the top 30 in approach shots. Expanding the frame by averaging the results for the top 40 golfers gives a crystal-clear picture of the pattern. The biggest contributor to scoring? Approach shots, which contribute 40% to total strokes gained.

> Among the top 40 PGA Tour pros, approach shots was the most important shot category, accounting for 40% of their scoring advantage.

Table 6.5 shows Tiger Woods's strokes gained each year over 10 years. His performance in individual categories varied quite a lot from year to year. But at no time during those 10 years did he fall below number five in approach shots; he was ranked number one in approach shots during six of the 10 years covered in the table.

Table 6.5. Tiger Woods's strokes gained by year: total strokes gained and breakdown by shot category from 2003 through 2012. Ranks each year are out of approximately 200 golfers with at least 30 rounds of PGA Tour ShotLink data in the year.

Year	Rank					Strokes gained per round					Rounds
	Total	Drive	Appr	Short	Putt	Total	Drive	Appr	Short	Putt	
2012	2	9	1	37	27	2.80	0.74	1.39	0.26	0.42	49
2011	29	136	4	89	49	1.09	-0.15	0.88	0.09	0.28	19
2010	48	123	4	160	91	0.71	-0.08	0.91	-0.20	0.08	29
2009	1	15	1	4	2	3.71	0.53	1.48	0.71	0.99	48
2008	1	8	1	3	4	4.14	0.61	2.01	0.67	0.85	11
2007	1	4	1	35	2	3.68	0.81	1.77	0.30	0.80	43
2006	1	4	1	23	21	3.78	0.92	1.98	0.39	0.49	37
2005	1	2	3	89	4	2.82	1.09	0.89	0.10	0.75	55
2004	1	21	5	9	3	3.06	0.48	1.12	0.51	0.95	54
2003	1	6	1	1	18	3.71	0.87	1.60	0.70	0.54	46

After approach shots, Table 6.4 shows that driving is the second-most-important category, contributing 28% to the total strokes gained among the top 40 golfers. Short-game shots contribute 17% and putting contributes 15%. The long game, which represents driving and approach shots combined, contributes 68% to total strokes gained; short game and putting combined contribute just 32%. Averaging just the top 10 or top 20 golfers gives similar results. The punch line doesn't change much when I look at results from each year. These results, computed from millions of shots in the PGA Tour's ShotLink database, show the importance of the long game compared to the short game and putting combined.

Among the top 40 PGA Tour pros, approach shots accounted for 40% of their scoring advantage, driving accounted for 28%, the short game 17%, and putting 15%.

Several points should not be overlooked. First, these are average results, whereas individual golfers come in all shapes and sizes. The short game and putting contribute more than 80% to Steve Stricker's scoring advantage, but only 11% to Sergio Garcia's. Differences like these give opposing sides of the putting-is-most-important debate plenty of ammunition. While results for individual golfers vary, the average over a number of golfers clearly shows the importance of the long game.

Second, the results are somewhat different when looking at winners of individual tournaments. We saw in chapter 2 that putting contributes 35% to victories on the PGA Tour, but here we see that putting contributes only 15% to total strokes gained. The two results are not inconsistent: Putting plays a relatively larger role in tournament victories compared to the play of the best golfers across all events.[13]

Third, and most crucially, the importance of the long game in explaining scoring differences doesn't imply that short-game skill and putting skill are not important. Rather, it implies that the best pros in the world are more equally matched in putting and the short game than they are in approach shots and driving. Golfers have to be great in all areas to play on the biggest stage in the world. Once on that stage, it is harder for pros to separate themselves based on putting and the short game compared to the long game.

Variability in skill across golfers, not the level of skill, is the key to measuring the importance of a skill. Here's an analogy to illustrate this point. A teacher grades students in a course by giving 40% weight to the midterm exam and 60% weight to the final exam. Based on the weighted average of

---

[13] Winning a tournament requires gaining approximately 3.7 strokes per round against the field. For Tiger to win, he has to gain, approximately, an additional 0.9 strokes per round compared to his usual play. Jim Furyk needs to gain an additional 1.9 strokes per round compared to his usual play. The additional gains during tournament wins often come more from putting than other parts of the game. Golfers generally don't start driving the ball 20 yards longer in the week of a tournament win, but they might have a "hot" putter and sink more putts than usual.

the midterm and final exams, the top 20% of the class will be given a grade of A in the course, the next 30% will be given a course grade of B, and so on. In other words, the students are graded on a curve. The teacher gives an easy midterm exam. It's so easy that all of the students get perfect scores. The final exam is harder and some students do better than others.

Even though the teacher gives a 60% weight to the final exam, it really accounts for 100% of a student's grade in the course. Why? Because equal midterm scores for all students mean that final exam scores are the only factor differentiating student performance. It's the same with golf. The number of long-game and short-game shots is analogous to the weights on the two exams. The part of the game that matters the most is the one with the most skill differences, not the one with the most shots. If all golfers score 100% on their putting exam, then only off-green shots determine the winner of a tournament. Variability is key: It's the *difference* in skill levels across golfers that determines a skill's importance.

Many pro golfers recognize the primacy of the long game. Rory McIlroy has commented, "Guys say you have to have a short game to win tournaments and it is not the case. Not at all." Jack Nicklaus added his support, saying: "I agree with Rory. I never practiced my short game because I felt like if I can hit 15 greens a round and hit a couple of par-fives in two and if I can make all my putts inside 10 feet, who cares where I chip it?"

How does an amateur stack up to a pro?

What does a typical 90-golfer look like, stats-wise, compared to a typical PGA Tour pro? Table 6.6 summarizes some of the key differences between the two. The scoring difference between a pro and an amateur is larger on par-five holes than par-four or par-three holes. Pros hit their drives about 70 yards farther and twice as straight as amateurs, though there is wide variation in these values across golfers. Pros hit their approach shots closer to the hole than amateurs across all shot categories.

Table 6.6. Comparison of a typical 90-golfer and a typical PGA Tour pro. "Greens hit" includes the green and the fringe of the green.

		90-golfer	Pro golfer
Average score	Par-3 holes	3.9	3.1
	Par-4 holes	5.2	4.1
	Par-5 holes	6.0	4.7
Driving	75% driving distance	225 yards	295 yards
	Driving accuracy	6.5 degrees	3.4 degrees
Approach	Median leave, 100–150 yards	12%	5.5%
	Median leave, 150–200 yards	14%	5.9%
	Greens hit, 100–150 yards	46%	80%
	Greens hit, 150–200 yards	26%	67%
Short game	Median leave, 0–20 yards	21%	14%
	Median leave, 20–60 yards	17%	11%
	Median leave, 60–100 yards	13%	6%
	Median leave sand, 0–50 yards	39%	16%
	Greens hit, 0–20 yards	93%	97%
	Greens hit, 20–60 yards	80%	91%
	Greens hit, 60–100 yards	64%	86%
	Greens hit sand, 0–50 yards	69%	92%

We can use Golfmetrics amateur data to determine what separates a 90-golfer from an 80-golfer, or a 100-golfer from a 90-golfer. As with pros, results for individual golfers vary, so in Table 6.7 I present results for typical amateur golfers. The 10-stroke difference between a typical 90-golfer and a typical 80-golfer breaks down this way: The drives of a typical 80-golfer are longer and straighter than those of a typical 90-golfer, and that contributes 2.5 strokes to the 10-stroke difference. In the approach shot category, the 80-golfer hits fewer skulled shots and fewer fat shots, and usually puts these shots closer to the hole than the 90-golfer.[14] This category contributes a whopping 4.0 strokes to the 10-stroke difference. Short-game shots contribute another 2.1 strokes, and putting contributes another 1.4 strokes.[15]

WHETHER THE ANALYSIS IS done using the strokes gained method detailed in this chapter, or the simulation method described in chapter 4, the results are the same: The long game explains two-thirds of the difference in scores between two typical amateur golfers. The short game and putting explain the remaining one-third. Golfers might see quick improvement in scores by working on their short game and putting, but they aren't crazy for taking full-swing lessons and working on their approach shots, or "ball striking" as it is usually called.

---

[14] Recall that the approach shot category included all shots outside of 100 yards from the hole, except for tee shots on par-four and par-five holes. This category includes layup shots and recovery shots.

[15] The results in Table 6.7 are based on simulation analysis. Strokes gained analysis gives similar results and thus provides an independent check of the results. The simulation analysis works this way: A model of a 90-golfer is built using records of shots taken by 90-golfers, and is validated against the data. The same is done for an 80-golfer. Then the 90-golfer model is simulated, but using the 80-golfer's drives. The resulting drop in score is recorded to assess the impact of driving on score. Then the 80-golfer's approach shots are plugged into the 90-golfer simulation to assess the impact of approach shots on score. This simulation approach makes it easy to calculate how each part of the game contributes to the 10-stroke difference in scores between the 90-golfer and the 80-golfer. Details are given in a 2013 Columbia Business School working paper by Broadie and Ko.

Table 6.7. Performance of amateur golfers: where strokes are gained between typical amateur golfers of different skill levels. For a typical amateur golfer to lower his score by 10 strokes requires, on average, a 2.8-stroke improvement in drives, 3.9-stroke improvement in approach shots, a 1.9-stroke improvement in short-game shots, and a 1.3-stroke improvement in putting. The long game, consisting of driving and approach shots, explains 67% of the difference in scores between a typical 100-golfer and a typical 90-golfer; the remaining 33% is explained by the short game and putting. Results are based on simulation analysis in Broadie and Ko (2013).

From	To	Driving	Approach	Short	Putt
90	80	2.5	4.0	2.1	1.4
100	90	2.6	4.0	2.0	1.4
110	100	3.4	3.7	1.7	1.2
	Average	2.8	3.9	1.9	1.3
	Fraction of total	28%	39%	19%	14%

> The long game explains two-thirds of the difference in scores between two typical amateur golfers; the short game and putting explain the remaining one-third.

Contrary to popular belief, this research proves that the long game explains two-thirds of the difference in scores between beginning and skilled amateurs, between amateurs and pros, and between average pros and the best pros. Academics call this a *robust* result: It holds for many different groups of golfers. It's the closest thing to a universal truth in golf.

Others have called these results heresy and sacrilege. But analysis of millions of golf shots disproves the conventional wisdom. There's no denying the importance of chipping and putting, but it's a good long game that sets the table for good scoring in golf. This anonymous quotation says it well: "If you can't putt you can't score, but if you can't drive you can't play."

> "If you can't putt you can't score, but if you can't drive you can't play."

Using strokes gained to diagnose strengths and weaknesses in your game

It's almost a tautology that the route to lower scores is maintaining strengths and improving weaknesses. "We golfers, it turns out, are bad at assessing the state of our skills," wrote golf journalist John Paul Newport. Strokes gained can be a big help in accurately diagnosing the strengths and weaknesses in a golfer's game. Here are a few illustrative stories.

In 2010, Luke Donald was ranked fifth in total strokes gained, in spite of ranking 175th in strokes gained driving. In 2011, he was the leading money winner on the PGA and European tours, and he finished the year ranked number one in the world. Putting is how Luke Donald became number one in the world, according to one golf writer. Really? He was number one in strokes gained putting in 2009, 2010, and 2011. Putting is a big part of Donald's success, but it doesn't explain his *rise* to number one. From 2010 to 2011, his total strokes gained increased by three-quarters of a stroke, with most of the gain coming from a half-stroke improvement in strokes gained driving. After his win at the PGA Tour's season-ending tournament, Luke told the media, "My long game has certainly improved a lot this year." And he was right! (For strokes gained details on Luke's game, see Table A-12 in the appendix.)

In 2011, Bo Van Pelt was ranked 22nd in total strokes gained, in spite of ranking 136th in strokes gained putting. In 2012, he was ninth in total strokes gained, and he tied Rory McIlroy for the most top-10 finishes with 10. From 2011 to 2012, his total strokes gained increased by 0.6 strokes; his strokes gained putting increased by 0.7 strokes. I asked Bo what explained his improved putting. He said that when he went to be fitted for a putter, he found out that he lined up his putts significantly better with a mallet-headed putter than with the blade-style putters he had been using. The switch improved his alignment and his path, and reduced his putter face rotation. He also decided to stick to one putter rather than switching putters after a poor putting round or tournament.

Sometimes strokes gained can shine a light on a golfer's strengths even when the golfer himself underestimates them. Justin Rose was ranked fourth in total strokes gained in 2012. In January 2013, Sean Foley, the coach of Tiger Woods, Hunter Mahan, and Justin Rose, asked Justin to rate his short game from the previous year. Justin replied that it needed some work. Armed with my strokes gained report, Sean said, "You had the best short game in 2012. You're like the homecoming queen who thinks she's a little fat!"

What does this mean if you are a typical 90-golfer? If you want to drop 10 strokes from your score, you won't be able to do it solely by improving one skill set, whether it is driving, approach shots, short game, or putting. If you're an atypical 90-golfer, say you have the long game of a scratch-handicap golfer but you're a horrendous putter, then certainly you could pick up more strokes by improving your putting than by improving your long game. Individual golfers can use strokes gained analysis to pinpoint specific areas of strength and weakness, and work on improving the area where they need it most. In addition, golfers can measure driving distances and accuracy and compare them with the amateur baseline. You can measure median leave or greens hit from different initial distances, and compare with the amateur benchmarks presented in this chapter. (In chapter 9, I will also introduce some games based on strokes gained that you can use to analyze and improve your ball striking, short game, and putting.)

The takeaway: The most important part of the game is the only area not represented by a putter, driver, or wedge. While strengths and weaknesses vary for every individual golfer, analysis of millions of golf shots shows that on average, approach shots contribute most to scoring. Ben Hogan might be rolling over in his grave at the thought.

19th Hole Summary

- Accuracy in degrees is independent of the shot distance and makes it easier to compare the accuracy of short hitters against that of long hitters.

- The average accuracy of a pro on the PGA Tour is 3.4 degrees from the desired line; a typical 90-golfer has an accuracy of about 6.5 degrees.

- A one-degree improvement in driving accuracy is about five yards closer to the target line on a 300-yard drive. The value of a one-degree improvement in driving accuracy is about three-quarters of a stroke per round for pros and about 0.9 strokes for a typical 90-golfer.

- The value of twenty additional yards in driving distance is about three-quarters of a stroke per round for pros and about 1.6 strokes for a typical 90-golfer.

- Driving distance is more important than driving accuracy.

- Across a range of golfers from amateurs to pros, longer hitters tend to be straighter hitters.

- PGA Tour pros hit half of their shots from 100 to 150 yards to within 5.5% of the initial distance to the hole; a typical 90-golfer hits half to within 12%. Expressed another way, from 125 yards, PGA Tour pros hit half of their shots to within 21 feet of the hole; a typical 90-golfer hits half to within 45 feet.

- Among the top 40 PGA Tour pros, approach shots accounted for 40% of their scoring advantage, driving accounted for 28%, the short game 17%, and putting 15%.

- Combining the driving and approach categories gives the long game, or all shots starting outside of 100 yards from the hole. The long game accounts for two-thirds of the scoring differences between the top PGA Tour pros and average tour pros. The short game and putting combine to explain the remaining one-third of scoring differences. The relative importance of the long game is the same between typical high-scoring and low-scoring amateur golfers.

PART II

GOLF STRATEGY

CHAPTER 7

PUTTING STRATEGY:
Using Data and Physics to Improve Your Putting

E ven though putting only accounts for a stroke or two of the difference in scores between a typical 100-golfer and a typical 90-golfer, putts might be the easiest strokes to erase from your scorecard. Physics can help to explain how factors such as green slope and putt angle affect distance control and the break of a putt. By examining putt scatter patterns, you can learn the strategies of the best putters in the world. And dynamic programming reminds us that the best putting involves not only thinking about whether the first putt is sunk, but also looking to where the misses finish.

Three ingredients are needed to sink a putt:

The first is *green reading*, or assessing the contours of the green, its slope and speed.

The second is *distance control*, which involves hitting the putt at the right speed for the green you are on.

The third is *directional accuracy*, or hitting the putt along the right line for the speed you've chosen.

These three elements relate to each other: The speed and slope of a particular green will affect how far the ball will roll and where it will end up. Within the range of choices that could lead to a holed putt, a good strategy can help you to choose those most likely to succeed.

ONE PLAYER TOLD ME he doesn't have his caddy help him read the greens because the caddy doesn't know how hard he plans to hit the putt. Green reading, speed, and line are inextricably linked. When putting, you've probably observed that the same putt can be sunk by hitting it softly and playing a lot of break or by hitting it harder and playing less break. Which is better, the die-it or jam-it strategy? In other words, is it better to have the ball tumble into the hole on its last roll, or is it better to have enough momentum for the ball to hit the back of the cup before falling? A putt breaks less when it is hit more firmly, and that potentially increases the chance of sinking the putt. But there is a trade-off, because a firmly hit putt that misses will finish farther from the hole, increasing the chance of missing the comebacker.

Like pieces of a jigsaw puzzle, green reading, distance, and direction all fit together to produce great putting. In this chapter, we'll examine the pieces and then put them together to gain insights about putting strategy.

Green slope: an important element of putting

Leadhands, nicknamed for putting as if he had weights at the end of his wrists, usually hits a downhill putt too hard and an uphill putt too softly. When facing a 20-foot putt, he doesn't recognize the gentle downhill slope, but thinks, "I left a similar length putt short on the last hole, so I better hit this one harder." He steps up and strokes: The putt rolls six feet past the hole. "Damn, I just tapped that," he mutters. Leadhands lines up the next one and leaves it short, racking up yet another three-putt.

When an amateur asks his partner or caddie for a read, a typical question is, "How much break do you see?" It is rare that you hear, "How steeply uphill is the slope for this putt?" Yet for most putts, and certainly for putts of any length, the most important judgment to make is the slope of the green, for slope determines both how hard or softly a putt needs to be hit and how much it will break. Mastering the art of green reading would help to reduce distance errors when putting.

One degree of slope corresponds to a rise of one foot over 60 feet of horizontal distance.[16] Two degrees of slope corresponds to a rise of two feet over 60 feet of horizontal distance. The slope can be very steep on the ramp between two tiers of a green, but holes aren't placed there because it would be unfair. The average slope near a hole at PGA Tour events is 1.1 degrees. Few holes have slopes less than 0.5 degrees, since there's usually some slope for drainage reasons. About 5% of greens have slopes of 2.0 degrees or greater.

Unfortunately for Leadhands, he is putting on a green with two

---

[16] More precisely, one degree of slope represents a rise of 1.05 feet over 60 feet, corresponding to a *grade* of 1.75% (i.e., 1.05/60).

One commercial device for measuring green slopes is the Breakmaster.

degrees of slope. If he is thinking of slope at all, it is likely that he underestimates its severity. When faced with a steep slope, amateurs are more likely to underestimate it than to overestimate it. This behavioral bias was identified in 1968 by Ward Edwards, who called it "conservatism." Edwards didn't have golf in mind, nor was he referring to anything political. By conservatism, he meant the tendency to underestimate large values and overestimate small values. In Leadhands's case, he knows that his first putt is downhill, but he doesn't realize how much, because like most people he has a natural tendency to underestimate extremes.

Green speed: another piece of the putting puzzle

Green speed is the distance, in feet, a ball travels on a level green when started at a velocity of approximately four miles per hour. A ball will travel farther on greens with less friction—those that are closely mown, firm, or very dry—so these greens are faster. The ball won't travel as far when there's more friction or resistance due to longer grass, bumps, or wetness, so these greens are slower.

In 1935, after seeing Gene Sarazen roll a putt off a speedy green during a U.S. Open at Oakmont, Edward Stimpson Sr. designed a wooden device to measure green speed. The distance a ball travels in feet on a green after rolling off his device is now called the Stimp reading of the green. In 1976, Frank Thomas, technical director of the USGA, redesigned the device out of aluminum, and used it at the U.S. Open at the Atlanta Athletic Club. The USGA has made its Stimpmeter available to golf course superintendents since 1978.

Green speeds have increased substantially in the past few decades. Today many municipal courses have green speeds around seven (that is, a golf ball will roll seven feet on a level portion of the green when started at a velocity of four miles per hour). These green speeds, typical through most of golf history, would be considered extremely slow by today's tournament standards. Though there is a great deal of variability due to climate, course maintenance, and types of grass, a Stimp reading of nine is now found on many good public and private courses. PGA Tour courses are even faster: The average Stimp reading of greens at PGA Tour events is 11. For some major tournaments, the Stimp reading might be as high as 13 or even 14.

If the slope at the hole on a fast green is too steep, bad things can happen. A golfer could hit a ball up to the hole, miss by a fraction, and have the ball roll back to his feet. The USGA learned this the hard way at the 1998 U.S. Open at the Olympic Club. Payne Stewart was leading the tournament on the 18th hole of the second round and faced an eight-foot putt for birdie. His putt barely missed the hole, and under normal green conditions, it would have finished one or two feet from the hole. But his putt kept moving slowly away from the hole and, 33 agonizing seconds later, finished 25 feet below. A combination of sun and wind had increased the speed of the green just to the critical value where putts don't stop. Stewart bogeyed the hole and went on to lose the tournament by one stroke.

Distance control: how hard to hit?

How hard should you hit a 20-foot downhill putt on a two-degree sloped green rolling 11 on the Stimpmeter? I find it useful to think of how far a putt would travel on a level green (zero degrees of slope) running at the same Stimp reading. I call this the *level green distance*. Suppose you tap a downhill putt on a two-degree sloped green rolling 11 on the Stimp-meter so it just dies at the hole 20 feet away. How far would the ball travel on a perfectly flat green, also with a Stimp reading of 11? Certainly less than 20 feet, but how much less? A little physics reveals that the answer is 10 feet. A 20-foot downhill putt, with this green speed and slope, needs to be hit as hard as a 10-foot putt on a level green. It's not enough to pace off the distance to the hole. You also need to judge the steepness of the green in order to determine how hard to hit the putt.

When Leadhands faced his six-foot comebacker, he was thinking about his most recent memory, that of hitting a putt too hard. Instead, he should have been thinking, "Wow, that downhill green was steeper than I had estimated. I need to make sure to hit this uphill one a little harder than normal because the green is so steep." How hard did he need to hit the uphill six-footer? Hard enough to travel nine feet on a level green. That's right—a golfer needs to hit an uphill six-footer almost as hard as a down-hill 20-footer for both to reach the hole (on a 2.0-degree, 11-Stimp green).

Amateur golfers are more likely to leave a long putt five feet short than they are to pull or push a putt by five feet. When reading putts, to get in or as close as possible to the hole it is important to focus on the amount of slope on the green. Golfers who ask, "Does this putt break to the left or right?" should also be asking, "How steep is this slope?"

Hitting downhill putts too hard and uphill putts too softly are common amateur putting errors. To reduce these errors, focus on estimating green slopes and understanding the impact of green slope on putt speed.

Table 7.1 summarizes level green distances by green slope and green speed. The table shows why fast greens are so much more difficult to putt than slow greens. For 20-footers on a seven-Stimp, 2.0-degree green, uphill putts need to be hit like 26-foot level putts, and downhill putts need to be hit like 14-foot level putts. In other words, putts under these conditions have an uphill-downhill ratio of about two to one. In contrast, 20-footers on a fast steep (13-Stimp, 2.0-degree) green have an uphill-downhill ratio of four to one. That's a big reason why fast greens require a lot more touch than slow greens. Another reason is that putts need to be hit softer on fast greens, bringing nerves more into play. (An offsetting factor is that closely mown and rolled greens are smoother than slower greens, which tend to be inconsistent and bumpy, so putts roll truer. Smooth greens, which also tend to be fast greens, take some of the luck out of putting.)

Table 7.1. Level green distances. The left panel shows the level green distances for a 20-foot putt by green slope (measured in degrees) and green speed (measured by the Stimpmeter, in feet). All putts are assumed to be straight uphill or straight downhill. Positive slopes indicate uphill putts; negative slopes indicate downhill putts. The right panel shows initial putt velocities in miles per hour for a putt to travel 20 feet for a given slope and Stimp reading. The velocities show that uphill putts need to be hit harder than downhill putts. Putts on slow greens need to be hit harder than putts on fast greens.

		Level green distance for a 20-foot putt				Velocity in mph for a putt to travel 20 feet			
		Stimp reading				Stimp reading			
	Slope	7	9	11	13	7	9	11	13
Uphill	2	26	28	30	32	8.0	7.2	6.7	6.4
	1	23	24	25	26	7.5	6.7	6.2	5.8
Level	0	20	20	20	20	6.9	6.1	5.5	5.1
	-1	17	16	15	14	6.4	5.5	4.8	4.3
Downhill	-2	14	12	10	8	5.8	4.7	3.9	3.3
Up-down ratio		1.9	2.3	3.0	4.0				

Scatter patterns: the target and the hole

Even though the ultimate goal is to get the ball in the hole, the target on a putt is usually not the hole itself. A putt that would roll one foot beyond the hole if the hole were covered will fall into an uncovered hole. You pick a target beyond the hole in order for the ball to fall into the hole when the hole gets in the way of the putt.

Setting the target at the hole, that is, zero feet beyond the hole, can be called the "die-it-in-the-hole" strategy. You'll often hear the advice "just lag it close" as another way to express it. For short putts, this strategy is far too conservative: It will lead to leaving 50% of putts short of the hole, with fewer made putts as a consequence. So let's start by restating that on short putts, choosing a target beyond the hole is necessary for best performance. But how much farther beyond the hole is a good strategy? Six inches? Three feet? How does the strategy relate to the length of the putt, green speed, and putt angle?

Analyzing a scatter pattern, which shows where many putts finish around the hole, can help pinpoint the ideal target from a given starting point. We can infer the putting strategy used by PGA pros by looking at the scatter pattern of their missed putts. The middle of a scatter pattern reveals the putter's intended target. If the target was five feet beyond the hole, then we'd expect to see missed putts centered on a spot about five feet beyond the hole. If a golfer intended to lag it just to the hole, we'd expect to see missed putts centered on the hole.[17]

A scatter pattern is more dispersed for long putts than short putts. Scatter patterns are more dispersed for amateurs than for pros.

Figure 7.1 shows a sample scatter pattern of missed 30-foot uphill putts taken by pros. The middle of the scatter pattern, or target, is marked with an X. The target is centered almost exactly on the hole, thus exposing that the putting strategy for most PGA Tour pros on 30-foot uphill putts is to lag it to the hole. Pros leave almost exactly 50% of these putts short of the hole, which is consistent with a target at the hole. A target that is one or more feet beyond the hole would lead to longer second putts and more putts to hole out, on average. A target that is one or more feet short of the hole would lead to fewer made putts and longer second putts.

---

[17] A better estimate of the golfer's target would be the middle of the scatter pattern of all putts, if we could see where the holed putts would have finished. Using the middle of only the missed putts could introduce a small bias in the estimate of the target.

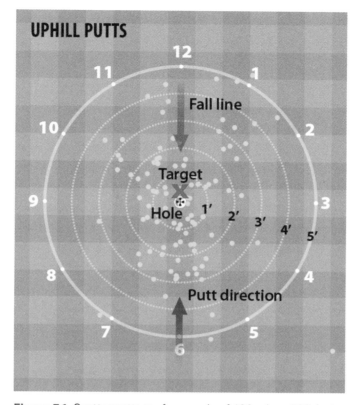

Figure 7.1. Scatter pattern of a sample of 100 missed 30-foot uphill putts for PGA Tour pros on greens between one and two degrees of slope, with an average slope of 1.4 degrees. The middle of the scatter pattern, or target, is marked with an X, which is centered almost exactly on the hole. This reveals the "average" putting strategy for PGA Tour pros on 30-foot uphill putts is to lag it to the hole.

For short putts, the main goal is to sink it, because a three-putt is not a big worry. In order to be sunk, the putt has to reach the hole. So the target needs to be set far enough beyond the hole so that almost all putts have a chance to go in. By setting the target beyond the hole, pros leave almost no putts short. Let's consider two short putts, a four-foot uphill and a four-foot downhill. How far beyond the hole should you set your target for these putts? Should the target be farther beyond the hole for the uphill putt or the downhill putt?

Figure 7.2 shows scatter patterns of missed four-foot putts taken by PGA Tour pros on greens with slopes between one and two degrees (that is, above average in steepness, though not extremely steep). The scatter pattern is more spread out for downhill putts than uphill putts, in part due to gravity: Uphill putts slow down quickly at the end of their path. For short putts, the scatter pattern needs to be positioned far enough beyond the hole to ensure that almost all putts reach the hole, so the target on a downhill putt needs to be set further beyond the hole than for an uphill putt. That is what the pros do.

Pros leave only about 1% of their four-footers short. In order for this to happen, the target for downhill putts needs to be farther from the hole than the target for uphill putts. Using the middle of each scatter pattern to infer the target, we see that pros send uphill putts 1.2 feet beyond the hole and downhill putts 2.2 feet beyond the hole. Of course, if the target is 2.2 feet beyond the hole, then some misses will roll three feet, four feet, or even farther beyond the hole.

Downhill putts: Target should be farther beyond the hole.
Uphill putts: Target should be closer to the hole.

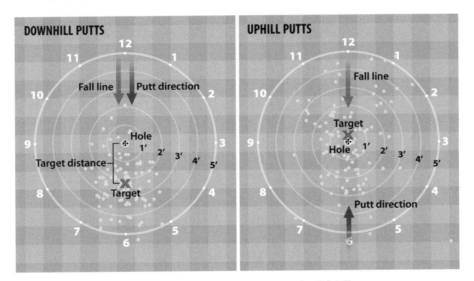

Figure 7.2. Scatter patterns of missed four-foot putts for PGA Tour pros on greens between one and two degrees of slope, with an average slope of 1.4 degrees. The left green shows downhill putts, with a target 2.2 feet beyond the hole. The right green shows uphill putts, with a target 1.2 feet beyond the hole. PGA Tour pros sink 87% of the four-foot downhill putts and leave 1.0% short; they sink 89% of the uphill putts and leave 1.2% short.

Now let's consider how the green slope affects what the target distance should be. For a four-foot downhill putt, should the target be farthest from the hole on a relatively flat (0.7-degree) green, a moderately sloped (1.4-degree) green, or a steeply sloped (2.3-degree) green? The steeper the green, the harder it is to control distance, and the larger is the scatter pattern, so the target should be farther from the hole to prevent leaving it short. For four-foot downhill putts, PGA Tour pros' scatter patterns reveal that they have a target 1.9 feet beyond the hole on relatively flat greens, 2.2 feet on moderately sloped greens, and 2.5 feet on steeply sloped greens.

The reverse happens for four-foot uphill putts. The steeper the green, the quicker the ball stops as it slows down and the smaller the scatter pattern, so the target should be closer to the hole. For four-foot uphill putts, PGA Tour pros' scatter patterns reveal a target 1.4 feet beyond the hole on relatively flat greens, 1.2 feet on moderately sloped greens, and 1.0 feet on steeply sloped greens.

- Downhill putts: the steeper the green, the farther the target should be beyond the hole.

- Uphill putts: the steeper the green, the closer the target should be to the hole.

The goal is to find a strategy that gets the ball in the hole with the fewest strokes. For long putts, pros set their target at, or very close to, the hole. This makes sense in order to give these putts some chance of going in the hole while also leaving the shortest next putt. For short putts, pros set the target far enough beyond the hole so that almost all putts reach the hole and have a chance of going in. Because distance is harder to control on downhill putts, the target should be farther beyond the hole than for comparable uphill putts. Similarly, for short downhill putts, the target should be farther beyond the hole on steeper and faster greens.

Figure 7.3 shows the targets set by PGA Tour pros for a range of putt distances and putt angles, on a green with a slope of 1.4 degrees, just slightly above average slope for a PGA Tour course. The targets represented in this graph were estimated from the middle of scatter patterns taken from Shot-Link data at a range of distances and conditions. As you can see from the figure, pros set their targets closer to the hole as putts get longer. Targets on uphill putts are closer to the hole than on any other kind of putt. Pros set their targets farther beyond the hole on downhill putts, and farthest for short downhill putts. Similar graphs showing pros' targets for flatter and steeper green slopes can be found in the appendix.

As the putt distance increases, the target should move closer to the hole.

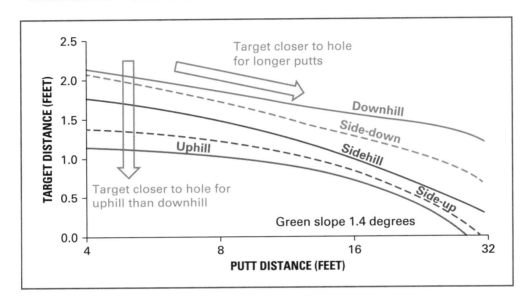

Figure 7.3. Target distances for PGA Tour pros on greens with slopes between one and two degrees at the hole and an average slope of 1.4 degrees. The target is farther from the hole on downhill putts than uphill. The target is farther from the hole on shorter putts than longer putts.

Observing how the pros set their putting targets can provide lessons for the rest of us. The scatter pattern for an amateur from 20 feet is similar to a pro from 30 feet, so targets should be comparable. An amateur's putting prowess from five feet is similar to a pro's from eight feet. Amateurs can use the pro targets after making a suitable distance adjustment.

Even though it isn't easy to distinguish between a target one foot versus two feet beyond the hole, the difference of a foot matters very much. Pros leave only about 1% of four-foot putts short, regardless of the green slope and putt direction. If they used a target for downhill putts of only one foot beyond the hole instead of two, they would leave 6% or 7% of these putts short, a dramatic difference in performance.

There has been much debate in the golfing community about how far beyond the hole is an optimal strategy. By analyzing pro data and the results from dynamic programming, and the intuition based on putt scatter patterns, we discover that a static "fixed distance beyond the hole" target strategy is not going to be effective. The right target changes with the green slope, green speed, and putt distance. To get your best score, then, you have to pay attention to conditions such as green slope and speed, and fit your putting strategy to the conditions.

The right amount of aggression

Why is leaving a four-footer 10 inches short of the hole worse than missing a four-footer six inches long, since both lead to the same two-putt outcome? Leaving too many putts short indicates a poor putting strategy—you haven't moved your scatter pattern or your target far enough beyond the hole. In the long run, this will mean fewer sunk putts. It's like leaving money on the table, to borrow a poker expression.

There's a trade-off between putting with enough aggressiveness to give the ball a chance to go in the hole versus too much aggressiveness, which leads to long comebackers. It's easy to get 100% of putts to the hole by whacking them, but not a good idea, because that aggressive strategy will lead to too many three-putts. Lagging five-footers to avoid a three-putt doesn't make sense either.

Die it or jam it? Neither is correct for short putts! Die-it risks leaving the putt short. Jam-it risks running the putt too far by the hole. An intermediate strategy makes sense for short putts, one that will have the ball rolling one to two and a half feet by the hole depending on the green slope and putt angle. As the putt distance increases, the die-it strategy makes more sense, especially for uphill putts. Your goal should be to minimize the number of putts taken, not to minimize the number of putts left short of the hole, or to avoid three-putts.

> Short putts: The target should be 1.0 to 2.5 feet beyond the hole, intermediate between the die-it and jam-it strategies.

We can look to the data to get a sense for the proper level of aggressiveness, which is different for short putts and long putts. What fraction of all 10-foot putts do PGA Tour pros leave short of the hole? The answer is 7%. The best putters on tour leave only 6% short, while the worst pro putters leave as many as 9% short. Amateurs do far worse: 90-golfers leave 16% of their 10-footers short of the hole. The data are clear: Better putters leave fewer putts short of the hole.

A useful alternative to the "die-it or jam-it" mentality is to ask, "How hard do I need to hit 10-foot putts so that I leave fewer than 7% of them short?" The 10-footers should be hit hard enough to have a chance to go in, but not so hard that you risk three-putting with any regularity.

As the distance of the putt increases, the chance of a one-putt declines, and the possibility of a three-putt increases. To properly balance these risks, golfers should be less aggressive on longer putts, and that's exactly what we see in the data. PGA Tour pros leave 17% of their 15-footers short of the hole, 26% of their 20-footers, and about 50% of their 50-footers. Die-it-at-the-hole is the proper strategy for long putts.

> Better putters leave fewer putts short of the hole. In fact, 90-golfers leave two to four times as many putts short as the best pro putters.

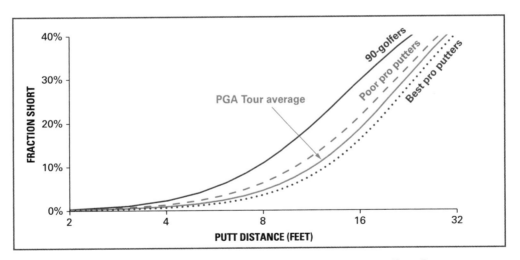

Figure 7.4. Fraction of putts left short by PGA Tour pros and amateur golfers. Poor putters leave more putts short than better putters. All golfers leave more putts short, on average, as the putt distance increases. Tour pros with strokes gained putting (SGP) of 0.5 putts per round or better are placed in the "best pro putters" category. These represent, approximately, the best 20 putters on tour in each year. Tour pros with SGP of -0.5 putts per round or less are placed in the "poor pro putters" category.

Table 7.2. Fraction of putts left short by PGA Tour pros and amateurs. For putts 15 feet and under, amateurs leave two to four times as many putts short as the best pro putters.

Putt distance	Best pro putters	PGA Tour average	Poor pro putters	90-golfer
4	1%	1%	1%	2%
5	1%	2%	2%	4%
6	2%	2%	3%	6%
7	3%	3%	4%	8%
8	3%	4%	6%	11%
9	5%	6%	8%	13%
10	6%	7%	9%	16%
11	8%	9%	12%	19%
12	9%	11%	14%	21%
13	11%	13%	15%	23%
15	14%	17%	20%	28%
17	18%	20%	23%	31%
20	23%	26%	28%	36%

As shown in Figure 7.4 and Table 7.2, for putts 15 feet and under, 90-golfers leave two to four times as many putts short as the best pro putters. To improve these numbers, amateurs need to set their targets farther beyond the hole and work on their distance control and putting strategy.

Putt like the pros

A simple tracking exercise can help you putt more like the pros. Putting targets are invisible; they cannot be directly observed, and it is difficult to think of adjusting your target to be six inches closer to or farther from the hole. In contrast, the fraction of putts left short is easy to count and provides a useful diagnostic for both pros and amateurs. Keep track of the fraction of putts you leave short in the three- to seven-foot range, the eight- to 11-foot range, and the 12- to 15-foot range. Compare your results with those of the pros shown in Table 7.2. Use this information to become a better putter.

How close do pros and amateurs leave long putts?

The first goal in putting is to sink it, but since few long putts are sunk, the next-most-important goal is to leave the putt close to the hole. How close to the hole does a PGA Tour pro leave a 40-foot putt? How about amateurs?

I bet you think amateurs are far worse than pros. Half of pros' 40-foot putts stop within three feet of the hole, an error of about 7.5%. Half of 90-golfers' 40-foot putts stop within four feet of the hole, an error of about 10%. Amateurs have surprisingly good distance control. It's true that the bad putts of amateurs don't fare as well as the bad putts of pros. One-quarter of pros' 40-foot putts stop more than 4.5 feet from the hole; one-quarter of amateurs' 40-foot putts stop outside of seven feet from the hole. It's also true that pros are putting on faster, but smoother, greens than amateurs.

Percentage distance error, the distance to the hole after the putt compared to the beginning of the putt, is a sensible measure of distance error for long putts, but not for short putts. A missed two-footer that finishes two feet from the hole has a 100% distance error, but the percentage error is meaningless. For short putts, I prefer to look at the percentage of putts that a golfer leaves short of the hole.

Directional accuracy and the putting wheel: understanding breaking putts

Our friend Leadhands hit a five-foot uphill left-to-right-breaking putt, as shown in Figure 7.5. He played one cup of break and the putt just missed on the high side, leaving a three-footer for his next putt. Should Leadhands play more or less than one cup of break on his next putt, assuming that he hits it with reasonable speed, unlike his first putt?

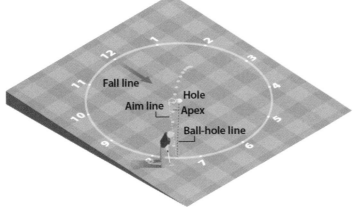

Figure 7.5.
A five-foot sidehill-uphill putt that missed on the high side and finished three feet from the hole. The golfer hit the putt too hard for one cup of break.

Had Leadhands hit the ball a little softer or played for a little less break, the putt would have dropped. The comebacker is shorter, only three feet instead of five, and shorter putts break less than longer putts. You might think that less than one cup of break on the second putt seems correct, or at most a half-cup outside the right edge. But physics shows that at the speed to go 18 inches beyond the hole, Leadhands should play almost one and a half cups of break. That's right, he should play more break, not less, than on the first putt. Leadhands would miss low if he played less than one cup of break at that speed, as shown in Figure 7.6. After playing too much break and missing on the high side, playing even more break on the next putt is counterintuitive, so what's going on here?

Downhill putts break substantially more than uphill putts, because of the physics of a ball rolling on the green.

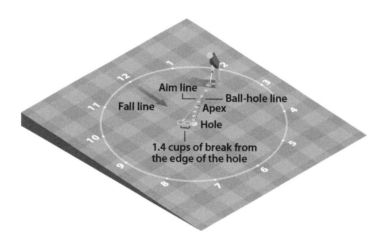

Figure 7.6. A three-foot sidehill-downhill putt that goes in the heart when played with 1.4 cups of break.

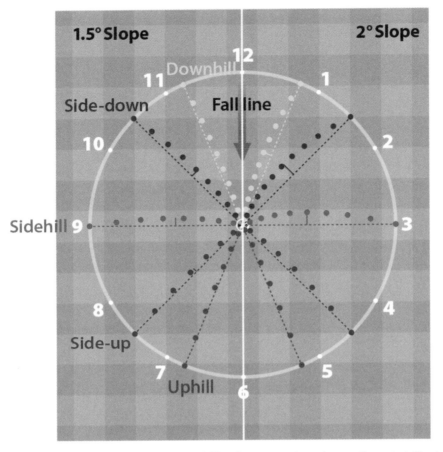

Figure 7.7. The putting wheel: Five-foot putt trajectories are illustrated. The left half-green has 1.5 degrees of slope and the right half-green has 2.0 degrees of slope. Downhill putts break more than uphill putts. Putts break more on steeper greens than on flatter greens. Similarly, though this is not shown, putts break more on faster greens than on slower greens.

> Downhill putts break substantially more than uphill putts.

The putting wheel in Figure 7.7 illustrates how the break of a putt depends on where on the clock face the putt starts. The clock is oriented so the fall line is at 12:00. All putts from 12:01 to 5:59 break right to left. All putts from 6:01 to 11:59 break left to right (they aren't shown here, to avoid clutter). A 9:00 putt has the same amount of left-to-right break as the right-to-left break of the 3:00 putt. Downhill putts break more than uphill putts starting from the comparable position on the clock: A putt from 1:00 breaks more than a putt from 5:00; a putt from 2:00 breaks more than a putt from 4:00. Comparing the left half-green and the right half-green in Figure 7.7, you can see that putts break more on steeper greens. Similarly, though this is not shown, putts break more on faster greens than on slower greens.

> Putts break more on steeper greens than on flatter greens.
> Putts break more on faster greens than on slower greens.

The putting wheel suggests an approach to green reading. The first step is to look at the green and try to find the fall line, illustrated by the 12:00 position on the clock. A ball at 12:00 that is rolled directly at the hole will fall into the hole without breaking left or right. If you walk in a circle around the hole, the 12:00 position is the point of highest elevation; the 6:00 position is the point of lowest elevation. After finding the fall line, see where your ball is positioned on the clock. You'll know that an uphill putt from 5:00 will break less than an uphill putt from 4:00. Then estimate the steepness of the green along the 12:00 to 6:00 fall line, because the slope affects the break of all putts around the clock face.

> Putting drill: A great drill is to drop balls in a circle, say, five feet from the hole, on the practice green. Practice trying to find the fall line. Then putt the balls into the hole and compare the breaks and trajectories with the putting wheel.

Breaking putts

Let's see if Leadhands has learned about breaking putts now. Figure 7.8 shows his five-foot downhill right-to-left-breaking putt. He played one and a half cups of break, which was not enough for this green speed and slope. He missed on the low side, leaving a three-footer for his next putt. Should Leadhands play the next putt inside or outside of the left edge of the hole?

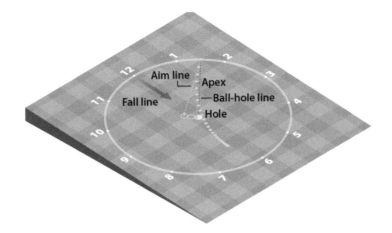

Figure 7.8. A five-foot downhill right-to-left putt that missed on the low side and finished three feet from the hole.

Previously Leadhands would have thought, "I just missed on the low side because I didn't play enough break. So on this next putt, I'm going to play a little extra break." Executing on that thought would lead to a three-putt. Now, armed with the knowledge of the putting wheel, Leadhands thinks, "This next putt is uphill, it's closer to the fall line, and it's a shorter putt than the last one. All of these factors mean there will be less break in this putt. I'm going to play the putt left-center, between the left edge and the center of the cup." This reasoning is correct and leads to a successful second putt, as illustrated in Figure 7.9.

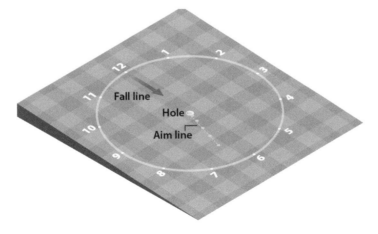

Figure 7.9. A three-foot putt from 6:30 that goes in the heart when played left-center.

When a pro misses a putt by a huge margin, green-reading errors are probably to blame. This play-by-play from the website of the 2012 Ryder Cup described one such error by Steve Stricker: "Stricker needs to win the hole to keep the hopes alive for the U.S. His approach hits the middle of the green, but too much, it rolls beyond Kaymer's ball. Stricker is a long way through the shadows: he's about 40 feet away. His putt starts left . . . and stays left. Misses by about eight feet, *on the wrong line all the way.* Kaymer needs a two-putt to give Europe the Ryder Cup win to retain the Cup. And Kaymer's putt goes too far as well, and leaves him with about six feet for his par. Now Stricker is up, putting for par. A must make . . . and he sinks it! Stricker saves par."

The mysterious case of missing low

The "low" side of the hole is the side with lower elevation, the left side of the hole on a right-to-left-breaking putt, or the right side on a left-to-right-breaking putt. My data show an impressive stat: Amateur golfers miss almost 70% of short putts on the low side of the hole. The proper fraction to miss on the low side should be about 50%. If a guy pees and consistently misses the bowl to the right, wouldn't he try to adjust his aim to compensate? It's a skill most males perfect at home, though you might not know it from their performance in public restrooms.

If you miss significantly more than 50% of putts on the low side, you are giving away strokes, making a systematic error that will lead to making fewer putts in the long run. It's often claimed that it is better to miss breaking putts on the "high" or "pro" side of the hole, but that's not true. Golfers who miss significantly more than 50% of putts on the high side are also giving away strokes, although this affliction affects very few golfers.

A useful stat to track is the fraction of makeable putts—say inside of 15 or 20 feet—that you miss on the high side, and the fraction that you miss on the low side. If you miss significantly more than 50% on one side or the other, that is a golden opportunity for improving your putting. To understand why so many golfers miss on the low side, we need to consider the physics of breaking putts.

The physics of breaking putts: aim at the apex, miss low

The top green in Figure 7.10 shows the path of a breaking putt. The *fall line* is the straight downhill direction that water would follow due to gravity. The clock face is oriented so that the downhill direction is from 12:00 to 6:00. The putt starts at 1:30 and gravity causes the putt to break from right to left, when viewed by a golfer looking from behind the ball to the hole. To sink the putt, the golfer needs to start the ball to the right of the ball-hole line. The *aim line* shows the initial direction of the putt. Golfers say this putt has "three cups of break," as illustrated by the dashed white circles. The putt's *apex* is the point on the trajectory that is farthest from the line joining the ball to the hole. The aim line lies to the right of the putt's path. Due to gravity, the putt starts breaking *immediately* after the putt is hit. Except at the starting point, the path of the putt is *always* below the aim line. The putts shown in Figure 7.10 are not freehand drawings. Equations from physics are used to determine the paths putts would take on a smooth, though sloped, surface.

Figure 7.10. Breaking putts illustrated. The fall line is the straight downhill direction. The putts start at 1:30 and break from right to left. The top green shows the path, in yellow, of a putt with three cups of break, measured from the edge of the hole. The path of the putt is always below the aim line, except at the starting point. The bottom green shows the path of a putt in red that misses low because it was aimed at the apex of the yellow putt.

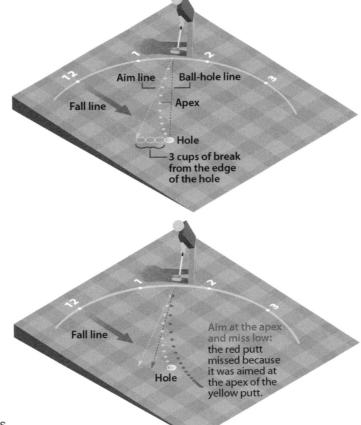

Have you ever heard the advice "Imagine the putt's path and then aim at the apex"? Aiming at the apex will lead to missing putts on the low side of the hole, as illustrated in the bottom green in Figure 7.10. To sink a breaking putt, you need to aim higher than the putt's apex.

> To sink a breaking putt, aim higher than the putt's apex.

The path of a putt after hitting it is visible, but the aim line is not. This makes it hard to learn from your own putts and to go to school on others' putts. You can, however, get useful feedback on a practice green by putting through a "gate" consisting of two tees placed a few inches in front of the ball, or by using the Putting Tutor, a learning device developed by renowned coach Dave Pelz. Both make it easier to visualize the putt's true aim line.

Missing on the low side can happen for the same reason amateurs leave many putts short: underestimating the slope of the green. You can perfectly visualize a putt, start it exactly on the aim line, and then miss low if the green slopes more than you expected.

In many sports you aim straight at the ultimate target. But on a breaking putt, the aim line points away from the hole, not directly at it. Even if you read the green properly, and aim on the proper line, your mind can influence you to change your putter path in midstroke, to hit at the ultimate target, the hole, and not away from it on the aim line.

The data clearly show that amateurs miss too many putts on the low side of the hole. Aiming beyond the apex of a putt, mastering the art of reading the green slope, and resisting the natural tendency to hit toward the hole are three of many possible ways to compensate for this phenomenon. Practicing with gates or other feedback devices can be an avenue to improvement. Keeping track of how many putts you miss low versus high is a useful way to assess whether you, like most golfers, suffer from this problem, and whether you are making progress toward solving it.

Going to school

Not all five-footers are created equal. A five-foot putt through a swale is more difficult than a five-footer on a nearly level green. The secret—the underappreciated fact—is that a five-foot second putt is much easier than a five-foot first putt. Why? Because the path of a first putt provides you with information about the fall line and the slope of the green to use on the second putt. Golfers refer to learning about the green by watching your first putt and the putts of others in your group as "going to school."

How important is going to school? Pro golfers sink 5% more second-putt five-footers than first-putt five-footers. This is a large difference, and it holds for uphill and downhill putts. First- and second-putt results are shown in Figure 7.11. It's possible that pro golfers are calmer and make better putting strokes on their second putts, but that explanation isn't very plausible. The most credible explanation is that going to school, that is, learning the slope and speed of the green by watching your first putt and the putts of others in your group, is a critically important factor in putting performance.

To improve putting performance, learn the green slope and speed by watching your first putt and the putts of others in your group.

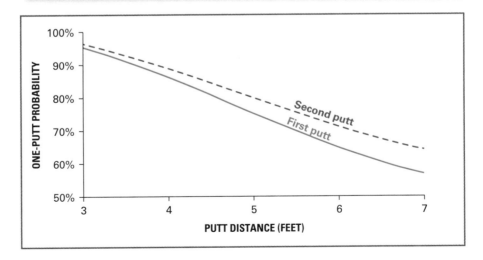

Figure 7.11. Pros sink many more second putts than first putts, and this illustrates the importance of green reading in putting performance.

Have you ever struck a putt, then immediately cringed and turned away in disgust at the realization that you just made an awful mistake? You may have thought that closing your eyes would prevent the poor putt and its accompanying regret from becoming indelibly etched in your mind and heart. By not looking at the path of your putt, though, you lost the benefit of additional learning about the fall line and the green slope on that hole. You made it harder on yourself for the next putt. School is important: If you observe your putts and the putts of others in your group, you will be better able to estimate the fall line, the steepness of the green, and the starting position of your putt on the clock face. You can use this information to sink more putts.

Phil Mickelson came to the final green in the 2004 Masters facing a downhill 20-foot putt for his first major win. As Mickelson explains, "I think the fortunate thing for me was that Chris DiMarco's bunker shot rolled three inches behind my line, behind my ball. Because it was such a fast putt, I had a great look at his entire putt, every inch of break." Phil went to school on DiMarco's putt and sank his 20-footer for a one-stroke victory.

Which are easier: uphill or downhill putts?

Perhaps you've heard a TV golf commentator say, "This putt is easy because it's right down the fall line. All he has to do is get it started and it will track right into the hole." Do you think downhill putts are easier than uphill putts?

One factor that affects downhill and uphill putts differently is gravity. Figure 7.12 shows five-foot uphill and downhill putts on a steeply sloped (2.5 degrees) green. These putts are straight up and straight down the fall line. The putts have no break and should be hit straight at the hole. Instead, both are hit two cups outside the right edge of the hole, representing 11 degrees of directional error. The downhill putt barely misses outside the right edge. The uphill putt misses by more than two cups wide of the right edge. Gravity helps to bend the downhill putt toward the hole. Gravity magnifies the direction error on the uphill putt. Even though both putts are started 11 degrees to the right of the correct aim line, the uphill putt misses by far more than the downhill putt due to gravity's effect. If this were the only effect, then downhill putts would be easier than uphill putts.

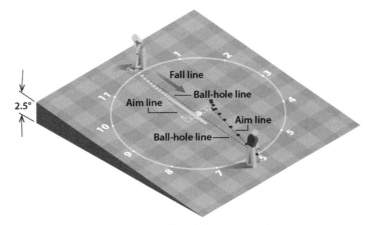

Figure 7.12. Paths of five-foot uphill and downhill putts on a green with 2.5 degrees of slope. Both putts are mistakenly hit two cups outside the right edge of the hole. The downhill putt just misses on the right edge while the uphill putt misses the hole by more than two cups from the right edge. Gravity helps downhill putts hold their line. Gravity magnifies direction errors on uphill putts. The downhill putt takes much more time to travel the same distance than the uphill putt.

What other factors affect uphill and downhill putts differently? The back of the cup is higher than the front of the cup on uphill putts, so it can act like a backboard on center-cut putts. This is a relatively minor factor. Distance control is certainly more difficult on downhill putts. But pros leave few five-footers short and they rarely three-putt from this distance, on either downhill or uphill putts. Distance control is a factor, but its effect is much less than that of gravity, especially on short putts. So are you convinced that downhill putts are easier?

Figure 7.13 shows five-foot uphill and downhill putts. This time two golfers hit their putts directly at the hole with no direction error. The fall line is at 12:00, and the downhill putt starts at 12:20 instead of 12:00, a difference of 11 degrees. Even though the downhill putt starts at 12:20, the golfer incorrectly believes the putt is straight down the fall line. He hits the putt straight at the hole and is surprised to see it break right to left and miss by more than a cup outside the left edge of the hole. The uphill putter starts at 5:40, and believes his putt is straight uphill. He hits the putt straight at the hole. The putt breaks right to left and barely misses the left edge of the hole. Physics easily demonstrates why, though both putts missed, the uphill one was much closer: Green-reading error affects downhill putts more than uphill putts.

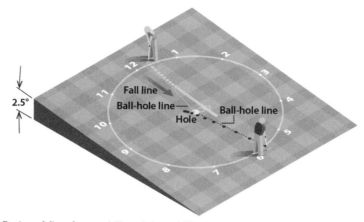

Figure 7.13. Paths of five-foot uphill and downhill putts on a green with 2.5 degrees of slope. The paths illustrate the effects of green-reading error for putts that are hit with no direction error. Both putts are hit directly at the hole in the mistaken belief that the putts are directly on the fall line. The downhill putt misses by more than one cup outside the left edge of the hole. The uphill putt barely misses on the left edge. Green-reading errors affect downhill putts more than uphill putts.

Gravity and green-reading errors both affect whether a putt drops in the hole. But green reading dominates the gravity effect and causes downhill putts to be more difficult than uphill putts.

> Green-reading errors cause downhill putts to be more difficult than uphill putts.

Earlier we saw that second putts are easier than first putts because of the learning effect. Table 7.3 gives PGA Tour putting results that show uphill putts are easier than downhill putts. Green-reading errors are largely responsible for these uphill-downhill differences. Improving your green-reading skills can result in improved putting results.

Remember that three-foot putt that Doug Sanders missed to fall into a tie with Jack Nicklaus for the British Open in 1970? Dan Jenkins wrote that golfer Gerald Micklem predicted Sanders's putt would miss because on that hole on that course, "It looks like it breaks left, but of course it breaks right." Arguably, faulty green reading cost Doug Sanders the British Open.

Table 7.3. One-putt probability, three-putt probability, and average number of putts by PGA Tour pros for uphill and downhill putts. The data are for green slopes between one and two degrees, with an average green slope of 1.4 degrees. Downhill putts start between 11:00 and 1:00; uphill putts start between 5:00 and 7:00. Pros make more uphill putts than downhill (until 15 feet), they three-putt uphill putts less often, and they average fewer putts to hole out on uphill than downhill putts from each distance. In short, uphill putts are easier for pros than downhill putts.

Putt distance	One-putt probability		Three-putt probability		Average number of putts	
	Downhill	Uphill	Downhill	Uphill	Downhill	Uphill
3	96%	96%	0%	0%	1.04	1.04
4	87%	89%	1%	0%	1.14	1.11
5	75%	80%	1%	0%	1.26	1.20
6	64%	69%	1%	0%	1.37	1.31
7	56%	62%	1%	0%	1.45	1.38
8	48%	53%	1%	0%	1.53	1.47
9	41%	48%	1%	0%	1.60	1.53
10	38%	43%	1%	0%	1.63	1.57
11	33%	36%	2%	0%	1.69	1.64
12	30%	33%	2%	0%	1.72	1.67
13	27%	29%	3%	0%	1.76	1.72
15	23%	25%	3%	0%	1.79	1.75
17	19%	19%	3%	1%	1.84	1.82
20	15%	15%	4%	1%	1.89	1.86

Which is easier: a longer uphill putt or a shorter sidehill putt?

Would you rather have a six-foot sidehill putt or an eight-foot uphill putt? Almost every golfer that I've asked, including tour pros, club pros, and low- and high-handicap golfers, says that the eight-foot uphill putt is easier.

We know that distance and angle are two important factors that affect putt difficulty. The distance effect says that shorter putts are easier than longer putts. The angle of a putt refers to where the putt starts on the clock face, whether it is uphill, sidehill, downhill, or somewhere in between. The putt angle effect says that uphill putts are easier than downhill or side- hill putts. Most golfers would agree that these two effects are obvious, and the data show both to be true. But the longer-uphill-versus-shorter-sidehill question asks which of these two effects is stronger.

Figures 7.14, 7.15, and 7.16 show the surprising results for greens that are relatively flat, moderately sloped, and steeply sloped at the hole location: A six-foot sidehill putt is easier than an eight-foot uphill putt in all cases. The distance effect dominates the putt angle effect except for the most steeply sloped greens. In putting, it is better to start closer to the hole than to have a longer putt from an uphill direction, except for the slickest and steepest greens.

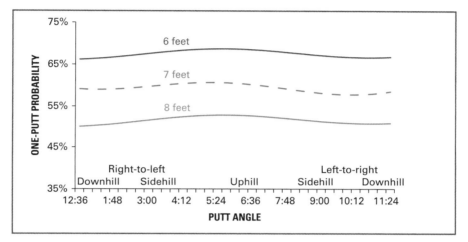

Figure 7.14. One-putt probabilities for PGA Tour pros for greens with slopes less than one degree at the hole (42% of hole locations are in this range), with an average slope of 0.7 degrees. On relatively flat greens, a six-foot sidehill putt is much easier than an eight-foot uphill putt. Putt angles are measured in hours and minutes on the clock face.

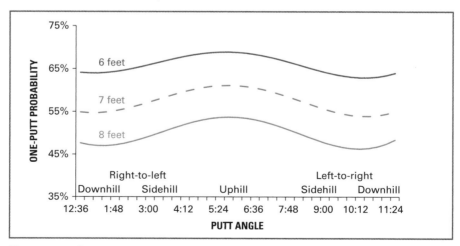

Figure 7.15. One-putt probabilities for PGA Tour pros for greens with slopes between one and two degrees at the hole (54% of hole locations are in this range), with an average slope of 1.4 degrees. On a moderately sloped green, a six-foot sidehill putt is easier than an eight-foot uphill putt. Putt angles are measured in hours and minutes on the clock face.

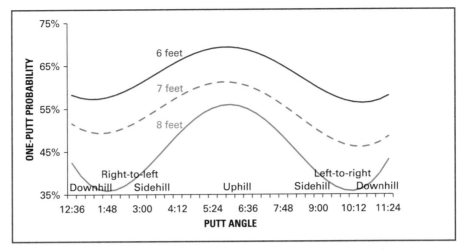

Figure 7.16. One-putt probabilities for PGA Tour pros for greens with slopes greater than two degrees at the hole (4% of hole locations are in this range), with an average slope of 2.3 degrees. On a steep green, a six-foot sidehill putt is more difficult than a seven-foot uphill putt but is still easier than an eight-foot uphill putt.

As you might expect, for right-handed golfers short left-to-right-breaking putts are more difficult than right-to-left-breaking putts. In the four-to-six-foot range, on moderate slopes, the make percentage for starting from 3:00 is almost 2% larger than that for starting from 9:00. The effect is smaller at other symmetrical positions on the clock face and is much smaller for larger distances. Although these calculations might slightly underestimate the effect, because they don't account for left-handed versus right-handed putters, the overall impact seems to be fairly small.

Putt distance is the primary factor that affects putt difficulty, which is the main reason that the strokes gained putting benchmark is based on putt distance.[18]

> Distance is the most important factor in putt difficulty: Except on a very fast steep green, a sidehill putt is easier than a two-foot-longer uphill putt.

[18] A slightly more accurate benchmark based on distance, putt angle, green slope, and green speed could easily be incorporated into the strokes gained putting calculation, but the marginal improvement may not be worth the added complexity.

The distance that separates good from great putters

If you need to sink a 20-footer to get into a playoff, or to win a bet against your buddy, then that's the most important putt to you at that moment. But over the course of a season, what length putt separates the best pro putters from the merely average pro putters? What length putt separates good amateur putters from poor amateur putters?

To be important, there has to be a performance difference between putters. One-footers aren't important because all pros make almost all of these putts. (There's always an exception, such as when In-Kyung [I. K.] Kim only needed to sink a one-foot putt to win the 2012 Kraft Nabisco Championship, a major on the LPGA Tour, and the putt lipped out.) And a putt has to happen enough times in a round to make a significant score difference possible. One golfer might be the best putter in the world from 80 feet, but those putts don't happen often enough to matter too much.

One-footers aren't the most important, because skill differences are too narrow. Eighty-footers aren't the most important, because they don't happen often enough. So what length putt is most important?

We can use the strokes gained putting stat to answer this question. Take each putt distance, look at the total strokes gained per round for the best putters, and compare with the PGA Tour average. This approach takes into account skill differences and the number of putts from each distance. Strokes gained shows that for the pros, the most important putt distance is five feet: This distance accounts for 9% of the total strokes gained of the best putters against the tour average. Next in importance are four and six feet, each accounting for another 8% of the total. Even three-footers account for 5% of the total. The range from three to seven feet accounts for 38% of the total strokes gained. The range from eight to 12 feet accounts for 24% of the total strokes gained. (Additional details are given in the appendix.)

Short putts, especially the three- to seven-foot range, are so important because the best putters sink more than the PGA Tour average and because there are so many of them. From five feet to 13 feet, the best putters sink about 5% more at each putt distance than the PGA Tour average. Five-footers win the importance contest because there are more five-footers than putts of any longer distance. Five-footers account for 5% of all putts.

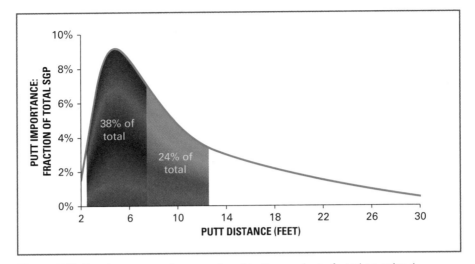

Figure 7.17. Putt importance is proportional to the product of strokes gained difference per putt and the number of putts per round. For a putt to be important, there needs to be a significant performance difference (that is, a difference in strokes gained per putt) and a large number of putts per round. The putt importance curve peaks at five feet: This distance accounts for 9% of the total strokes gained of the best putters against the tour average.

For amateur golfers the results are very similar. The most important putt distance for amateurs is four feet. This distance accounts for 13% of the total strokes lost against pro putters. The range from three to seven feet accounts for 46% of the total strokes lost. Short putts are slightly more important for amateurs than they are for pros. The moral to the story: short putts matter a lot!

> For pros, five feet is the most important putt distance; for amateurs it's four feet. Short putts matter a lot!

How many putts over 21 feet does a PGA Tour golfer sink in a four-round tournament? Five? Seven? If you watch golf on TV, it appears that pros sink putts from all over the planet with great regularity.

But the average number of such long putts sunk by the pros is only 1.5. The best putters on the PGA Tour only sink 1.7 per four-round tournament. Are you surprised? I know I was. TV distorts our view because putts that are made are shown repeatedly on the highlight reel, while missed putts aren't. As the PGA Tour promos say, "These guys are good," but they aren't that good. This information helps to calibrate expectations about your own putting. If you don't sink a single putt over 21 feet in a round, it doesn't mean you've had a bad putting round. This fact also helps to explain why short putts are more important than long putts.

This doesn't mean you should only practice short putts. But over large groups of golfers, what separates the best pro putters from the average pro putters, and what separates pro putters from amateur putters, are the short putts.

Par putts versus birdie putts: an illusion?

Do pros perform differently when putting for par than when putting for birdie? *Sports Illustrated* underwrote a putting study of PGA Tour golfers and published the results in a 1989 article. The article said, "Curiously, when putting from the same distances, the pros were consistently more successful at making putts for pars than putts for birdies." Every stroke counts the same on the scorecard, so how could this be? In the article, Tom Kite was quoted as saying, "There shouldn't be any difference. I know I don't approach a par putt any differently than a birdie putt." Yet that's what the data appeared to show.

Although *Sports Illustrated* commissioned the project, they left the data collection and analysis to the PGA Tour. In a manual precursor to the ShotLink system, 11,000 putts were measured using surveying equipment, then recorded on paper, and finally transferred to a computer for analysis. The person who performed the analysis was Steve Evans, who is now the senior vice president of information systems for the PGA Tour. Among many other responsibilities, he now oversees the collection, analysis, and distribution of the PGA Tour's ShotLink data.

The 1989 article reported that PGA Tour golfers made 55% of their six-footers. In the ShotLink era, 2003–2012, PGA Tour golfers made 67% of their six-footers, a dramatic increase. When I spoke with Steve Evans, he attributed the increase to five factors: better agronomy, which leads to smoother greens, deeper fields, more time spent practicing putting, better teaching of putting by coaches, and fewer shoes with spikes.

Even though 11,000 putts might sound like a lot, it represents less than 1% of the putting data in the ShotLink database. Devin Pope and

Maurice Schweitzer analyzed the ShotLink data for the par-birdie effect. In their 2011 *American Economic Review* article, they concluded that "professional golfers hit birdie putts less accurately than they hit otherwise similar par putts." In 2011, I asked Mark Calcavecchia about the effect and he said, "It's just human nature." Intrigued by these results, I looked into the data myself. Sure enough, for putts between four and seven feet, pros sink 3.6% more par putts than birdie putts. But that figure doesn't take into consideration that par putts in this range tend to be second putts, while birdie putts tend to be first putts. We already know that second putts are easier than first putts because of the learning effect.

After controlling for first-putt–second-putt differences, and controlling for uphill, downhill, and sidehill differences, the par-birdie effect is reduced by more than half. Looking at all putt distances, taking into account differences in strokes gained (not just the one-putt probabilities) and the frequency of putts, I calculate an effect of 0.1 strokes per round. But even this computation overestimates the birdie-par effect. A short first putt for par can happen after chipping from off the green, so the golfer gets to see the path of the chip before hitting his putt. Before putting, a golfer often gets to see the putts of other golfers in the group putting along a similar line.

It seems likely that the par-birdie effect is less than 0.1 strokes per round. Far more important, in my estimation, is the performance increase to be gained from going to school. Watch your putts and the putts of others in your group and read the contours of the green, especially near the hole.

19th Hole Summary

- Green reading, distance control, and directional accuracy are three key elements of putting.

- The slope and speed of the green have a dramatic effect on how hard uphill and downhill putts need to be struck. Amateurs often hit downhill putts too hard and uphill putts too soft.

- "Going to school," learning from your first putt and the putts of others in your group, is a great way to read the green.

- The amount a putt breaks depends on a putt's angle to the fall line, so it is important to find the location of the fall line.

- Aiming for a spot beyond the hole gives your putt the best chance of falling in. For short putts, the target should be farther from the hole on downhill putts, closer on uphill putts.

- For putts under 15 feet, focus on leaving few putts short of the hole, while not overdoing it by banging putts way beyond the hole. Poor putters leave more putts short of the hole.

- For downhill putts, the steeper the green slope the farther the target distance should be from the hole. An occasional downhill miss that goes three or four feet beyond the hole is to be expected.

- For long putts, focus on getting the ball to stop as close to the hole as possible, whatever the putt angle. Better to take a downhill putt a foot or two closer than a longer uphill putt.

- For both pros and amateurs, three to seven feet is the distance range that most separates good putters from average putters.

CHAPTER 8

TEE-TO-GREEN STRATEGY:
How Data and Optimization Can Lower Your Score

Hall of Fame golfer Ray Floyd wrote, "The reason people don't shoot lower scores, to be blunt, is that most people don't know how to PLAY. Not how to swing, or how to hit the ball farther; how to play the game. . . . But here is the hard truth: If somehow I was given your physical game and we had a match, I would beat you 99 times out of 100 because I know how to play the game better than you do."[19] Floyd played with hundreds of amateurs in pro-am tournaments throughout his career, and he says when it comes to strategy, most golfers don't have a clue. This chapter takes you through several strategic situations so you can learn how to develop a game plan to shoot lower scores.

Is golf so different from other sports? Football coaches develop game plans to take advantage of the opposing team's weaknesses. Baseball managers have a strategy toolkit that includes lineups, pitching changes, and defensive alignment. Coaches, managers, and players in many sports engage in constant strategy sessions to try to maximize their chances of winning. Although we don't always think of it, in golf a good game plan also increases our chances of a better score against old man par.

Too often, TV announcers and golf pundits make judgments based on hindsight. Zach Johnson was praised for his strategy of laying up on every par-five hole en route to his 2007 Masters win. But Rickie Fowler was widely criticized for laying up on the par-five on the 15th hole of the

---

[19] Raymond Floyd, *The Elements of Scoring: A Master's Guide to the Art of Scoring Your Best When You're Not Playing Your Best* (New York: Simon and Schuster, 2000).

last round of the 2010 Phoenix Open, which he went on to lose by one shot. Golf Channel announcer Brandel Chamblee called it "the most shocking play I have seen in 2010." In response, Fowler sent a series of tweets to his Twitter followers: "I love how people and the media keep giving me a hard time about 15 last week, where, if I would have gone for it and hit it in the water . . . they would have said 'O he should have laid up,' or if I hit my wedge close and made a bird and gone on to win I'm a genius."

Fowler was exactly right: One good outcome doesn't prove that a strategy was the best choice, and one bad outcome doesn't mean it was a poor decision.

A good strategy is one that gives you the best chance of success. Two important ingredients—shot patterns and hole features—can be combined with simulation to identify the strategy with the best chance of success. Then by considering several strategic situations, we can learn how to develop an optimized game plan to shoot lower scores.

Shot patterns and hole features: two main ingredients of strategy

Good golf decisions depend on two main ingredients: a golfer's shot pattern (the range of outcomes that can happen on any golf shot) and the features of the golf hole (the width of the fairway, placement of hazards, and the shape of the green). Understanding how these ingredients are used to weigh, for example, the risk of sending a shot into a hazard against the reward of hitting a par-five in two will help you achieve your lowest score. Golfers come in all shapes and sizes, and both general principles and specific decisions vary for different types: high- and low-handicappers, short and long hitters, inconsistent and consistent golfers. There are hundreds of books on golf instruction, but *Every Shot Counts* is unique in using golf shot data and scientific analysis to develop strategies to lower your golf scores.

A shot pattern is the range of outcomes that can happen on any golf shot. When you hit a shot, you observe only one outcome, but you need to plan for the range of outcomes that could happen, taking into account the likelihood of each. The outcome of a shot pattern also depends on the features of the hole. A shot that travels 30 yards right of the fairway could have a clear path to the pin on one hole and be out of bounds on another. A good decision considers both a golfer's shot pattern and the features of the hole in order to properly balance the inevitable risk-reward trade-offs.

A golfer's strategic choice is where to position his shot pattern. The most likely outcome of the shot is the golfer's *target* and is, roughly, the middle of the shot pattern. The target represents the final resting position of the shot, not the landing position. By moving the shot pattern left or right, the golfer is also moving the target left or right. Many golfers think in terms of a target, but the target carries with it the entire shot pattern. The golfer can move the target somewhat shorter or longer, for example, by swinging harder, gripping down, changing the length of the backswing, or changing clubs. The target distance, that is, the distance from the ball to the target, can't exceed the distance a golfer can hit the ball with the selected club in the prevailing wind, temperature, and course conditions.

A golfer's *aim* is the initial intended line of the shot and it differs from the golfer's target. A golfer who slices the ball might aim 20 yards left of his target, hit a 20-yard left-to-right slice, and finish at the target. The target represents the most likely finishing position of the shot, while the aim refers to the initial intended direction of the shot.

Golf strategy is about choosing the position of a target and its associated shot pattern. That's a different view from that of many golfers who think of strategy as whether to play a draw, cut, or straight shot. Or whether to play a lofted shot or a bump-and-run shot. It's true that those decisions are a part of strategy, but I'm focusing on the prior, more fundamental question of target choice—how aggressive or conservative to be. On an approach shot, for example, if the golfer chooses to center the shot pattern on a pin tucked near the edge of a green close to a bunker, many shots will finish close to the hole but many others will land in the sand. If, instead, the golfer chooses to center the shot pattern on the middle of the green, fewer shots will land in the sand, and more shots will finish on the green, but some will be farther from the hole. There is a delicate balancing act between the rewards of getting close to the hole and the risk of missing the green.

In the previous chapter we saw how this approach works for putting. The strategic choice on a putt is how far from the hole to place the target. The putting target is also the middle of a shot pattern, though for putts we used the term "scatter pattern." The lag-it strategy corresponds to positioning the target at the hole—in other words, centering the scatter pattern on the hole. With this choice, about half of the putts finish short of the hole, with the remaining half finishing in the hole or beyond it. The jam-it strategy corresponds to setting the target quite a bit beyond the hole, thus insuring that almost all of the scatter pattern lies beyond the hole so almost no putts are left short.

The question is the same with shot strategy: Which target is the best choice? Finding the best choice is an optimization problem. In the real world, you can't replay a shot until you learn the best strategy. With the speed of computers today, though, and the record of golfers' actual shots in the ShotLink and Golfmetrics databases, the optimization problem can be solved by simulating many targets and picking the one with the best outcomes.

Tee shot with out of bounds: when to be aggressive

An amateur golfer hits his last two drives in the fairway. Brimming with confidence, on the next hole he aims straight down the middle of the fairway and watches in dismay as his tee ball slips out of bounds. "Where did that come from? I haven't hit a shot like that all day," he thinks. Resigned to a disappointing score, the golfer plays on, while trying to figure out what went wrong with that swing. "Maybe I didn't get all my weight to the left side. Whatever. If I had just aimed a little more to the left, I'd still be in play. If I'd just made a better decision before I swung the club, I wouldn't be facing a double bogey or worse." Let's revisit the problematic tee shot and see how the golfer might have benefited from a better strategy.

The golfer was playing the hole shown in Figure 8.1, a 400-yard par-four with out of bounds (OB) down the entire right side. The left side of the hole had only rough that came into play. Bunkers were located to the left and right of the green and because the green was deeper than it was wide, a shot from the middle of the fairway was the best angle to approach the green. From the tee, what target would you have chosen? Straight down the middle? Left-center of the fairway? Think about it before you read on.

Now that you've chosen your target, what percentage of your tee shots do you think will end up out of bounds? Many golfers hate this question, because it forces them to consider an outcome that they want to block

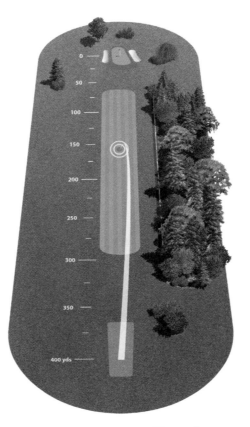

Figure 8.1. 400-yard par-four hole: The hole has out of bounds (OB) down the entire right side of the hole beyond the fence, and has rough on the left side of the hole. The figure shows the most likely drive when the target is the middle of the fairway.

from their minds. But unless you are Tom Kite, who went years without hitting a ball out of bounds on the PGA Tour, it is something that you should consider. The answers I've heard range from a low of 5% to a high of 30%, with most answers in the 10% to 25% range.

How can you figure out the optimal target, the one that minimizes your average score? How does that optimal target correspond to an optimal percentage out of bounds? We could have a golfer play the hole 100 times using the middle of the fairway as a target and record the average score, then pick another target, have him play the hole 100 times using the new target and record the average score, repeat the process with a few more targets and identify the best target as the one with the lowest average score. No way that's going to happen. And even if it did, how long would it take to get the results? How would we account for golfer fatigue? Changing wind and ambient conditions? How could we be sure the golfer was really hitting to the intended target?

Here's the beauty of simulation: I can perform this very multitarget

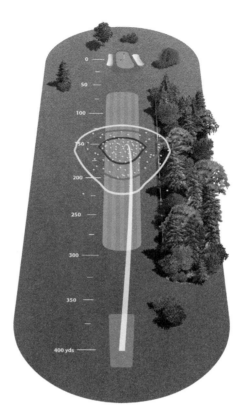

Figure 8.2. 80-golfer shot pattern: The shot pattern of a typical 80-golfer with a target in the middle of the fairway. The shot pattern is summarized by three contours. The blue inner contour contains 50% of the tee shots. The red middle contour contains 90% of the tee shots, and the yellow outer contour contains 98% of the tee shots. With the target in the middle of the fairway, the average score is 4.7, with 7% of tee shots finishing out of bounds.

experiment, using thousands of plays of the hole as data, in just a few minutes of computer time. So we can have confidence in the results, the simulation is carefully calibrated with the raw shot-level data to faithfully represent the play of actual golfers in each phase of the game.

The simulated tee shot pattern of a typical 80-golfer with a target in the middle of the fairway is shown in Figure 8.2. On this hole, with this target, the 80-golfer's average score on the hole is 4.7. The average score was computed using simulation, as described in chapter 4, which, in turn, is based on actual amateur golfers' shots recorded in data from Golfmetrics. With the target in the middle of the fairway, the data show, 7% of tee shots will land out of bounds. Recall that out of bounds is a stroke and distance penalty, which means a golfer hits shot three from the tee if the first shot goes OB, with shot two representing the penalty of bringing the ball back to the tee.

Each target has a corresponding average score. The golfer doesn't have to select the middle of the fairway as the target, but is free to move it to the left or right. The golfer can also move the target closer to the tee, for example, by choosing a 3-wood instead of a driver. Computer simulation clearly shows that the shorter-target strategy leads to higher scores in this case, so let's focus on the direction decision.

What target produces the lowest average score on the hole? Moving the target to the right will lead to more shots going out of bounds, with a corresponding increase in the golfer's average score. Moving the target to the left moves the entire shot pattern to the left. With this change, some out-of-bounds shots move to the right rough (a good thing), some shots in the right rough move to the fairway (also good), and some shots in the fairway move to the left rough (not so good). The myriad outcomes from simulating many shots show that a small move of the target to the left will lead to a lower score, because the penalty for an out-of-bounds shot is larger than the penalty for being in the rough. With a larger penalty for missing right than left, it is better to move the target to the left, away from the out of bounds.

But how far left is best? An optimization based on simulating thousands of plays of the hole for each possible target finds that the optimal target for a typical 80-golfer is the left edge of the fairway. With this target choice, the 80-golfer's average score is 4.6, compared with 4.7 when the target is the middle of the fairway. Only 1.5% of tee shots finish out of bounds, compared with 7% when the target is the middle of the fairway. Figure 8.3 shows the optimal position of the shot pattern, with the large 98% contour missing the out of bounds on the right. With the optimal target, fewer shots finish in the fairway, but the trade-off is worth it. In other words, the strokes saved by hitting fewer tee balls out of bounds outweighs the strokes lost by hitting more tee balls in the rough.

The difference between a target in the middle of the fairway and the optimal target is an average of 0.1 strokes for a typical 80-golfer. It doesn't sound like much, but it's a big deal. If a golfer could save 0.1 strokes by using a better strategy on 18 holes, that's a savings of almost two strokes per round. That's huge! And it comes for free—without having to make any swing changes.

When Phil Mickelson hired short-game coach Dave Pelz in 2003, he told Pelz, "I want to be a quarter of a shot better per round in the majors." He wanted to be one shot better at the end of four rounds. Coincidentally

Figure 8.3. 80-golfer optimal target: The optimal target for a typical 80-golfer is near the left edge of the fairway. With this target choice, the average score is 4.6, compared with 4.7 when the target is the middle of the fairway. Only 1.5% of tee shots finish out of bounds, compared with 7% when the target is the middle of the fairway.

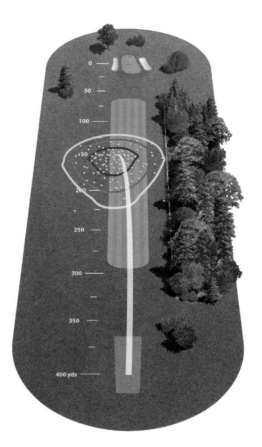

or not, Phil did win his first major the next year, by one stroke. Saving fractions of a shot through better strategy can add up to a lot of strokes over the course of a season.

There isn't a single optimal strategy that every golfer can apply to a hole, because it depends on the individual golfer and his shot pattern. Let's see how the strategy for a typical 100-golfer compares to that for a typical 80-golfer.

The tee shot pattern of a typical 100-golfer with a target in the middle of the fairway is shown in Figure 8.4. The 100-golfer's tee shot pattern is wider than the 80-golfer's and significantly closer to the tee. This observation is consistent with the longer-hitters-tend-to-be-straighter result shown in Figure 6.3 in chapter 6. On this hole, with this target, the 100-golfer's average score is 5.9, nearly a double-bogey average. With the target in the middle of the fairway, 15% of tee shots land out of bounds.

Figure 8.4. 100-golfer shot pattern: The shot pattern of a typical 100-golfer with a target in the middle of the fairway. The shot pattern is summarized by three contours. The blue inner contour contains 50% of the tee shots. The red middle contour contains 90% of the tee shots, and the yellow outer contour contains 98% of the tee shots. With the target in the middle of the fairway, the average score is 5.9, with 15% of tee shots finishing out of bounds.

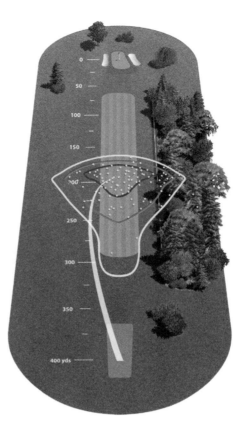

What's the best target for a typical 100-golfer? I had no idea until I crunched the numbers. Then I was shocked at the results. I double- and triple-checked to be sure. The surprising result was that the average-score-minimizing target for a typical 100-golfer is a few yards into the left rough, as shown in Figure 8.5. That's right, a typical 100-golfer should choose a target so far left that it's not even in the fairway.

To be clear, the golfer isn't aiming into the left rough and playing for a slice so the ball finishes in the middle of the fairway. For a slicer, a target in the left rough means aiming even farther left so that a left-to-right-curving shot will, most likely, finish just in the left rough. For a drawer of the ball, a target in the left rough means aiming, say, down the left side of the fairway so that a right-to-left-curving shot will, most likely, finish just in the left rough.

With the target in the left rough, the 100-golfer hits the fairway much less often than with the middle-of-the-fairway target. Only 2% of tee

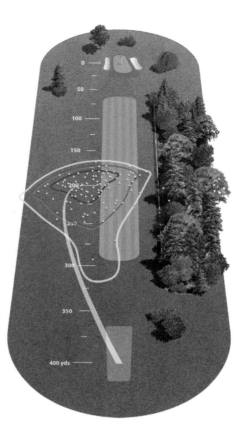

Figure 8.5. 100-golfer optimal target: The optimal target for a typical 100-golfer is a few yards into the left rough. With this target choice, the average score is 5.7, compared with 5.9 when the target is the middle of the fairway. Only 2% of tee shots finish out of bounds, compared with 15% when the target is the middle of the fairway.

shots finish out of bounds, though, compared with 15% when the target is the middle of the fairway. Most important, with the left-rough target, balancing all the possible outcomes, the simulation predicts that the 100-golfer's average score drops to 5.7 from 5.9.

Why is the optimal target so far left for a 100-golfer? Because of the stroke and distance rule for hitting out of bounds, which is effectively a huge, two-stroke penalty. When there is a safe route to play the hole, hitting out of bounds should be avoided at nearly all costs. The wider the shot pattern, the farther left the target needs to be to avoid the out of bounds. For 80-golfers and 100-golfers, the optimal target is shown by simulation to result in an OB fraction of only about 2%. That's less than once in 50 plays of the hole!

The difference between a target in the middle of the fairway and the optimal target in the left rough is an average of 0.2 strokes for a typical 100-golfer. Similar savings across 18 holes add up to three and a half

Figure 8.6. Pro golfer shot pattern: The shot pattern of a pro golfer with a target in the middle of the fairway. The shot pattern is summarized by three contours. The blue inner contour contains 50% of the tee shots. The red middle contour contains 90% of the tee shots, and the yellow outer contour contains 98% of the tee shots. With the target in the middle of the fairway, the average score is 4.15, with 4% of tee shots finishing out of bounds.

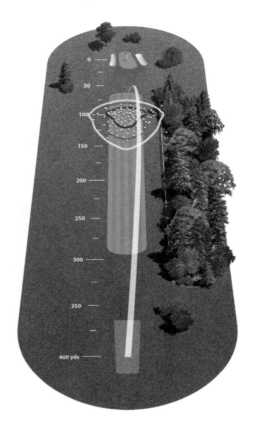

strokes per round, not even including the potential savings from better strategy on other shots. Higher-handicap golfers can save even more strokes from a better strategy than lower-handicap golfers.[20]

The shot pattern of a typical pro golfer with a target in the middle of the fairway is shown in Figure 8.6. Pros drive it longer and straighter than amateurs, and you can see the result in the shot pattern, just as we saw it in Figure 6.3 on page 104. The pro golfer's tee shot pattern is narrower than the 80-golfer's and significantly farther from the tee. With a target in the middle of the fairway, the pro's average score is 4.15, with 4% of tee shots landing out of bounds.

As shown in Figure 8.7, the optimal target, chosen for its average-score-minimizing properties, for a typical pro golfer is the left-center of

---

[20] There's a consistent theme to various results in this book. Shorter drivers benefit more from an extra 20 yards of driving distance than longer drivers. Poor putters benefit more from a larger hole than good putters. Higher-scoring golfers benefit more from improved strategy.

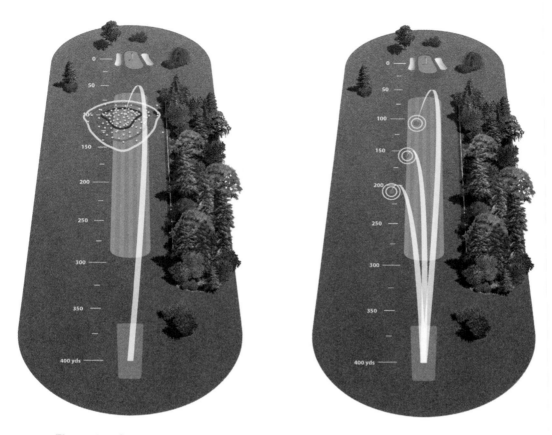

Figure 8.7. Optimal targets: The left illustration shows the optimal target for a typical pro golfer in the left-center of the fairway. With this target choice, the average score is 4.05, compared with 4.15 when the target is the middle of the fairway. Only 0.7% of tee shots finish out of bounds, compared with 4% when the target is the middle of the fairway. The right illustration shows the optimal targets for the pro, 80-golfer, and 100-golfer.

the fairway. By shading the target a little to the left, the pro's average score drops from 4.15 to 4.05, with 0.7% of tee shots landing out of bounds.

As illustrated in Figure 8.7, the optimal target changes depending on golfer skill, which is summarized by their shot pattern. A common feature of the optimal target for the three levels of golfer is less than 2% of tee shots finishing out of bounds for all skill levels. For more accurate drivers, the optimal target is more aggressive, meaning closer to the middle of the fairway. For directionally challenged drivers, the optimal target is more conservative, meaning farther from the middle of the fairway and farther from the out-of-bounds area.

> Optimal strategies change with a golfer's skill: More accurate drivers should choose a more aggressive target.

Many have said that you should choose a conservative target and then swing aggressively. It is possible to be too conservative, for the optimal fraction to hit out of bounds is not zero. Hitting 0% out of bounds implies choosing a target so far away from the out of bounds, and so far away from the center of the fairway, that the average score would be higher. Extremely conservative and extremely aggressive strategies, on average, waste strokes. My advice is to choose an optimal target and then swing aggressively.

> Choose an optimal target and then swing aggressively.

Better golfers are better strategists

So far, we've used simulation results to compare the merits of different strategies. But are golfers good strategists? Do all golfers learn intuitively that the best way to play the game is to consider the current state of their abilities? To check, I examined the amateur Golfmetrics data to see how many shots go out of bounds on our sample hole. Then, using ShotLink data, I examined how many pros' shots go out of bounds on similar holes. The results are summarized in Table 8.1. Pros play optimal, or nearly optimal, strategies on this type of hole. In contrast, amateur golfers hit four to seven times more shots out of bounds than they would if they chose an optimal strategy. The results shown in Table 8.1 are averages over dozens of golfers. Some individual golfers hit 25% of their tee shots out of bounds—more than 10 times the optimal fraction.

Ray Floyd was right: Weekend golfers are poor strategists. I can only

Table 8.1. Are golfers good strategists? The table shows the percentage of shots that finish out of bounds by the golfer, by the target, and in the data. "Target middle" means the target is in the middle of the fairway. On this hole, amateur golfers hit four to seven times more shots out of bounds than is optimal. Pros play optimal, or nearly optimal, strategies on this type of hole (the difference between 0.5% and 0.7% is not statistically significant).

Golfer group	Target middle	Target optimal	Data
Pro golfer	4%	0.7%	0.5%
80-golfer	7%	1.5%	6%
100-golfer	15%	2.0%	14%

Amateur golfers are poor strategists: They hit many more shots out of bounds than is optimal.

speculate why. In their foursome, golfers might see one shot out of four go out of bounds. They might incorrectly conclude that what does happen is what should happen. Perhaps golfers are overconfident in their ability to avoid the trouble. Perhaps there's a fear of your buddy saying, "Aiming that far left? What a wimp!" Perhaps golfers don't fully appreciate the two-shot penalty for hitting out of bounds. The simplest explanation might be the most likely—golfers derive more pleasure from a drive in the fairway with the possibility of a par or birdie, even if it carries a greater chance of a double or triple bogey.

Tee shot with hazard: adjusting the target

It's likely that you have played similar holes where out of bounds comes into play on the tee shot, but every hole is unique. The out of bounds might be farther away or closer to the fairway. For an 80-golfer, the left edge of the fairway target is *not* the lesson to apply to other similar holes. The lesson is that when out of bounds is in play off the tee, and there is a safe play away from the out of bounds, choose a target so that the chances of hitting the ball out of bounds are slim.

How slim? Even when the out-of-bounds fence is only a few paces from the fairway, a 100-golfer should hit 3% or fewer tee shots out of bounds. More accurate drivers should hit even fewer out of bounds: 2% or less for 80-golfers and 1.5% or less for pros.

This way of thinking—combining shot patterns and hole features—applies to playing the same hole under changing conditions from day to day. On windy days, tee shot patterns expand. In order to still hit, say, 2% or fewer tee shots out of bounds, an expanded shot pattern calls for a more conservative target choice, so choose a target farther from the out of bounds.

Now let's consider a hole of a similar length, but instead of trees and an out-of-bounds area, there is a lateral water hazard all of the way along the right side of the hole. If a golfer hits into the lateral hazard, he gets to hit his next shot from the place where the ball crossed the hazard line, under penalty of one stroke (unlike out of bounds, which is a stroke and distance penalty, or effectively a two-stroke penalty).

On a hole with a lateral hazard, how should a golfer change his target? How many shots should find the water? Not surprisingly, simulation results show that a reduced penalty calls for a more aggressive target.

What is surprising to many is the small fraction of tee shots that should optimally find the hazard. Simulation results show that a pro should choose a target far enough from the water so that only 2% of tee shots find the water, 80-golfers should choose a target so that only 3% find the water, and 100-golfers should choose a target so that only 5% find the water. These values decrease if the lateral water hazard is farther from the fairway.

Many amateur golfers treat out-of-bounds and lateral hazards the same, and attempt to avoid both equally, but this wastes strokes. The larger penalty for an out-of-bounds hazard calls for a more conservative strategy than a lateral hazard. Still, most amateur golfers don't pay lateral hazards enough respect, let alone out of bounds. Improving strategy may be the quickest, easiest way for amateur golfers to lower their scores.

> Optimal strategies change with hole features: Larger penalties call for more conservative play; smaller penalties call for more aggressive play.

Long and crooked: the "driver versus iron" question

Many golfers are under the mistaken impression that good golf strategy is synonymous with boring play. I want to convince you that a conservative strategy isn't always the best strategy.

You may have heard this advice for golfers playing a long par-four hole, who can't reach the green in two shots: Take three shots, using a 5-iron off the tee, followed by another 5-iron, and then a short iron to reach the green. The first two iron shots will likely finish in the fairway, or at least stay out of trouble, leaving an easy third iron shot from 100 yards or so to the green. You'll have a chance to one-putt for par and will rarely do worse than a bogey, or so it is claimed.

This logic doesn't hold up when scrutinized with actual data. For most golfers, the conservative "three-shot strategy" will lead to higher scores, not lower ones. Not to mention making the game less fun.

Why is the three-shot strategy flawed? By using an iron for the first two shots on a long par-four hole, the golfer is, for sure, giving up a lot of distance, and the lost distance translates to higher scores. Playing an iron off the tee might give up 60 yards compared with a driver, and playing an iron on the second shot might give up another 40 yards. Instead of being close to the green for the third shot, the golfer guarantees a third shot of at least 100 yards to the green.

It is true that iron shots are less likely to find the rough and worse trouble, but that must be weighed against giving up, say, 100 yards on the first two shots on the hole. Using simulation, I find that the three-shot strategy costs the 90-golfer about two to three strokes per round. The loss will vary depending on the features of a particular hole, but unless there are severe hazards on both the left and right sides of the hole, the three-shot strategy rarely pays off. On many long par-four holes, going for maximum distance on the first shot is a better bet for amateurs.

The Golf Digest U.S. Open Challenge was an event that was inspired by Tiger Woods's comment that a 10-handicap golfer couldn't break 100 at a U.S. Open course. The event was first held in 2008 on the 7,600-yard Torrey Pines South Course. The amateur foursome included John Atkinson, who played to a handicap index of 8.1. His conservative strategy was to go for accuracy over distance, so he hit hybrids off the tees, focusing on staying in the fairway to avoid the long rough. Apparently he thought the control gained by using his hybrid was worth more than the loss of distance. He gave up 50 or so yards on his tee shots, and often had to hit from deep rough anyway, and that wasn't a recipe for success. Atkinson stuck with his game plan for the entire 18 holes. In his round, he started off with four bogeys, failed to make a single par, and ended up shooting 114.

Of course, this single outcome doesn't prove the folly of Atkinson's strategy, but simulation analysis predicts a higher average score with this conservative approach. We've seen the importance of distance off the tee, and giving up 50 yards a tee shot for a bit more accuracy is a poor trade. Make no mistake, there are holes where sacrificing some distance off the tee is sensible, for instance, to hit the fat part of the fairway rather than risking hitting into penal bunkers a few yards ahead. And the calculation changes for different golfers because an iron off the tee by a pro goes farther than the drive of most amateurs. But on many holes, long and crooked is better than short and crooked.

Layup strategy: the data say go long

From your position in the fairway, the green is too far for you to reach in one shot. Your natural impulse might be to pull out a fairway wood and bang the ball as far as possible. Then you remember Tom Watson's advice: "Don't just fire your layup shot as far as you can. You probably will be better off 90 yards from the flag than 45 yards." Heeding his advice, you reach into the bag for a mid-iron or hybrid. Until you remember former tour golfer and current teacher of many tour pros Stan Utley's advice: "Anytime you have a chance to get closer to the hole, I think you have a better chance to hit that shot closer than one from 100 or 120 yards." What is your best strategy?

In a way, both Watson and Utley are right—the best play depends on the percentages, and the percentages may be different for Tom Watson and Stan Utley, or for a pro and an amateur. In order to play the percentages, you have to know the percentages.

Golf strategy requires thinking ahead. To decide whether to lay up to, say, 80 yards or to 30 yards from the hole on this shot, you need to know your likely results for the next shots. Although I don't know your personal stats, I do have records of thousands of shots by golfers of all skill levels playing under actual course conditions. The fascinating results are that most golfers will score worse from 80 yards from the hole than from 30, even if every layup to 30 yards lands in the rough, and every layup to 80 yards lands in the fairway. For example, the data in Table 8.2 show that 90-golfers take significantly fewer strokes to finish a hole from 30 yards in the rough (3.1 average) than from 80 yards in the fairway (3.4 average). These numbers mean that most 90-golfers would be better off laying up closer to the hole, even if their ball ends up in the rough. The gain depends on the features of the hole, but saving 0.3 strokes is common.

Here's another way to think about it. Imagine that your layup finished in the fairway 30 yards short of the hole. I'll give you the option to pick up your ball, walk backward to 80 yards, drop your ball without penalty, and play from there. Would you do it? Many people think their chances of success are better from 80 yards than from 30 yards, because they believe it's easier to hit a good shot with a full swing than with a partial swing. But the data in Table 8.2 show that golfers' instinct on this point is often wrong.

There are exceptions. Hazards close to the green change the risk-reward balance. Why take the risk with water in play at 30 yards but not a bit farther back? Pin placement matters: If the pin is tucked just over a front bunker, better golfers might want a longer shot to hit beyond the hole and spin it back. Individual skill matters: If you suffer the dreaded "chip yips," or if you are sure you're better from 80 yards than 30 yards, then lay farther back—and book a lesson with your pro to improve your wedge play. But for most people, going to 30 yards is a better bet.

Table 8.2. Average number of strokes for golfers to complete a hole from 30 and 80 yards. Results from the rough do not include shots from behind trees or other obstacles. For each golfer category except pros, the average number of strokes to finish a hole is higher from 80 yards in the fairway than from 30 yards in the rough. These results suggest that laying up to 30 yards is usually a better strategy than laying up to 80 yards.

Golfer group	30 yards to the hole		80 yards to the hole	
	Fairway	Rough	Fairway	Rough
PGA Tour pro	2.5	2.7	2.7	3.0
80-golfer	2.7	2.8	3.1	3.2
90-golfer	2.9	3.1	3.4	3.5
100-golfer	3.1	3.4	3.7	3.8
110-golfer	3.3	3.7	3.9	4.1

The 2012 U.S. Open winner, Webb Simpson, learned this lesson by studying his own numbers. For readers of *Golf Digest,* Simpson wrote, "Get as close as you can. Unless there's water guarding the pin, I try to get as close to the green as possible on my second shot. I used to lay up to 90 or 100 yards, but I studied my stats, and I'm just as good or better from, say, 60 yards. So now I go for it. If I get it around the green, great, but even with a half wedge my odds are at least as good as they are from 100 yards. Also, I've worked on my chipping, so anywhere near the green is an up-and-down opportunity." Indeed, from 100 yards in the fairway, pros get up and down about 28% of the time. From 60 yards in the fairway it's 36%, and from 30 yards it's 52%.[21] There are large potential savings from laying up closer to the hole.[22]

Recovery strategy: when is the risk worth it?

A pro just sliced his drive into the trees. From this position he has two options. The safe play is to chip back to the fairway, leaving 200 yards to the hole. There's a good chance he'll make a bogey. The risky, but potentially more rewarding, option is to thread a punch shot through the trees toward the green. If he pulls it off, he'll be in the fairway 100 yards from the hole with a better chance of saving par. If he fails, his ball could hit the trees, go just about anywhere, and bring double bogey or worse into the picture. What should he do? What would you do?

If this is the last hole of a tournament and the pro needs to save par to get into a playoff, probably the risky strategy makes sense. If the pro is leading and a bogey still wins, then the safe play makes sense. But what about the more common situation in which there are many holes left in the tournament and the pro wants to make the lowest score, on average?

Rather than a full-blown simulation, which depends on the specific features of the hole, I offer a simpler analysis for general guidance. There

---

[21] See Table A-23 in the Appendix.

[22] Here's another way to see it. Suppose a tour pro had the option of either taking the tour average score on all par-five holes throughout the season or placing his second shot in the fairway 100 yards from the hole (a perfect layup every time) and continuing from there. Which is better? The tour average on par-five holes is 4.7. The "perfect layup option" leads to an average score of 4.8 (two shots to lay up and then an average of 2.8 strokes to complete the hole). Giving up an average of 0.1 strokes on every par-five hole would place the pro at a significant disadvantage to the field.

are three main outcomes to consider. First, the safe play to the fairway leads to an average of 4.2 strokes to hole out. This counts one for the recovery chip and 3.2 for finishing the hole from there (see Table 5.2). Second, a successful outcome of the risky punch through the trees leads to an average of 3.8 strokes to hole out: This counts one for the punch shot and 2.8 for finishing the hole from there. The third outcome to consider is the unsuccessful risky shot. Let's assume the ball rattles around the trees and settles back in about the same spot. After that, the pro will play the safe chip back to the fairway. Taking the risk and failing leads to an average of 5.2 strokes to hole out: one for the unsuccessful punch, one for the safe chip to the fairway, and 3.2 for finishing the hole from there.

If the probability of a successful punch shot is greater than 72%, then the risky recovery leads to a lower average score. The 72% value is not a magical constant written in stone. It just provides some general guidance in this situation. In order for the risky play to gain 0.2 strokes relative to the safe play, and not just break even, a success rate of 86% is required.

The right decision depends on the specific circumstances. A good lie and a wide enough opening through the trees could give a high enough chance of success for the risky play to make sense. A more difficult lie or a smaller opening and the risky play could be a poor choice.

RECOVERY SHOT RISK ANALYSIS:
comparison of average strokes to hole out

- Safe chip (to 200 yards in the fairway): 4.2

- Risky recovery, successful (to 100 yards in the fairway): 3.8

- Risky recovery, unsuccessful (same spot in the trees): 5.2

Compared to the safe chip, a successful risky recovery gains an average of 0.4 strokes while an unsuccessful risky recovery loses an average of 1.0 stroke. The risky recovery needs to be successful at least 72% of the time to produce a lower average score.

The breakeven probability is 72%, because the 72% chance of a gain of 0.4 strokes matches the 28% chance of a loss of one stroke (0.72 [0.4] = 0.28 [0.1]).

Phil Mickelson hit a famous successful recovery shot in the 2010 Masters that led to a birdie and a victory. Many golf pundits called it a poor decision with a good outcome. He had a good lie in the wood chips and a wide opening, so, even before he hit the shot, it appeared to me to be a reasonable choice. The circumstances were quite different on the last hole of the 2006 U.S. Open at Winged Foot where Phil hit an infamous unsuccessful recovery shot. That he didn't pull off the shot suggests that he attempted a shot with far less than the required high probability of success. Commenting on his decision afterward, he said, "I am such an idiot."

Now let's assume instead that if the risky punch shot fails, the ball hits a tree and ricochets out of bounds. Taking the risk and failing leads to an average of 6.2 strokes to hole out: one for the unsuccessful punch, one for the out-of-bounds penalty stroke, one for the safe chip to the fairway, and 3.2 for finishing the hole from there. In this case, the probability of a successful punch shot needs to be greater than 84% to give a lower average score than the safe play.[23] In order for the risky play to gain 0.2 strokes relative to the safe play, and not just break even, a success rate of 92% is required.[24]

We see that the pro requires, roughly, between a 70% and a 90% chance of success to make the risky play worthwhile. Amateurs, however, are known to attempt the risky play with a slim chance of success. It may make for a fun story to tell in the grill room after the round in the rare event the risky play succeeds, but that strategy throws away strokes.

How to tell your chance of success in this situation? Go to the course when it is empty, drop 10 balls in the trees (in slightly different spots and lies), and attempt the risky recovery shots. Count how many balls find the fairway and how many finish in a comparable or worse position. This test has two benefits. The first is practicing punch shots. The second is giving you a more realistic assessment of your chance of success in similar situations.

[23] The breakeven probability is 84% because the 84% chance of a gain of 0.4 stroke matches the 16% chance of a loss of two strokes (0.84 [0.4] = 0.16 [2.0]).

[24] We saw in Table 8.1, referring to tee shot on the par-four hole, that the pro should hit less than 1% of his tee shots out of bounds. So why isn't a 99% success rate required for the risky recovery shot with out of bounds in play? The answer is that the safe play isn't a great alternative in the recovery situation, but is a very good option in the par-four tee shot situation.

19th Hole Summary

- Good golf decisions depend on two main ingredients: a golfer's shot pattern and the features of the golf hole. A golfer's best strategy is to choose a target that maximizes the chance of success on that hole for his skill level.

- Tee shots that land in the rough cost about one-tenth to one-quarter of a stroke; shots into a recovery situation cost about one-half of a stroke; shots into water or a lateral hazard cost a full stroke; and shots that land out of bounds cost two strokes.

- The bigger the penalty associated with a hazard, the more the target should be moved away to avoid it.

- Amateur golfers turn out to be poor strategists, often hitting more aggressively or more conservatively than they should. Improving strategy, then, may be amateurs' best and quickest road to a lower score.

- Optimal strategies change with a golfer's skill. More accurate golfers should choose a more aggressive target. That usually means aiming closer to the middle of the fairway on tee shots or closer to the hole on approach shots.

- Optimal strategies change with course and weather conditions. Windy days and sidehill lies both lead to larger shot patterns and call for more conservative targets.

- The most conservative strategy is not the same as the optimal strategy. On most holes, choosing an iron off the tee instead of a driver gives way strokes.

- Unless there is danger close to the hole, or the pin location dictates otherwise, the data show that most golfers score better by laying up closer to the hole than by laying back to 80 or 100 yards.

CHAPTER 9

PRACTICE WITH A PURPOSE: Golf Games and Drills to Measure and Improve Performance

Strokes gained is a great tool to measure golf performance, but average golfers don't have the benefit of the PGA Tour's ShotLink system to automatically record our shots. Still, many good players track their performances as an integral part of their practice routine by playing games and doing drills. Like piano exercises, golf practice games and drills are both varied and repetitive. They connect your brain to your muscles[25] while giving you numbers to show how you stack up against all kinds of other golfers.

Luke Donald continually strives to improve his game, in part through efficient and effective practice. In addition to working on technique during practice, Luke plays many games that involve scoring and rating shots on a numerical scale. In this chapter, I present golf games and skills tests that anyone can use to measure performance on practice greens, short-game areas, and the course. I also offer some new stats that any golfer can use to measure performance without resorting to full strokes gained calculations.

Most of these games involve assigning points for certain outcomes: holing a putt or hitting a shot close to the hole. Rather than pick an arbitrary set of points, I want the points to promote good practice habits. In putting, this might mean penalizing putts that finish short of the hole in order to emphasize the importance of distance control.

---

[25] Scientists have found that myelin, the insulation that wraps around nerve fibers, is the brain's mechanism for creating muscle memory. When Sean Foley was asked to explain Justin Rose's rise in the world rankings, his one-word answer was "myelin."

How will you know how you are doing? I've used real data—ShotLink data for professionals and Golfmetrics amateur data—to come up with performance grading charts that let you compare your shots with those of other golfers, from the best pros in the world to middling amateurs. Even when practicing by yourself, you'll know if you are putting better than Luke Donald or worse than a 100-golfer. You'll know how your short game stacks up against Phil Mickelson's. A side benefit of performance grading is that it allows you to handicap a competition with a friend or pro to make it a fair contest. The scoring of each practice game is simple, with no need for lengthy or complicated calculations.[26]

10-foot putting games

For practicing 10-foot putts, try the 10-foot-10-point game, in which the goal is to reach 10 points as quickly as possible.

10-foot-10-point game

Goal

To win by getting 10 points in the fewest holes possible.

Rules

- Drop a ball between nine and 11 feet from the hole.
- Putt until you hole out.
- Keep track of the number of holes played.

Scoring

- Add two points if you sink the first putt.
- Zero points if you take two putts to hole out, first is long.
- Lose one point if you take two putts to hole out, first is short.
- Lose three points if you take three or more putts to hole out.
- Lose the game if your score drops to minus 10 points.

Final result

Number of holes to reach 10 points.

[26] For the mathematically inclined reader, I also choose points so that scores in the games are highly correlated with strokes gained. This means that better game scores translate to better golf scores in a nearly linear manner.

Each time you hole out counts as one hole played. Keep track of how many holes it takes you to finish, by reaching either 10 points or minus 10 points. The points, summarized in Table 9.1, are designed to reward good putting: A one-putt gains points and a three-putt loses points. The most likely outcome, a two-putt, neither gains nor loses points, unless the first putt is short of the hole. The penalty for leaving the first putt short is to remind you to focus on distance control and getting the ball to the hole. You can't get away with ramming the first putt way beyond the hole, because a three-or-more-putt hole carries the greatest penalty.

Table 9.1. Points for the 10-foot putting games: Putt from 10 feet (and nine and 11 feet), starting from different positions on the clock face (uphill, downhill, and sidehill). Note: The same point system will be used for five- and 15-foot putts.

Outcome	Points
One-putt	2
Two putts, first putt long	0
Two putts, first putt short	-1
Three or more putts	-3

Three important details will help you to get the most out of the game. First, after you finish the first hole, move to a *different* hole on the practice putting green. Every putt should be played as read-once-and-hit-once. Hitting putts from the same place isn't how golf is played. It doesn't help with your green reading. Hitting twice from the same place is easier than real golf, doesn't help with your green reading, and makes it harder to accurately measure your performance. So unless the putting green is crowded, walk to a new hole after each holed putt.

Second, start each hole from a different position on the clock face. You don't have straight uphill putts all day on the course, so you don't want to attempt only straight uphill putts on the practice green. On the first hole, pick a random position on the clock face, say a 3:00 sidehill putt. On each succeeding hole, start from a different position on the clock face, say a 7:00 uphill putt followed by a 10:00 sidehill-downhill putt. Make sure to hit all of the positions on the clock face equally. Don't just alternate uphill and downhill putts.

Third, vary the distance to each hole within a two-foot range, so start between nine and 11 feet away. Research shows that you'll become better at 10-footers by practicing nine-, 10-, and 11-footers instead of practicing 10-footers only. So vary your initial putt distances between nine and 11 feet, making sure not to have more nine-footers than 11-footers.

Now figure out how you stack up against other golfers. This is the grading part of your putting exam. PGA Tour putters almost always win the game—they reach 10 points before minus 10 points. An average PGA Tour putter wins in about 14 holes. The best tour putters win in about 11 holes, with a range between five and 30 holes.[27] The worst PGA Tour putters take about 17 holes to win. A typical 80-golfer takes about 24 holes to win, while a 90-golfer takes about 43 holes to win. If you consistently win in just 10 holes, your putting performance is better than that of the best putters on tour. The complete grading scorecard is given in Table 9.2.

Table 9.2. 10-foot-10-point grading scorecard.

Golfer group	Median holes to win
Best tour putter	11
Average tour putter	14
Worst tour putter	17
80-golfer	24
90-golfer	43
100-golfer	loses more often than wins
110-golfer	loses more often than wins

Throughout this chapter, pro results are based on actual play in tournament competition on difficult courses. Amateur results are based on play on "regular" courses, not on a practice green or short-game area. Scores might be slightly better in a relaxed practice session on a practice green where the subtle contours and breaks are known.

You can play the 10-foot-10-point game by yourself or against one or more friends. If you play against friends, alternate who starts putting to each hole and make sure you each start from different clock-face positions.

[27] The best putters are those who gain 0.5 strokes per round or more with their putting, which includes about the top 20 putters in a given year. The worst putters are those who lose 0.5 strokes per round or more with their putting.

For example, you start at 10:00 and your friend starts from 5:00. On the next hole, you start at 8:00 and your friend at 4:00. The key is to mix it up on every hole, changing the positions on the clock face and varying the distances between nine and 11 feet. The first person to reach minus 10 points loses. The first person to reach 10 points wins.

Higher-handicap golfers might get frustrated trying to win at the 10-foot-10-point game. The 10-foot-10-*hole* game is a slight variation to speed things up. The goal of the 10-foot-10-hole game is to see how many points you can score in 10 holes. Rules and scoring are the same as for the 10-foot-10-point game. Use the scorecard in Table 9.3 to grade your performance in this game against golfers of all skill levels.

Table 9.3. 10-foot-10-hole grading scorecard.

Golfer group	Average points
Best tour putter	8
Average tour putter	7
Worst tour putter	6
80-golfer	4
90-golfer	2
100-golfer	-1
110-golfer	-3

The grading scorecards in Tables 9.2 and 9.3 can be used to handicap matches between two or more players. For example, a five-point handicap would make it a fair competition between an 80-golfer and a 100-golfer in the 10-foot-10-hole putting game.

Variations: 5-, 10-, and 15-foot putting games

Putting games from various starting distances can be played using the same rules and point system as the 10-foot games. For 5-foot games, start between four and six feet from the hole. For 15-foot games, start between 14 and 16 feet from the hole. Remember to use the read-once-putt-once rule, and putt to a different hole each time. Vary the starting distances in a two-foot range, and vary the starting positions around the clock face.

Table 9.4. 5-, 10-, and 15-foot grading scorecard.

Golfer group	Median holes to win			Average points in 10 holes		
	5-foot 15-point	10-foot 10-point	15-foot 5-point	5-foot	10-foot	15-foot
Best tour putter	10	11	11	16	8	4
Average tour putter	10	14	14	15	7	3
Worst tour putter	11	17	18	14	6	1
80-golfer	13	24	21	12	4	0
90-golfer	14	43	NA	10	2	-2
100-golfer	18	NA	NA	8	-1	-4
110-golfer	23	NA	NA	6	-3	-6

The grading scorecard in Table 9.4 shows golfers of different levels' scores for 5-, 10-, and 15-foot games. From a 15-foot starting distance, it would take too long to get to 10 points (for the best pro putters it takes 25 holes, for 80-golfers more than 70 holes), so the game is played to just five points. That is, getting to five points wins and getting to minus five points loses. For the 5-foot game, getting to just 10 points is too easy, so the game is played to 15 points.

The spiral game

David Orr, the director of instruction at Campbell University PGA Golf Management in North Carolina, relayed the spiral game to me. He's coached the putting of Justin Rose, Edoardo Molinari, and many other professionals and amateurs. This game focuses on the most important putting distances and involves the added pressure of having to start all over after a miss.

Spiral game: two feet to six feet

Goal
To sink five putts in a row from varying angles and distances.

Rules
- Position five balls in a clockwise spiral around a hole, starting at two feet and ending at six feet.
- Place the two-footer at a random clock position, say 3:00, the three-footer at 5:30, the four-footer at 8:00, the five-footer at 10:30, and the six-footer at 1:00.
- Try to sink all five putts in a row.
- If you miss a putt, reposition all five balls, preferably around a different hole, starting from a different clock-face position and in a counterclockwise spiral, and start again. For example, place the two-footer at 8:00, the three-footer at 5:30, the four-footer at 3:00, the five-footer at 12:30, and the six-footer at 10:00.
- Keep track of the number of missed putts.

Scoring
- Win when you successfully sink all five putts in a row.
- Final score: the number of putts missed before winning.

The grading scorecard in Table 9.5 shows median scores for golfers where the farthest ball is placed six to 10 feet from the hole. Half of the time, a 100-golfer will have three or fewer misses before winning in the two-foot-to-six-foot spiral game. More than half of the time, a pro golfer will have a score of zero, meaning zero misses before winning the two-to-six-foot spiral game.

The game quickly becomes very hard for longer distances. In the two-foot-to-eight-foot spiral game, balls are placed at two, three, four, five, six, seven, and eight feet from the hole. Half of the time, a 100-golfer will have fifty misses before winning the two-foot-to-eight-foot spiral game (I wouldn't recommend it).

Table 9.5. Spiral game grading scorecard.

	Median number of misses until win				
Golfer group	2-feet to 6-feet	2-feet to 7-feet	2-feet to 8-feet	2-feet to 9-feet	2-feet to 10-feet
Best tour putter	0	0	1	3	7
Average tour putter	0	1	2	4	12
Worst tour putter	0	1	3	8	23
80-golfer	1	3	11	40	>100
90-golfer	2	5	19	60	>100
100-golfer	3	14	50	>100	>100
110-golfer	4	15	77	>100	>100

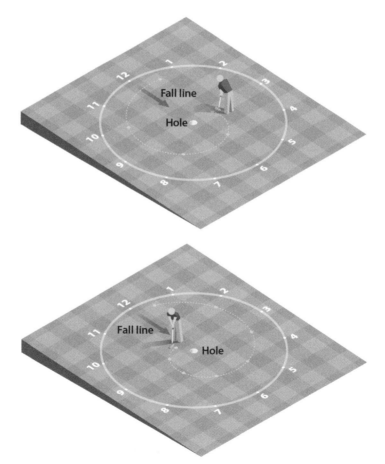

Figure 9.1. Spiral game illustrated. The top green shows putts in a clockwise spiral from two feet through six feet, starting at 3:00. The bottom green shows putts in a counterclockwise spiral from two feet through nine feet, starting at 11:00. The clock face is oriented so 12:00 represents the straight downhill direction illustrated by the fall line.

20-, 30-, and 40-foot putting games

As the putt distance increases, avoiding a three-putt becomes increasingly important. In longer-distance putting games, points are no longer subtracted for leaving putts short. Instead, one-putts receive the largest reward and three-putts lose points.

Longer-distance putting games are played in the same way as shorter-distance putting games, but with a larger variation in the distances. For 20-foot games, putts can start between 15 and 25 feet from the hole. For 30-foot games, putts can start between 25 and 35 feet; for 40-foot games, putts can start between 35 and 45 feet. As before, use the read-once-putt-once rule (putt to a different hole each time), and vary the starting positions around the clock face. The point system for the 20-, 30-, and 40-foot putting games is summarized in Table 9.6.

20-foot-15-point game

Goal

To win by getting 15 points in the fewest holes possible.

Rules

- Drop a ball between 15 and 25 feet from the hole.
- Putt until you hole out.
- Keep track of the number of holes played.

Scoring

- Add five points if you sink the first putt.
- Add one point for a two-putt if the first finishes within three feet of the hole, whether long or short.
- Zero points for a two-putt if the first putt is outside of three feet.
- Lose three points if you take three putts or more to hole out.
- Lose the game if your score drops to minus 15 points.

Final result

Number of holes to reach 15 points.

Table 9.6. Points for the 20-, 30-, and 40-foot putting games.

Outcome	Points
One-putt	5
Two putts, first putt within 3 feet	1
Two putts, first putt outside 3 feet	0
Three or more putts	-3

For the 20-foot-15-point game, getting to 15 points wins and getting to minus 15 points loses. The grading scorecard is given in Table 9.7. If you play and win in 15 holes, your performance is typical for an 80-golfer.

The goal of the 20-foot-10-hole game is to see how many points you can score in 10 holes. Use the scorecard in Table 9.7 to grade your performance in this game against golfers of all skill levels. The grading scorecard in Table 9.7 can be used to handicap matches between two or more players. For example, a four-point handicap would make it a fair competition between a 90-golfer and a 100-golfer in the 20-foot-10-hole putting game, since the 90-golfer is expected to win by four points.

Table 9.7. 20-, 30-, and 40-foot grading scorecard.

Golfer group	Median holes to win			Average points in 10 holes		
	20-foot 15-point	30-foot 10-point	40-foot 5-point	20-foot	30-foot	40-foot
Best tour putter	10	11	7	15	10	5
Average tour putter	11	12	8	14	8	4
Worst tour putter	12	14	10	12	7	2
80-golfer	15	18	NA	10	4	-1
90-golfer	20	29	NA	7	0	-5
100-golfer	35	NA	NA	3	-4	-9
110-golfer	42	NA	NA	-1	-7	-14

Green-reading skill drill: finding the fall line

Green-reading skill is arguably as important as putting technique, yet few golfers practice green reading. Here's a new green-reading drill that you won't find in any instruction book or magazine. It focuses on finding the fall line, the straight downhill direction in which water would flow due to gravity.

Green-reading skill drill

Goal
To reduce your "fall line error," the amount by which you misread the fall line.

Rules
- Pick a hole on your practice green or on the course.
- Before you've seen any putts roll to the hole, read the green to estimate where a six-foot putt (that's about two putter lengths) will roll straight downhill into the hole.
- Place a coin to mark the location you've identified as the fall line six feet from the hole.
- Stroke a putt from just in front of the coin straight to the hole.
- If the putt rolls on a straight line into the hole, you've correctly identified the fall line.
- If the putt breaks either way, putt from a slightly different starting position until you locate the fall line.

Scoring
- When you find the true fall line, measure the distance between the coin, which is your initial fall line estimate, and the true fall line. This distance is your fall line error.
- If the putt rolls on a straight line into the hole the first time, you've correctly identified the fall line and your score is zero.

Tip: If you walk in a circle around the hole, the fall line position is the point of highest elevation. There is no grading scorecard for this drill.

Figures 9.2.
Fall line drill. The top green shows the first two steps: estimating the position of the fall line and then putting directly at the hole to see any break. The bottom green shows the final two steps: finding the true fall line and then measuring the error.

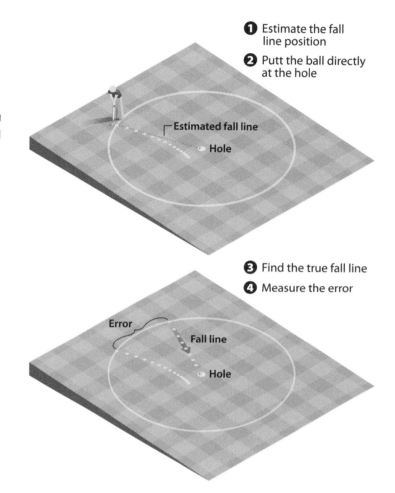

❶ Estimate the fall line position

❷ Putt the ball directly at the hole

Estimated fall line

Hole

❸ Find the true fall line

❹ Measure the error

Error

Fall line

Hole

Repeat the green-reading skill drill for other holes on the practice green or on the course. Instead of using an actual hole, you can also use a tee as a target for this drill. Keep a record of your fall line error and also record whether the slope near the hole is small, moderate, or steep. It is harder to estimate the fall line when the slope is small than when it is steep. You'll find that your fall line green-reading error decreases as you practice this drill. Once you know how to identify the fall line, it becomes easier to estimate the break for putts that start away from the fall line, using the putting wheel shown in Figure 7.7 on page 144.

Short-game games

Short-game games help you to sharpen skills on shots taken from a distance of 40 yards or less. These games are played from 10, 20, 30, and 40 yards, starting from the fairway, rough, and sand, using the same rules and the same point system.

Short game: 20-yard fairway game

Goal

To score the most points in five shots.

Rules
- Drop a ball between 15 and 25 yards from the hole in the fairway and hit the shot.
- Repeat for a total of five shots, choosing a range of difficulties.

Scoring
- Add five points for each holed shot.
- Add two points for each shot that stops on the green within six feet of the hole.
- Add one point for each shot that stops on the green between six and 12 feet from the hole.
- Zero points for each shot that lands on the green but outside 12 feet from the hole.
- Lose one point for each shot that misses the green.

Final result

The total points in five shots.

Table 9.8. Points for the 10- to 40-yard games.

Outcome	Points
Hole out	5
Within 6 feet	2
Between 6 and 12 feet	1
On green, outside 12 feet	0
Miss green	-1

Since short-game shots vary considerably in difficulty for a given distance, shots should be chosen to reflect a range of difficulty. Some shots should be easy chips with a lot of green to work with. Some fairway or rough shots should have a bunker between the ball and the hole, requiring a lofted pitch or lob shot. Some shots should be short-sided, meaning the distance from the ball to the edge of the green is greater than the distance from the edge of the green to the hole. Some shots should be to a hole that slopes toward the golfer and others to holes that slope away from the golfer.

Every shot should be played from a different distance within a 10-yard range. Hitting two shots in a row from the same distance to the same hole isn't how golf is played on the course and doesn't help as much to develop touch around the green as hitting from different distances. In 20-yard games, hit shots between 15 and 25 yards from the hole. For example, hit one shot from 15 yards, the next from 25 yards, then from 20 yards, 25 yards, and 15 yards. In the 30-yard games, hit shots between 25 and 35 yards from the hole.

Table 9.9. Fairway 10- to 40-yard grading scorecard.

Golfer group	Average number of points in 5 shots			
	10 yards	**20 yards**	**30 yards**	**40 yards**
Best tour short game	10	8	6	5
Average tour short game	9	7	5	4
Worst tour short game	8	6	4	3
80-golfer	7	5	3	2
90-golfer	6	4	2	1
100-golfer	5	3	1	0
110-golfer	4	2	0	-1

Table 9.10. Rough 10- to 40-yard grading scorecard.

Golfer group	Average number of points in 5 shots			
	10 yards	**20 yards**	**30 yards**	**40 yards**
Best tour short game	8	5	4	3
Average tour short game	7	4	3	2
Worst tour short game	6	4	2	1
80-golfer	5	3	1	0
90-golfer	4	2	0	-1
100-golfer	3	1	-1	-2
110-golfer	2	0	-2	-3

Table 9.11. Sand 10- to 40-yard grading scorecard.

Golfer group	Average number of points in 5 shots			
	10 yards	20 yards	30 yards	40 yards
Best tour short game	6	6	4	3
Average tour short game	5	5	3	2
Worst tour short game	4	4	3	1
80-golfer	1	1	1	0
90-golfer	1	0	-1	-2
100-golfer	0	-1	-2	-3
110-golfer	-3	-3	-4	-5

The grading scorecards in Tables 9.9 to 9.11 show how golfers of varying skill levels stack up against each other. The pro results in the tables are based on play in tournament competition on difficult courses, with hard and fast greens from tight lies in the fairway or thick rough around the greens. The amateur results are based on play on regular courses, often in small-money matches and sometimes in competition. The fairway grading scorecard in Table 9.9 shows that the average score from 40 yards in the fairway for an average PGA Tour pro is four points in five shots. Playing the game multiple times, the pro will score two or three points 30% of the time, four points 20% of the time, and five or six points 30% of the time. Pros will score seven or more points about 10% of the time. A 90-golfer's average score is one point in five shots in the 40-yard fairway game.

Median-leave games

Like short-game games, median-leave games test your ability to take shots from various distances and from a range of conditions. Median-leave games measure performance using the middle, or median, remaining distance of a group of shots. Why median remaining distance and not average remaining distance? First, when you are out on the course, it is easier to measure one median distance than to measure lots of distances and take the average. Second, the average distance can be disproportion-ately affected by a single poor shot. These fairway, rough, and sand games can be played on a practice area. Alternatively, you can record shot out-comes from your play on an actual course to track your performance and to see how it stacks up against that of pros or amateurs.

20-yard fairway median-leave game

Goal

To score the most points in five shots.

Rules

- Drop five balls between 15 and 25 yards from the hole in the fairway and hit the shots.

Scoring

- Pick up the two shots that are closest to the hole and the two that are farthest from the hole.
- Measure the distance of the remaining shot to the hole in feet. This is the median distance, meaning it is the middle of the five distances to the hole.

Final result

The median distance, in feet, of the five shots.

The five shots should all be different. One way to do this is to hit to a single hole from five different positions around the green. For a 20-yard game, the distances can vary between 15 and 25 yards, but the average distance should be 20 yards. If you are attempting 40-yard shots, the actual initial distances can vary between 35 and 45 yards. The median remaining distance of five shots is the third-closest to the hole. You can also measure the median remaining distance using the fourth-closest of seven shots, the fifth closest of nine shots, and so on.

The grading scorecards for the fairway, rough, and sand median-leave games are given in Tables 9.12 to 9.14. For example, in the 20-yard fairway game, if your median distance is nine feet, then your performance ranks between those of an 80-golfer and a 90-golfer. The scorecards readily show the skill differences between different groups of golfers. On a 100-yard fairway shot, a pro's median leave is 16 feet while a 90-golfer's median leave is 37 feet. On a 10-yard sand shot, a pro's median leave is seven feet while a 90-golfer's median leave is 19 feet. Needless to say, this is why pros play golf for a living and amateurs have real jobs.

I've received requests from multiple pros to create a performance table for the very best golfers, so that's what I've done in Tables 9.12 to 9.14. In these scorecards, the "very best pro" refers to the three pros each year with top scores in each particular distance category. For example, for initial distances between 60 and 100 yards, each year I find the best three pros, measured by strokes gained for shots starting 60 to 100 yards from the hole, and compute the median remaining distance to the hole. For initial distances between 100 and 150 yards, each year I find the best three pros, measured by strokes gained for shots starting 100 to 150 yards from the hole, and compute their median remaining distance to the hole. If you want to be the best in the world, your scores should be consistently better than the "very best pro" scorecard numbers.

You can use the scorecards in Tables 9.12 to 9.14 to see how you stack up against the very best. Say you're practicing on the course (or short-game area) and you want to benchmark your shots against those of the very best pros. On the first hole, you drop a ball at 50 yards in the fairway and hit the shot. The fairway median-leave scorecard shows that the median remaining distance for the very best pros is nine feet. Give yourself one point if your shot finishes within nine feet and subtract one point if it finishes outside of nine feet. On the next hole, you drop a ball at 40 yards in the rough and hit the shot. The rough median-leave scorecard shows that the median remaining distance for the very best pros is 11 feet. Give yourself one point if your shot finishes within 11 feet, and subtract one point if it finishes outside of 11 feet. Next, drop a ball 20 yards from the hole, in the sand. Give yourself one point if your shot finishes within six feet (the median remaining distance for the very best pros as shown in the sand median-leave scorecard) and subtract one point if it finishes outside of six feet. Keep track of your total points in the game.

If your final total was positive, your shots were better than those of the very best pros. If your final total was negative, you've got some work to do. You can also play this game against another golfer and use the difference in total points to determine the final score.

Table 9.12. Fairway median-leave game grading scorecard.

Distance to hole (yards)	Median remaining distance (feet)					
	Very best pro	Average pro	80-golfer	90-golfer	100-golfer	110-golfer
10	3	4	5	6	6	7
20	5	6	7	10	11	12
30	6	8	12	16	19	22
40	8	10	16	21	24	26
50	9	12	20	23	28	34
60	10	13	21	25	31	40
70	10	13	23	31	37	41
80	12	14	24	33	39	43
90	12	15	26	35	41	44
100	13	16	28	37	46	56
110	15	17	29	44	53	57
120	15	18	31	47	58	63
130	17	19	35	49	63	76
140	18	21	39	50	66	86
150	21	23	42	56	73	93
160	22	25				
170	25	28				
180	27	31				
190	31	34				
200	34	37				
210	37	42				
220	41	47				

Table 9.13. Rough median-leave game grading scorecard.

Distance to hole (yards)	Median remaining distance (feet)					
	Very best pro	Average pro	80-golfer	90-golfer	100-golfer	110-golfer
10	4	5	6	8	10	11
20	8	9	11	15	19	21
30	10	12	16	20	24	29
40	11	15	17	25	31	37
50	14	17	21	28	35	41
60	15	19	22	33	40	42
70	16	21	27	36	44	53
80	18	22	28	37	46	54
90	19	24	29	40	50	57
100	24	26	32	41	52	64
110	26	28	37	43	58	75
120	29	31	38	50	66	86
130	31	33	40	51	70	91
140	32	35	41	56	75	96
150	37	38	47	57	88	110

Table 9.14. Sand median-leave game grading scorecard.

Distance to hole (yards)	Median remaining distance (feet)					
	Very best pro	Average pro	80-golfer	90-golfer	100-golfer	110-golfer
10	5	7	17	19	22	26
20	6	8	18	24	29	34
30	9	11	20	31	41	48
40	11	16	34	52	62	67

Table 9.15. Grading scorecard for fairway and rough. Note: the median leave is expressed as a fraction of the initial distance.

Fairway

Distance to hole (yards)	Median leave: remaining distance relative to the initial distance					
	Very best pro	Average pro	80-golfer	90-golfer	100-golfer	110-golfer
10–20	9%	11%	13%	17%	20%	22%
20–60	7%	9%	13%	16%	20%	23%
60–100	5%	6%	10%	13%	16%	19%
100–150	4%	5%	9%	13%	16%	19%
150–200	5%	6%	10%	14%	18%	23%

Rough

Distance to hole (yards)	Median leave: remaining distance relative to the initial distance					
	Very best pro	Average pro	80-golfer	90-golfer	100-golfer	110-golfer
10–20	14%	17%	19%	26%	32%	36%
20–60	10%	13%	16%	22%	27%	30%
60–100	7%	9%	12%	16%	20%	23%
100–150	8%	8%	10%	13%	18%	25%
150–200	9%	9%	13%	18%	25%	34%

If you keep track of your shots when you play a round on the course, then you will be able to group the shots into larger distance categories and to compute the median distance as a fraction of the initial distance. For example, say you have five fairway shots between 100 and 150 yards to the hole. Suppose the remaining distances, as a fraction of the initial distances, sorted from smallest to largest, are 3%, 10%, 11%, 13%, and 30%. The median value, 11% in this case, is the middle of the five percentages. Compare this value with the scorecard given in Table 9.15. The reason for using percentages is that they are much closer to constant over different distances. For example, for an 80-golfer, the median remaining distance from 100 yards in the fairway is 28 feet, and from 150 yards it is 42 feet. These absolute distances are quite different, but expressed as percentages, both are about 9% of the initial distance.

Table 9.16. GIR and GIRP scorecard: GIR is the number of greens hit in regulation per round. GIRP is the number of greens and fringe hit in regulation plus one stroke per round. Hitting a green on a par-five hole in three or fewer strokes counts as a green in regulation (GIR). Hitting the green or fringe on a par-five hole in four or fewer strokes counts as a "green or fringe in regulation plus one" (GIRP). The table gives average values for GIR and GIRP per round by golfer group. Amateurs scoring 85 or above would do better to track their GIRPs.

Golfer group	GIR	GIRP
PGA Tour pro	11.6	17.3
75-golfer	8.9	17.0
80-golfer	7.0	15.4
85-golfer	5.3	13.8
90-golfer	3.9	12.3
95-golfer	2.8	10.8
100-golfer	1.9	9.5
105-golfer	1.2	8.1
110-golfer	0.8	6.8

Greens or fringe in regulation plus one (GIRP)

A standard golf stat for measuring tee-to-green performance is greens in regulation, or GIR. A hole counts as a GIR, or "greenie," if the golfer reaches the green on a par-three in one shot, a par-four in one or two shots, or a par-five in three or fewer strokes. The way to remember this is that a hole's par includes a nominal two putts, so a greenie is counted if a green is reached in par minus two strokes or less. A ball that is a few inches off the green, that is, a ball on the "fringe" of the green, does *not* count as being on the green for the GIR stat. Since golfers average more than one shot per round from the green fringe, it is important to follow a consistent convention when computing GIR.

Table 9.16 shows that PGA Tour pros hit an average of 11.6 greens per round en route to shooting an average score of 71. A golfer shooting 90 hits an average four greens per round, while a golfer shooting 100 averages just two greens per round. Tracking the standard GIR stat can be quite frustrating for beginning golfers, because hitting a green in regulation is a relatively rare event.

For recreational golfers, I propose a new stat called GIRP: greens or fringe in regulation plus one. If a golfer reaches the green or fringe of a par-three hole in one or two shots, it counts as a GIRP. Similarly, if a golfer reaches the green or fringe of a par-four hole in three shots or less, or a par-five hole in four shots or less, it counts as a GIRP. Tracking GIRPs has the advantage of helping recreational golfers set and achieve more realistic goals. Hitting a par-three hole in one shot is simply not a realistic goal for many golfers, but hitting it in two shots is realistic. Likewise, hitting a par-four hole in three shots or a par-five hole in four shots are realistic goals. According to Table 9.16, golfers who average 10 or more GIRPs per round should be regularly breaking 100. Tracking GIRPs can help you plan your strategy on a hole. When water or another hazard is in play, taking one more shot to get to the green while avoiding the hazard often leads to lower scores.

Tracking GIRPs can help you diagnose your strengths and weaknesses. Table 9.16 shows that a 95-golfer averages nearly 11 GIRPs per round. If you have eight GIRPs and shoot 95, it means that your short game and putting were much better than expected and you should focus practice on your driving and approach shots. Strokes gained can identify strengths and weaknesses with much more accuracy, but tracking GIRPs is still informative and is much simpler to do.

Tracking awful shots

Awful shots—tops, chunks, shanks, and others—add up faster than many golfers think. A typical 100-golfer loses 10 strokes per round due to these swings. As Ben Hogan said, "Golf is not a game of good shots. It is a game of bad shots. The guy who misses the best is going to win." A simple and often effective idea is to review your shots after each round, recalling both the best shots (always a good confidence booster) and the worst shots (to help with the next practice session). Track awful shots to see if you are hitting more than your share.

I define an awful shot using the strokes gained measure of shot quality: Any shot with a strokes gained between -0.8 and -1.3 is classified as an awful shot. Awful shots include advancing the ball less than 80 yards, hitting into a penalty situation, hitting into a position where a recovery is needed for the next shot, skulling a chip over the green, hitting into

Table 9.17. Awful shot scorecard: Off-green strokes lost per round to awful shots. Count one for each awful shot and count two for each double-awful shot and add the numbers to get your awful total. The long-game and short-game columns break the awful total down by where the awful shots occur, outside 100 yards from the hole or inside 100 yards (excluding putts on the green).

Golfer group	Awful total	Long game	Short game
PGA Tour pro	0.7	0.5	0.2
75-golfer	1.4	1.1	0.3
80-golfer	2.5	1.7	0.8
85-golfer	3.9	2.6	1.3
90-golfer	5.6	3.8	1.8
95-golfer	7.5	5.1	2.4
100-golfer	9.7	6.7	3.0
105-golfer	12.1	8.5	3.6
110-golfer	14.8	10.6	4.2

the sand from 50 yards out, or a complete whiff. In short, these are shots where a single swing makes almost no progress to the hole. Worse still are double-awful shots: those shots with strokes gained less than -1.3. These are single swings that lose about two strokes, and include shots out of bounds, lost balls, or balls hit into water where the drop is taken close to the initial position.

While some awful shots are caused by execution errors, others are due to poor strategy. Choosing a target too close to out of bounds, trying to thread a recovery shot through a small opening rather than chipping back onto the fairway, or attempting to cut off too much of a dogleg can cause a serious loss of strokes. For both pros and amateurs, more than twice as many awful shots occur in the long game compared to the short game. Why? Balls are more likely to encounter trees, water, out of bounds, and other hazards on long shots. There are more land mines to step on outside of 100 yards than when you are nearer the green.

To see how your game stacks up, in each round you play score one for each awful shot and score two for each double-awful shot. Add the numbers to get your *awful total* and compare with the numbers in the awful shot scorecard in Table 9.17. A typical 90-golfer loses eight times as many strokes due to awful shots as a pro. Consistency is the name of the game. If you shoot 90 and have an awful total of more than six, you need to work on consistency.

Most likely, you will find that to achieve your best score, it is less important to hit great shots than it is to avoid awful shots. For most amateur golfers, reducing the number of awful shots is the single easiest way of shaving strokes off your scorecard.

19th Hole Summary

- Three key steps to lowering golf scores: measure, analyze, and improve.

- Strokes gained can be used to measure the performance of golfers on the golf course, and to identify areas of strength and weakness.

- The best golfers practice with games like those described in this chapter on the putting green, short-game area, or the course. Many of these games were designed with point systems so that you can measure your performance.

- Using gaming scorecards, a single game can be used to analyze your performance relative to those of golfers of many skill levels. More important, tracking points through time allows you to see your own progress, or slippage, in a given skill.

- Once you've identified one or more areas of your game to work on, see your local golf professional for a lesson and for help in designing a game- and drill-based practice plan.

- For most amateur golfers, reducing the number of awful shots is the single easiest way of shaving strokes off your scorecard.

- The pros I've talked to all practice with a purpose. Improvement comes from deep practice, not just wishful thinking or beating balls on the range.

CHAPTER 10

THE 20TH HOLE: Summing Up and Looking Ahead

For years, like many other golfers, I used to record traditional stats on my scorecard: fairways, greens, and putts. I'd look at it after the round and then throw it away. I didn't learn much more about why I played well or poorly from the traditional stats than from my score alone.

Not only were traditional stats of little use in helping me understand my game, they couldn't answer the other questions I was curious about: What does it take to drop 10 strokes from a player's score? How much is 20 yards of extra driving distance worth? Is it better to hit a putt hard to take out some of the break or to play more break and die it into the hole?

This book is the fruit of years of exploring these and other golf questions, bringing to bear the mathematical tools that I use as a professional academic in assessing and managing financial risk. Little did I realize that analyzing the game of golf would become a continuing journey, as each answer would lead to interesting new questions that I'd be working on years later.

I wouldn't have been able to produce the insights in this book without detailed shot information—where shots started and where they finished—that only became available in the past several years. Some of the data I had to generate myself with a program called Golfmetrics, which I used to collect and analyze detailed golf shot data, mostly from amateurs. The PGA Tour's ShotLink data, collected at their tournaments starting in 2003, provided a wealth of information about professional play. My deep gratitude goes out to the folks at the PGA Tour for their active decision to share data with academic researchers, starting in 2007. For me, it was a lucky confluence of events.

But the right way to analyze the data wasn't at all clear.

It quickly became apparent that measuring golf performance would require comparing skills that had been thought of as apples and oranges. Bombing a drive down the middle of the fairway requires strength and timing. Hitting a chip shot requires precise contact for the ball to travel the desired distance. Sinking a downhill double-breaking 20-foot putt requires green-reading skill and putting touch. One appeal of golf is the many different skills required, yet this also makes it challenging to figure out a method for measuring the relative importance of different parts of the game.

The linchpin of this research was the strokes gained concept, which allowed me to work with the new mountain of shot-level data to compare parts of the game that had never been measured with the same stick.

Let me repeat a brief explanation of strokes gained: If a stroke starts on a tee where, according to historical data, the average score is four, and if it finishes at a position in the fairway where the average strokes to hole out is 2.8, then the tee shot has moved the ball 1.2 strokes closer to the hole with just one stroke. The single tee shot has gained 0.2 strokes compared to an average tee shot, so it has a "strokes gained" of 0.2.

Strokes gained recognizes that sinking a 20-foot putt represents a better performance than sinking a three-foot putt, even though they both count as a single stroke on the scorecard. Strokes gained assigns a number to this intuition. Though strokes gained has roots in some fancy mathematics developed at the dawn of the computer age, there is an elegant simplicity to a stat that, at its core, merely involves subtracting two numbers.

Analyzing this data with the strokes gained method brought forth a number of surprising facts. For instance, strokes gained shows with mathematical precision that putting accounts for just 15% of the difference in scores between the top golfers in the world and the field. In the rarefied air of the PGA Tour, though, strokes gained reveals an incredible variety of putting skill levels among pro golfers. Putting contributes almost 40% to the scoring advantage of Luke Donald, Steve Stricker, and Zach Johnson. For Rory McIlroy, Ernie Els, Sergio Garcia, and Adam Scott, on the other hand, putting partially negates their tee-to-green scoring advantage.

A look beyond the top golfers in the world reveals a remarkable regularity: Putting accounts for about 15% of the difference in scores between the best pros and average pros, between pros and amateurs, and between beginning and skilled amateurs. As we saw in chapter 2, when pros "up their game" in order to win a tournament, putting accounts for more of the increase than other parts of the game, but it would be easier to find a live unicorn than an 80-golfer who could consistently compete on the PGA Tour if only he had tour-average putting ability.

Another insight that appeared when the data were analyzed using the strokes gained method was that about two-thirds of the difference in scores between pros and amateurs is due to shots starting outside of 100 yards from the hole. Through the consistent lens of strokes gained, we uncover the importance of the long game generally, and approach shots in particular. A golfer who is a genius at putts or drives won't necessarily be a great scorer, but a genius at approach shots is likely to make his mark.

Take for example Greg Ward, probably the best putter in the world that you've never heard of, and Jason Zuback, the longest driver. Ward was inducted into the Professional Putters Association Hall of Fame in 2002 and he was twice honored as the PPA player of the decade. Zuback won the World Long Drive Championship five times and was inducted into the Long Drivers of America Hall of Fame in 2003. He regularly hits drives over 400 yards and straight enough to stay inside the 40- to 50-yard-wide fairways used in the competitions. Yet neither man has top-level skills throughout the game, or the overall scores of a pro. Neither Ward nor Zuback would stand a chance if he attempted to compete on the PGA Tour.

On the other hand, if there were a world championship for approach shots between 150 and 200 yards, I'd venture to guess that the winner could compete on the top professional tours. A performance advantage in these shots leads to a big scoring advantage on the PGA Tour, as we saw from the strokes gained analysis in chapter 6. Superior performance in these shots requires an excellent repeatable swing in order to control the shot distance, direction, trajectory, and ball spin to stop the ball close to the hole from a range of lies in the fairway and rough. A golfer with a swing that's good for shots between 150 and 200 yards is usually good at shorter and longer shots as well.

As we saw in chapter 6, from 2004 to 2012 the best golfer on the PGA Tour from 150 to 200 yards was Tiger Woods. He hits his approach shots three to four feet closer to the hole than the PGA Tour average, for a scoring advantage of 1.3 strokes per round. Even if Tiger were tour average in all shots except approach shots, he'd still rank in the top 10 of PGA Tour golfers. Approach shots are that important.

While the importance-of-the-long-game principle applies for all groups of golfers, from the best pros to the worst amateurs, individual golfers have unique areas of strength and weakness. To get better, golfers need to understand where they stand. "As painful as it is," major-winner Mark Brooks recently said, "recognize what your deficiencies are and work on them until they are no longer deficiencies." But recognizing weaknesses is harder than many people think, especially without a good yardstick to measure with. Some amateurs incorrectly believe they are poor putters because they count every stroke taken with a putter, even if it is from 10 yards off the green. Some think they have an adequate long game because they remember the best shot they ever hit, while others only compare themselves to their buddies. Using strokes gained analysis, golfers can now gain a better understanding of their own game and how to improve it.

The PGA Tour has now been collecting its great ShotLink data for more than a decade. For years they have been publishing dozens of new stats on their website: proximity to the hole starting from 125 to 150 yards in the fairway, scrambling from 20 to 30 yards, one-putt percentage in round three of a tournament, and many more. But their "core" stats, like greens in regulation and fairways hit (that is, driving accuracy), didn't change until much more recently: They only rolled out the new strokes gained putting stat in May 2011.

Strokes gained putting is just the tip of the golf stats iceberg. In the future, an entire strokes gained family can be used to measure and compare driving, approach shots, and short-game play. These new stats will fill the golf stats vacuum with quality information. I look forward to a day in the not-too-distant future when shot data are automatically collected and a golfer can give his pro or coach objective information about his game: what is improving and what needs fixing.

Sea changes are underway in many sports—football, basketball, and soccer—allowing major league teams to use data and analytics to assess player skills and determine lineups and strategy. Detailed shot data can be used in a similar way to improve golf strategy. Pros are better than amateurs at all types of golf shots, but they are also better at skills that don't involve a club: green reading, putting strategy, and tee-to-green strategy. Many amateurs overestimate their skill, underestimate the effect of hazards, and choose highly risky shots that lead to too many "awful shots" and dropped shots on the scorecard. Playing smarter golf, without any swing changes, can lead to lower scores immediately.

I have been able to investigate both hunches and conventional wisdom in the light of statistical scrutiny, but I have also learned that taking an evidence-based approach doesn't mean there is a mathematical formula for the right strategy. Golfers will always have to assess the unique circumstances of each shot: the lie, the wind conditions, the pin location, the contours of the green, and their own ability to hit a shot with a given trajectory and spin.

Numbers aren't a substitute for the drama of the game, but they can enhance the fan experience. Instead of the announcer's saying a player is facing a difficult pitch shot, I look forward to the day when we will be told that half of similar shots end up 20 or more feet from the hole. We could be informed "that shot on 17 to four feet just gained 0.8 strokes for Els." Many sports have box scores that announcers use in wrapping up the action. At the conclusion of a golf tournament, I anticipate we'll hear announcers tell us how much driving, approach shots, short game, and putting contributed to the victory.

What should golfers do as a result of all this information? First, just sit back and appreciate the game of golf from a slightly different vantage point. A data-driven scientific approach to golf doesn't subtract from the beauty and fun of golf. Rather, it gives me, and I hope it will give you, a framework for understanding golf performance and strategy, and for evaluating which factors contribute to the final score and how to think about making the best decisions for you on the golf course.

Golf isn't a game of putting, nor is it a driving match. Henry Cotton, who won three British Opens between 1934 and 1948, summed up its essence. Cotton famously said, "Every shot counts." A data-driven approach expands our understanding while showing that golf isn't a mystical game beyond our comprehension. Golf can be analyzed, taken apart, and the resulting insights can help you play better. The revolution is just beginning.

APPENDIX

Chapter 2. Numbers Talk

Tournament-by-tournament putting contribution to victory (PCV) results for Tiger Woods, Phil Mickelson, and Vijay Singh are given in Tables A-1 and A-2. Figure A-1 gives a chart of their tournament-by-tournament PCV results.

Table A-3 gives the top 25 PGA Tour tournament winners ranked by putting contribution to victory. These golfers won largely because of their putting. Table A-4 gives the bottom 25 PGA Tour tournament winners ranked by putting contribution to victory. These golfers won largely because of exceptional off-green play and in spite of their putting. Table A-5 gives the middle 25 PGA Tour tournament winners ranked by putting contribution to victory. These tournaments illustrate the typical contribution of putting to victories.

Table A-1. Tiger Woods's putting contribution to victory (PCV). Tiger's average strokes gained putting in his victories is 1.14 putts. His average margin of victory is 4.09 strokes versus the field. Tiger's average putting contribution to victory is 28% (1.14/4.09). Putting contributed slightly less to Tiger's victories than the overall average PCV of 35%. Put another way, Tiger's off-green play contributed more to his victories than the average victory.

Rank	Year	Tournament	Strokes gained putting (SGP)	Off-green strokes gained	Winning score versus field (SVF)	Putting contribution to victory (SGP/SVF)
1	2009	Arnold Palmer	1.87	1.57	3.44	54%
2	2009	AT&T National	1.89	2.28	4.16	45%
3	2005	Buick Invitational	1.75	2.13	3.88	45%
4	2007	Wachovia	1.95	2.58	4.53	43%
5	2007	Buick Invitational	1.33	1.96	3.29	40%
6	2007	TOUR Championship	1.55	2.52	4.08	38%
7	2007	BMW Championship	1.48	2.79	4.27	35%
8	2009	WGC-Bridgestone	1.32	2.54	3.86	34%
9	2012	Arnold Palmer	1.44	2.98	4.43	33%
10	2008	Buick Invitational	1.86	3.90	5.76	32%
11	2009	Buick Open	1.07	2.51	3.59	30%
12	2006	Buick Open	1.28	3.06	4.35	30%
13	2006	WGC-Bridgestone	1.07	2.60	3.67	29%
14	2009	BMW Championship	1.51	3.68	5.19	29%
15	2008	Arnold Palmer	1.00	2.44	3.44	29%
16	2006	Buick Invitational	0.73	2.07	2.80	26%
17	2005	Ford at Doral	1.14	3.44	4.58	25%
18	2006	Ford at Doral	0.86	2.81	3.67	23%
19	2005	WGC-NEC	0.61	2.26	2.87	21%
20	2006	Deutsche Bank	1.15	4.46	5.61	21%
21	2007	WGC-Bridgestone	0.76	4.02	4.79	16%
22	2009	Memorial	0.55	3.87	4.42	12%
23	2012	Memorial	0.04	3.89	3.93	1%
24	2007	WGC-CA	-0.79	4.29	3.50	-23%
		Average	1.14	2.94	4.09	28%

Table A-2. Vijay Singh's and Phil Mickelson's putting contribution to victory (PCV). Vijay's average putting contribution to victory is 20% (0.77/3.92). Phil's average putting contribution to victory is 27% (1.10/4.12). Both are less than the overall average PCV of 35%. Vijay's wins typically occur in spite of his putting.

Rank	Golfer	Year	Tournament	Strokes gained putting (SGP)	Off-green strokes gained	Winning score versus field (SVF)	Putting contribution to victory (SGP/SVF)
1	Vijay Singh	2006	Barclays Classic	2.97	0.78	3.75	79%
2	Vijay Singh	2004	New Orleans	2.48	1.40	3.89	64%
3	Vijay Singh	2007	Mercedes-Benz	1.36	2.03	3.39	40%
4	Vijay Singh	2004	Chrysler Championship	1.63	3.15	4.78	34%
5	Vijay Singh	2007	Arnold Palmer	1.26	2.80	4.05	31%
6	Vijay Singh	2005	Buick Open	1.33	3.11	4.44	30%
7	Vijay Singh	2005	Sony Open	0.89	2.76	3.65	24%
8	Vijay Singh	2005	Wachovia	1.04	3.70	4.74	22%
9	Vijay Singh	2004	Buick Open	0.99	3.54	4.53	22%
10	Vijay Singh	2008	Barclays	0.30	2.11	2.41	12%
11	Vijay Singh	2004	Bell Canadian Open	0.34	3.64	3.98	9%
12	Vijay Singh	2008	Deutsche Bank	0.38	3.99	4.37	9%
13	Vijay Singh	2004	LUMBER Classic	-0.08	3.57	3.49	-2%
14	Vijay Singh	2005	Shell Houston Open	-0.08	3.63	3.55	-2%
15	Vijay Singh	2004	Shell Houston Open	-0.16	3.96	3.81	-4%
16	Vijay Singh	2004	Deutsche Bank	-0.37	5.21	4.84	-8%
17	Vijay Singh	2008	WGC-Bridgestone	-1.14	4.19	3.05	-37%
			Average	0.77	3.15	3.92	20%
1	Phil Mickelson	2009	TOUR Championship	1.62	1.18	2.80	58%
2	Phil Mickelson	2005	BellSouth Classic	1.58	1.90	3.48	45%
3	Phil Mickelson	2005	FBR Open	1.57	3.25	4.82	33%
4	Phil Mickelson	2008	Colonial	1.11	2.72	3.83	29%
5	Phil Mickelson	2006	BellSouth Classic	1.77	4.99	6.76	26%
6	Phil Mickelson	2009	Northern Trust Open	0.78	2.58	3.35	23%
7	Phil Mickelson	2008	Northern Trust Open	0.92	3.19	4.11	22%
8	Phil Mickelson	2007	Deutsche Bank	0.76	2.97	3.74	20%
9	Phil Mickelson	2007	PLAYERS	0.77	3.23	4.00	19%
10	Phil Mickelson	2011	Shell Houston Open	0.77	3.97	4.74	16%
11	Phil Mickelson	2009	WGC-CA	0.47	3.20	3.66	13%
			Average	1.10	3.02	4.12	27%

Table A-3. Top 25 PGA Tour tournament winners ranked by putting contribution to victory. These golfers won largely because of their putting. Putting performance is measured by strokes gained putting (SGP) per round. Winning performance is measured by the winner's average score versus the field (SVF) per round. The putting contribution to victory is the ratio SGP/SVF. Off-green strokes gained is the score versus the field (SVF) minus strokes gained putting (SGP).

Rank	Golfer	Year	Tournament	Strokes gained putting (SGP)	Off-green strokes gained	Winning versus field (SVF)	Putting contribution to victory (SGP/SVF)
1	Bill Haas	2011	TOUR Championship	2.05	-0.26	1.79	114%
2	Daniel Chopra	2008	Mercedes-Benz	2.47	-0.03	2.44	101%
3	Luke Donald	2012	Transitions	2.60	0.38	2.98	87%
4	J. J. Henry	2006	Buick Championship	3.30	0.76	4.06	81%
5	Matt Kuchar	2009	Turning Stone Resort	2.54	0.63	3.17	80%
6	Vijay Singh	2006	Barclays Classic	2.97	0.78	3.75	79%
7	Ben Curtis	2006	Booz Allen	3.57	0.96	4.53	79%
8	Wes Short Jr.	2005	Michelin	2.28	0.72	3.01	76%
9	Kenny Perry	2008	John Deere Classic	2.28	0.79	3.07	74%
10	Stuart Appleby	2004	Mercedes	2.66	1.03	3.69	72%
11	Geoff Ogilvy	2010	Tournament of Champions	1.72	0.67	2.38	72%
12	Lucas Glover	2011	Wells Fargo	2.65	1.05	3.70	72%
13	Jeff Maggert	2006	FedEx St. Jude	3.09	1.32	4.41	70%
14	Nick Watney	2011	AT&T National	2.74	1.23	3.97	69%
15	Steve Flesch	2007	Turning Stone Resort	2.19	1.03	3.22	68%
16	Jerry Kelly	2009	New Orleans	2.28	1.13	3.41	67%
17	Stuart Appleby	2005	Mercedes	1.64	0.83	2.48	66%
18	Luke Donald	2011	Children's Miracle Network	2.01	1.04	3.05	66%
19	Stewart Cink	2004	MCI Heritage	2.16	1.18	3.33	65%
20	Carl Pettersson	2006	Memorial	2.58	1.42	4.00	64%
21	Stewart Cink	2004	WGC-NEC	2.46	1.38	3.84	64%
22	Jim Furyk	2006	Canadian Open	2.41	1.36	3.77	64%
23	Vijay Singh	2004	New Orleans	2.48	1.40	3.89	64%
24	K. J. Choi	2011	PLAYERS	2.05	1.20	3.25	63%
25	Aaron Baddeley	2006	Heritage	2.57	1.51	4.08	63%

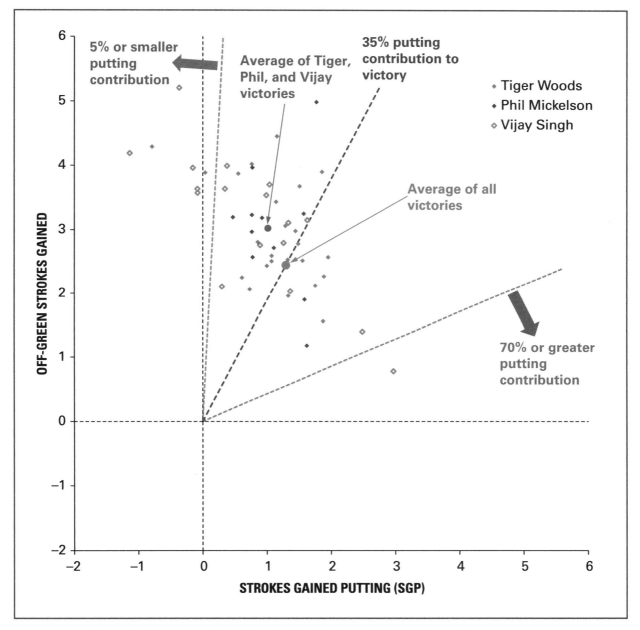

Figure A-1. Victories of Tiger Woods, Vijay Singh, and Phil Mickelson: off-green strokes gained per round plotted against strokes gained putting per round (SGP). The sum of off-green strokes gained and strokes gained putting is the winner's average score versus the field (SVF), or total strokes gained per round versus the field. The putting contribution to victory is the ratio SGP/SVF. The average putting contribution to victory for these 61 victories was 25%.

Table A-4. Bottom 25 PGA Tour tournament winners ranked by putting contribution to victory. These golfers won in spite of their putting. Putting performance is measured by strokes gained putting (SGP) per round. Winning performance is measured by the winner's average score versus the field (SVF) per round. The putting contribution to victory is the ratio SGP/SVF. Off-green strokes gained is the score versus the field (SVF) minus strokes gained putting (SGP).

Rank	Golfer	Year	Tournament	Strokes gained putting (SGP)	Off-green strokes gained	Winning score versus field (SVF)	Putting contribution to victory (SGP/SVF)
291	Scott Stallings	2011	Greenbrier Classic	0.21	2.88	3.09	7%
292	Nick Watney	2009	Buick Invitational	0.25	3.78	4.03	6%
293	Bubba Watson	2011	Farmers Insurance	0.25	3.95	4.20	6%
294	Sergio Garcia	2004	Buick Classic	0.19	3.16	3.35	6%
295	Jason Gore	2005	LUMBER Classic	0.22	3.61	3.83	6%
296	Rory Sabbatini	2006	Nissan Open	0.19	3.49	3.68	5%
297	Dustin Johnson	2012	FedEx St. Jude	0.17	3.32	3.49	5%
298	Woody Austin	2007	St. Jude Championship	0.25	5.17	5.42	5%
299	Chris Couch	2006	New Orleans	0.05	3.47	3.52	2%
300	Tiger Woods	2012	Memorial	0.04	3.89	3.93	1%
301	Ben Crane	2010	Farmers Insurance	0.02	2.98	3.00	1%
302	Scott Verplank	2007	Byron Nelson	-0.05	3.84	3.79	-1%
303	Sean O'Hair	2011	Canadian Open	-0.08	3.60	3.52	-2%
304	Vijay Singh	2004	LUMBER Classic	-0.08	3.57	3.49	-2%
305	Vijay Singh	2005	Shell Houston Open	-0.08	3.63	3.55	-2%
306	Brett Wetterich	2006	Byron Nelson	-0.11	3.68	3.57	-3%
307	Vijay Singh	2004	Shell Houston Open	-0.16	3.96	3.81	-4%
308	Mark Hensby	2004	John Deere Classic	-0.22	3.57	3.35	-7%
309	Vijay Singh	2004	Deutsche Bank	-0.37	5.21	4.84	-8%
310	Jason Dufner	2012	Byron Nelson	-0.39	4.22	3.84	-10%
311	Steve Flesch	2007	Reno-Tahoe Open	-0.81	4.99	4.18	-19%
312	Tiger Woods	2007	WGC-CA	-0.79	4.29	3.50	-23%
313	Sergio Garcia	2004	Byron Nelson	-0.71	3.55	2.84	-25%
314	Sean O'Hair	2009	Quail Hollow	-0.82	3.99	3.17	-26%
315	Vijay Singh	2008	WGC-Bridgestone	-1.14	4.19	3.05	-37%

Table A-5. Middle 25 PGA Tour tournament winners ranked by putting contribution to victory. Putting performance is measured by strokes gained putting (SGP) per round. Winning performance is measured by the winner's average score versus the field (SVF) per round. The putting contribution to victory is the ratio SGP/SVF. Off-green strokes gained is the score versus the field (SVF) minus strokes gained putting (SGP).

Rank	Golfer	Year	Tournament	Strokes gained putting (SGP)	Off-green strokes gained	Winning score versus field (SVF)	Putting contribution to victory (SGP/SVF)
145	David Toms	2006	Sony Open	1.96	3.46	5.42	36%
146	Trevor Immelman	2006	Western Open	1.31	2.31	3.62	36%
147	Jonathan Byrd	2011	Tournament of Champions	1.11	1.97	3.09	36%
148	Fred Funk	2005	PLAYERS	1.11	1.98	3.09	36%
149	Ryan Palmer	2004	FUNAI Classic	1.21	2.22	3.43	35%
150	Tiger Woods	2007	BMW Championship	1.48	2.79	4.27	35%
151	Zach Johnson	2008	Valero Texas Open	1.35	2.59	3.94	34%
152	Tiger Woods	2009	WGC-Bridgestone	1.32	2.54	3.86	34%
153	Parker McLachlin	2008	Legends Reno-Tahoe Open	1.63	3.15	4.79	34%
154	Vijay Singh	2004	Chrysler Championship	1.63	3.15	4.78	34%
155	Rory Sabbatini	2009	Byron Nelson	1.50	2.93	4.43	34%
156	Adam Scott	2006	TOUR Championship	1.19	2.32	3.51	34%
157	Ernie Els	2004	Memorial	1.76	3.44	5.20	34%
158	Fred Funk	2004	Southern Farm Bureau	1.15	2.26	3.42	34%
159	Geoff Ogilvy	2005	Chrysler Tucson	1.00	1.98	2.98	34%
160	John Senden	2006	John Deere Classic	1.28	2.54	3.82	33%
161	Joey Sindelar	2004	Wachovia	1.04	2.08	3.12	33%
162	Hunter Mahan	2010	Phoenix Open	0.98	1.95	2.93	33%
163	Mark Wilson	2007	Honda Classic	1.06	2.15	3.21	33%
164	Ernie Els	2010	WGC-CA	1.23	2.51	3.74	33%
165	Harrison Frazar	2011	FedEx St. Jude	1.39	2.85	4.24	33%
166	Geoff Ogilvy	2008	WGC-CA	1.07	2.22	3.29	33%
167	Tiger Woods	2012	Arnold Palmer	1.44	2.98	4.43	33%
168	Phil Mickelson	2005	FBR Open	1.57	3.25	4.82	33%
169	Ryan Palmer	2008	Ginn sur Mer Classic	0.88	1.83	2.71	33%

Chapter 3. Strokes Gained Putting

The gold standard for putting rounds, the largest SGP versus the field round from 2003 to 2012, belongs to J. J. Henry in his second round of the FBR Open in 2006. Henry shot a 61 while gaining an astonishing 8.6 strokes on the greens versus the PGA Tour benchmark. The field gained 0.3 strokes to the benchmark, so J. J. gained 8.3 strokes on the greens relative to the field. Table A-6 contains the details. His 61 was 9.5 strokes better than the field average of 70.5. Putting contributed 87% (8.3/9.5) to his score relative to the field.

Table A-6. Putting results for J. J. Henry in round two of the 2006 FBR Open at the TPC Scottsdale Stadium course. He gained 8.6 strokes relative to the PGA Tour benchmark while the field gained 0.3 strokes. His strokes gained putting versus the field of 8.3 was the best single-round putting performance in 2003–2012.

Hole	1	2	3	4	5	6	7	8	9	Out
Distance (feet)	29	26	31	16	42	6	5	6	8	
Tour avg putts	2.0	1.9	2.0	1.8	2.1	1.3	1.2	1.4	1.5	15.2
Henry's putts	1	2	2	1	2	1	1	1	1	12
Strokes gained	1.0	-0.1	0.0	0.8	0.1	0.3	0.2	0.4	0.5	3.2

Hole	10	11	12	13	14	15	16	17	18	In	Total
Distance (feet)	8	16	28	2	27	26	13	27	9		
Tour avg putts	1.5	1.8	2.0	1.0	2.0	1.9	1.7	1.9	1.6	15.4	30.6
Henry's putts	1	1	1	1	1	1	2	1	1	10	22
Strokes gained	0.5	0.8	1.0	0.0	1.0	0.9	-0.3	0.9	0.6	5.4	8.6

SGP to benchmark	8.6
Field average SGP	0.3
SGP to field	8.3

The best putting rounds in the years 2003–2012 as ranked by SGP to the field are given in Table A-7. The list is headed by J. J. Henry's round in 2006. While many great putters are on the list, some notables are missing because of the focus on putting performance in a single round. Joe Durant, owner of one of the worst putting rounds, also appears on this exclusive list of the best putting rounds. Some of the best rounds ever, as measured by the SGP to the field, have 25 or more putts in a round. For example, Nathan Green took 27 putts with an SGP of 6.3 in the 21st-best putting round. The number of putts was large because his putts started a long way from the hole—an average of 24 feet away. Kenny Perry took 22 putts with an SGP of 6.3 in the 22nd-best round. The number of putts was small because he started an average of 14 feet from the hole. The difference in their initial putt distances was huge. By taking initial putt distances into account, strokes gained putting provides a much more accurate measure of putting performance.

Table A-7. Best 40 putting rounds in the ShotLink era from 2003 through August 2012. Rounds are ranked by strokes gained putting to the field (SGP) in the rightmost column.

Rank	Date	Golfer	Avg distance of first putt (feet)	Putts	Strokes gained putting (SGP)
1	2/3/2006	J. J. Henry	18.0	22	8.32
2	7/8/2010	Paul Goydos	19.9	22	7.36
3	8/27/2005	Darron Stiles	19.8	25	6.96
4	3/18/2012	Scott Piercy	17.2	23	6.93
5	7/26/2012	Charl Schwartzel	17.0	24	6.81
6	7/31/2011	J. P. Hayes	16.2	23	6.79
7	2/24/2005	Steve Stricker	15.5	22	6.66
8	10/1/2004	Woody Austin	12.6	22	6.64
9	9/15/2005	Mark O'Meara	14.4	21	6.62
10	6/10/2004	David Frost	21.4	26	6.60
11	10/24/2009	Matt Bettencourt	14.0	22	6.58
12	7/8/2010	Steve Stricker	20.8	25	6.58
13	3/22/2012	Chris Stroud	18.9	25	6.51
14	9/23/2005	Dan Forsman	22.3	26	6.51
15	3/31/2011	Jimmy Walker	17.3	23	6.45
16	7/7/2011	Kris Blanks	20.6	25	6.42
17	8/23/2007	Brian Gay	12.6	20	6.40
18	10/31/2004	Joe Durant	22.0	25	6.38
19	10/27/2005	Dean Wilson	19.3	24	6.36
20	7/23/2009	Kevin Na	15.9	24	6.35
21	10/7/2011	Nathan Green	23.7	27	6.34
22	6/29/2007	Kenny Perry	14.4	22	6.29
23	9/5/2005	Tim Herron	21.2	25	6.28
24	4/30/2005	Daniel Chopra	13.4	22	6.26
25	1/26/2003	Pat Bates	22.3	26	6.25
26	3/31/2012	Hunter Mahan	21.4	26	6.17
27	7/10/2008	Chris Riley	14.4	23	6.16
28	3/17/2006	Mark O'Meara	18.8	24	6.15
29	3/5/2006	Fredrik Jacobson	18.0	24	6.14
30	11/1/2007	J. P. Hayes	18.4	25	6.12
31	10/12/2007	John Daly	17.5	24	6.12
32	8/24/2012	Charl Schwartzel	20.0	26	6.12
33	8/22/2003	Guy Boros	13.0	22	6.11
34	1/26/2012	Marc Turnesa	17.3	25	6.08
35	10/2/2003	Heath Slocum	15.9	23	6.07
36	8/29/2008	Mike Weir	12.3	21	6.07
37	5/5/2005	Fred Funk	19.7	25	6.06
38	4/30/2010	J. P. Hayes	16.3	25	6.02
39	10/21/2010	Robert Garrigus	20.6	26	6.02
40	9/30/2004	Brenden Pappas	18.8	24	6.01

In order to understand how good a particular putting round is, it is helpful to look at all putting rounds, not just the best putting rounds. For example, how good is a putting round that gains one stroke on the field? It might not seem very impressive, but Table A-8 shows that it is better than 72% of putting rounds on tour. A putting round that loses one stroke to the field is in the bottom 30% of putting rounds.

Table A-8. Frequency of SGP to the field for individual professional putting rounds. For example, a putting round that gains 1.5 strokes against the field is better than 81% of rounds on the PGA Tour. A putting round that loses 2.5 strokes to the field is better than only 8% of rounds on the PGA Tour, that is, it is worse than 92% of rounds.

Strokes gained putting (SGP)	Fraction of rounds worse	Strokes gained putting (SGP)	Fraction of rounds worse
5.5	99.9%	-0.5	38%
5.0	99.8%	-1.0	28%
4.5	99.5%	-1.5	19%
4.0	99%	-2.0	12%
3.5	98%	-2.5	8%
3.0	96%	-3.0	4%
2.5	93%	-3.5	2%
2.0	88%	-4.0	1%
1.5	81%	-4.5	0.6%
1.0	72%	-5.0	0.3%
0.5	61%	-5.5	0.1%
0.0	50%		

Most improved putter awards

Whose putting improved the most from 2011 to 2012? Table A-9 shows Derek Lamely heading the list, with a putting improvement of one stroke per round. Unfortunately, his improved putting wasn't enough to make up for the rest of his game, which led to his making the cut in only five of 21 tournaments he entered. The resurgence of Ernie Els, Sergio Garcia, and Jim Furyk in 2012 is due in large part to their improved putting. The average improvement of the top 10 most improved putters is 0.73 strokes per round. Table A-9 shows that the vast majority of the gain comes from putts 21 feet and under. It is very difficult for pros to gain many strokes on the field in putts 22 feet and over.

Table A-9. Most improved putters from 2011 to September 2012 as measured by SGP.

Rank	Golfer	Total SGP improvement	SGP Improvement		
			0–6 ft	7–21 ft	22+ ft
1	Derek Lamely	1.00	0.29	0.41	0.30
2	Jeff Maggert	0.90	0.43	0.32	0.14
3	Phil Mickelson	0.79	0.00	0.54	0.24
4	Dustin Johnson	0.76	0.44	0.25	0.07
5	Ernie Els	0.70	0.48	0.41	-0.19
6	Tom Gillis	0.69	0.47	-0.09	0.31
7	Bo Van Pelt	0.68	0.35	0.22	0.11
8	James Driscoll	0.62	0.19	0.08	0.34
9	Sergio Garcia	0.61	0.27	0.24	0.09
10	Jim Furyk	0.59	0.44	0.22	-0.08
	Average	0.73	0.34	0.26	0.13

Strokes gained to the average field

The main putting stat used by the PGA Tour is strokes gained putting to the field. This is computed by adjusting strokes gained putting to the tour average by the difficulty of the greens measured by how well the field putted each round. But some tournaments—for example, World Golf Championships and the TOUR Championship—have smaller fields composed of better-than-tour-average putters. Especially in these tournaments, the field might putt better than the PGA Tour average putting benchmark, not because the greens are easier, but because the golfers are better putters than the tour average. Adjusting the putting results by the performance of the field would unfairly penalize these golfers.

For regular full-field events, it is reasonable to assume that the average putting of the field primarily reflects the difficulty of the greens. But in general, it is difficult to simultaneously estimate the difficulty of the greens and the skill of the putters. Good putting results for the field could be due to easier-than-average greens or more highly skilled putters in the field. That's where some fancy math comes in to disentangle the two effects. The technique we use is called fixed-effect regression, but it is really just an extension of ideas from algebra, which allows you to solve for two unknowns simultaneously when given enough information.

This regression approach allows us to use putting data to simultaneously estimate difficulty of greens and the putting skill of golfers. The resulting stat is called strokes gained putting to the average field, because it measures putting skill to the average field, taking into account the difficulty of the greens. The PGA Tour stat, strokes gained putting to the field, measures putting skill relative to the field in each round. Both stats give similar results, but strokes gained putting to the average field is a little more accurate. It also explains why some of the results presented in this chapter will differ slightly from those on the PGA Tour website.

Although described only for strokes gained putting, the same adjustments for the difficulty of a particular round and the strength of the field are made to strokes gained driving and all other strokes gained computations in the book.[28]

Chapter 6. Distance, Accuracy, and the Secret of Tiger Woods

Tables A-10 to A-18 give "career-at-a-glance" results for the very best pros through the lens of strokes gained. Table A-10 shows Tiger's career in the ShotLink era. Incredibly, he ranked first in total strokes gained every year from 2003 through 2009 (though 2008 was based on only 11 rounds due to his injury). He was never out of the top five in strokes gained approach shots, even in his off years of 2010 and 2011.

The next tables give strokes gained results for Jim Furyk (Table A-11), Luke Donald (Table A-12), Phil Mickelson (Table A-13), Rory McIlroy (Table A-14), Vijay Singh (Table A-15), Ernie Els (Table A-16), Sergio Garcia (Table A-17), and Steve Stricker (Table A-18).

Luke Donald was ranked 29th in the world in January 2010 and ninth in January 2011. In 2011, he improved his total strokes gained by another three-quarters of a stroke per round, rising to world number one in June 2011. Table A-12 shows that virtually all of this improvement came from his long game: Driving contributed about a half stroke and approach shots another quarter of a stroke. Strokes gained analysis shows that his tee-

[28] For more details on the adjusted strokes gained computations, see Broadie, M., 2012, "Assessing Golfer Performance on the PGA TOUR," *Interfaces*, Vol. 42, No. 2, pp. 146–65.

to-green play was not "mid-rung"—he was number one in strokes gained approach shots in 2011.

Table A-16 shows that Ernie Els's struggles in 2011 were mostly due to the decline in his putting of more than one stroke per round. His resurgence in 2012, including a win at the British Open, was due in large part to his improved putting. Steve Stricker was the comeback player of the year in 2006. Table A-18 shows that his short game has been stellar throughout his career, and his improved play in 2006 was almost entirely due to better long-game play. Stricker was also named comeback player of the year in 2007 when his approach play improved further. Luke Donald, Ernie Els, and Steve Stricker are great examples of the maintain-your-strengths-and-improve-your-weaknesses approach to lower scores.

Table A-14 shows that Rory McIlroy was ranked first in total strokes gained in 2012 with a gain of 3.0 strokes per round. He gained 0.4 strokes per round with his short game and putting, compared to Phil Mickleson's 1.2 strokes per round. If Rory could improve his short game and putting to Phil's level, while maintaining his long game, he'd gain 3.8 strokes per round. Put another way, Rory's long game combined with Phil's short game and putting would rival Tiger's total strokes gained in 2003 and 2006 through 2009. That's how good Tiger was in those years.

Table A-10. Tiger Woods strokes gained by year: total strokes gained and breakdown by shot category from 2003 through 2012. Ranks each year are out of approximately 200 golfers with at least 30 rounds of PGA Tour ShotLink data in the year.

| Year | Rank | | | | | Strokes gained per round | | | | | |
	Total	Drive	Appr	Short	Putt	Total	Drive	Appr	Short	Putt	Rounds
2012	2	9	1	37	27	2.80	0.74	1.39	0.26	0.42	49
2011	29	136	4	89	49	1.09	-0.15	0.88	0.09	0.28	19
2010	48	123	4	160	91	0.71	-0.08	0.91	-0.20	0.08	29
2009	1	15	1	4	2	3.71	0.53	1.48	0.71	0.99	48
2008	1	8	1	3	4	4.14	0.61	2.01	0.67	0.85	11
2007	1	4	1	35	2	3.68	0.81	1.77	0.30	0.80	43
2006	1	4	1	23	21	3.78	0.92	1.98	0.39	0.49	37
2005	1	2	3	89	4	2.82	1.09	0.89	0.10	0.75	55
2004	1	21	5	9	3	3.06	0.48	1.12	0.51	0.95	54
2003	1	6	1	1	18	3.71	0.87	1.60	0.70	0.54	46

Table A-11. Jim Furyk strokes gained by year: total strokes gained and breakdown by shot category from 2003 through 2012.

Year	Rank					Strokes gained per round					Rounds
	Total	Drive	Appr	Short	Putt	Total	Drive	Appr	Short	Putt	
2012	5	53	4	22	22	2.09	0.27	1.01	0.33	0.48	66
2011	36	84	9	47	134	0.94	0.10	0.71	0.23	-0.10	70
2010	3	63	11	2	22	2.03	0.23	0.67	0.64	0.49	60
2009	3	80	14	6	4	2.13	0.15	0.65	0.53	0.80	65
2008	6	46	13	76	28	1.62	0.33	0.71	0.13	0.44	75
2007	10	53	10	9	105	1.68	0.31	0.74	0.59	0.04	66
2006	2	17	3	14	3	2.94	0.58	1.10	0.45	0.81	68
2005	4	68	1	4	31	2.26	0.21	1.11	0.55	0.39	68
2004	22	29	42	101	16	1.49	0.41	0.43	0.05	0.60	31
2003	4	43	11	7	13	2.55	0.39	0.99	0.58	0.59	59

Table A-12. Luke Donald strokes gained by year: total strokes gained and breakdown by shot category from 2003 through 2012.

Year	Rank					Strokes gained per round					Rounds
	Total	Drive	Appr	Short	Putt	Total	Drive	Appr	Short	Putt	
2012	3	124	11	3	2	2.21	-0.06	0.77	0.58	0.91	48
2011	1	89	1	6	1	2.71	0.08	1.18	0.49	0.95	52
2010	5	175	3	10	1	1.95	-0.38	0.92	0.45	0.96	53
2009	13	182	23	12	1	1.48	-0.47	0.51	0.42	1.03	61
2008	2	164	47	1	2	1.96	-0.25	0.40	0.89	0.92	28
2007	18	84	46	30	20	1.36	0.13	0.39	0.34	0.49	50
2006	4	84	8	1	12	2.43	0.13	0.87	0.83	0.61	43
2005	5	59	4	1	17	2.23	0.23	0.86	0.64	0.50	40
2004	21	102	20	24	57	1.50	0.11	0.72	0.40	0.27	60
2003	95	151	93	39	84	0.25	-0.25	0.09	0.31	0.10	63

Table A-13. Phil Mickelson strokes gained by year: total strokes gained and breakdown by shot category from 2003 through 2012.

Year	Rank					Strokes gained per round					Rounds
	Total	Drive	Appr	Short	Putt	Total	Drive	Appr	Short	Putt	
2012	8	110	20	4	7	1.86	0.00	0.66	0.55	0.64	60
2011	6	51	2	9	140	1.63	0.28	1.03	0.44	-0.11	58
2010	10	38	8	15	117	1.49	0.40	0.75	0.39	-0.05	57
2009	19	20	48	7	119	1.29	0.52	0.31	0.50	-0.05	48
2008	1	17	6	9	50	2.25	0.51	0.91	0.54	0.27	59
2007	3	43	7	5	59	2.06	0.38	0.77	0.69	0.23	52
2006	5	11	6	44	66	2.13	0.65	0.99	0.29	0.20	49
2005	8	41	22	9	47	1.81	0.38	0.61	0.52	0.30	50
2004	10	8	15	31	125	1.80	0.67	0.81	0.36	-0.04	50
2003	47	89	101	22	60	0.82	0.11	0.02	0.44	0.24	50

Table A-14. Rory McIlroy strokes gained by year: total strokes gained and breakdown by shot category from 2009 through 2012.

Year	Rank					Strokes gained per round					Rounds
	Total	Drive	Appr	Short	Putt	Total	Drive	Appr	Short	Putt	
2012	1	2	2	35	73	2.97	1.22	1.34	0.27	0.15	40
2011	12	1	50	101	139	1.42	1.14	0.35	0.04	-0.11	18
2010	22	3	19	158	125	1.19	0.90	0.57	-0.19	-0.09	40
2009	67	38	36	116	155	0.47	0.39	0.40	0.00	-0.32	22

Table A-15. Vijay Singh strokes gained by year: total strokes gained and breakdown by shot category from 2003 through 2012.

Year	Rank					Strokes gained per round					Rounds
	Total	Drive	Appr	Short	Putt	Total	Drive	Appr	Short	Putt	
2012	43	33	22	39	179	0.91	0.41	0.61	0.25	-0.37	82
2011	40	37	52	43	131	0.86	0.36	0.34	0.25	-0.08	72
2010	30	25	2	33	195	1.05	0.49	0.93	0.31	-0.68	57
2009	70	33	30	68	186	0.40	0.40	0.46	0.14	-0.61	51
2008	4	3	7	7	177	1.80	0.80	0.80	0.57	-0.38	63
2007	9	12	17	19	107	1.75	0.63	0.64	0.45	0.03	82
2006	6	25	10	8	90	2.07	0.53	0.86	0.57	0.10	84
2005	2	3	7	5	64	2.58	1.04	0.79	0.55	0.20	84
2004	2	1	3	7	126	2.85	1.10	1.17	0.62	-0.04	85
2003	2	1	12	8	66	3.07	1.36	0.95	0.54	0.21	64

Table A-16. Ernie Els strokes gained by year: total strokes gained and breakdown by shot category from 2003 through 2012.

Year	Rank					Strokes gained per round					Rounds
	Total	Drive	Appr	Short	Putt	Total	Drive	Appr	Short	Putt	
2012	35	51	19	89	101	1.01	0.28	0.67	0.05	0.00	65
2011	71	69	8	55	194	0.48	0.18	0.76	0.20	-0.66	59
2010	7	44	9	37	28	1.75	0.35	0.71	0.28	0.42	55
2009	16	25	6	24	152	1.37	0.46	0.88	0.33	-0.30	54
2008	25	80	2	43	190	1.10	0.14	1.14	0.28	-0.46	36
2007	2	17	2	27	104	2.16	0.57	1.20	0.35	0.04	44
2006	8	18	24	2	96	1.94	0.57	0.55	0.74	0.07	51
2005	3	5	10	36	29	2.37	0.97	0.74	0.27	0.40	30
2004	3	3	12	6	78	2.47	0.81	0.84	0.65	0.16	41
2003	10	9	9	25	159	1.90	0.77	1.00	0.42	-0.29	32

Table A-17. Sergio Garcia strokes gained by year: total strokes gained and breakdown by shot category from 2003 through 2012.

Year	Rank					Strokes gained per round					Rounds
	Total	Drive	Appr	Short	Putt	Total	Drive	Appr	Short	Putt	
2012	14	31	43	25	19	1.64	0.43	0.39	0.32	0.50	44
2011	19	12	37	33	123	1.31	0.66	0.41	0.30	-0.07	45
2010	92	47	74	93	166	0.21	0.34	0.18	0.05	-0.36	36
2009	28	23	8	150	113	1.08	0.48	0.77	-0.15	-0.01	44
2008	2	10	3	21	111	1.95	0.55	1.04	0.39	-0.04	56
2007	4	82	3	21	39	1.97	0.14	1.07	0.43	0.33	55
2006	21	28	5	105	148	1.43	0.49	1.00	0.07	-0.13	43
2005	6	1	11	28	159	1.95	1.10	0.72	0.32	-0.19	52
2004	8	7	1	28	200	1.94	0.73	1.33	0.37	-0.49	50
2003	112	39	63	120	196	0.04	0.44	0.29	-0.03	-0.67	28

Table A-18. Steve Stricker strokes gained by year: total strokes gained and breakdown by shot category from 2003 through 2012.

Year	Rank					Strokes gained per round					Rounds
	Total	Drive	Appr	Short	Putt	Total	Drive	Appr	Short	Putt	
2012	12	45	8	16	57	1.75	0.32	0.83	0.40	0.21	54
2011	2	76	34	2	2	2.18	0.17	0.43	0.72	0.87	53
2010	1	52	4	3	15	2.36	0.30	0.87	0.64	0.55	56
2009	2	46	5	3	56	2.23	0.33	0.88	0.72	0.30	62
2008	14	173	43	1	26	1.31	-0.32	0.43	0.75	0.46	58
2007	5	117	5	6	25	1.96	-0.04	0.91	0.68	0.41	65
2006	17	145	65	3	20	1.47	-0.09	0.32	0.73	0.50	54
2005	129	216	160	3	9	-0.05	-1.16	-0.19	0.61	0.68	59
2004	144	216	137	10	12	-0.22	-1.27	-0.08	0.48	0.66	61
2003	141	201	102	5	97	-0.32	-0.99	0.02	0.63	0.02	45

Table A-19 shows the top 40 golfers in strokes gained approach (SGA) per round on the PGA Tour from 2004 through 2012 broken down by shot category. Tiger Woods is ranked first in strokes gained for shots starting between 150 and 200 yards from the hole. He's ranked first for shots starting between 200 and 250 yards from the hole. But from 100 to 150 yards, the top golfers are Tom Lehman, Rory McIlroy, and Kris Blanks. Average strokes gained of the top 40 golfers in SGA shows that shots from 150 to 200 yards contribute 44% (0.24/0.55) of the total gain in SGA. These are the most important shots for tour pros and this is the reason that the median leave for shots from 150 to 200 yards is a good measure of overall approach shot skill.

Table A-19. Strokes gained approach (SGA) per round broken down by shot category: top 40 golfers in SGA on the PGA Tour from 2004 through 2012. Ranks are out of 240 golfers with at least 200 rounds from 2004 to 2012, with the exception of Rory McIlroy, who has only 120 rounds of ShotLink data (and so has an asterisk by his name). Approach shot categories 100–150, 150–200, and 200–250 do not include sand shots or recovery shots, or shots greater than 250 yards from the hole. These "other" approach shots are not included for space reasons.

	Rank				Strokes gained per round			
Golfer	Total SGA	100–150	150–200	200–250	Total SGA	100–150	150–200	200–250
Tiger Woods	1	10	1	1	1.28	0.20	0.62	0.30
Robert Allenby	2	5	5	3	0.88	0.23	0.35	0.23
Jim Furyk	3	7	2	11	0.78	0.21	0.38	0.17
Ernie Els	4	17	8	10	0.77	0.15	0.34	0.17
Sergio Garcia	5	20	11	9	0.75	0.14	0.28	0.17
Rory McIlroy*	6	2	12	12	0.73	0.27	0.27	0.17
Phil Mickelson	6	4	19	40	0.72	0.24	0.23	0.10
Adam Scott	7	21	13	12	0.71	0.14	0.25	0.16
Vijay Singh	8	6	7	77	0.70	0.21	0.35	0.06
Luke Donald	9	30	4	28	0.65	0.12	0.36	0.11
Chad Campbell	10	27	3	55	0.61	0.13	0.37	0.08
Tom Lehman	11	1	17	86	0.60	0.29	0.24	0.06
Scott Verplank	12	72	6	17	0.58	0.07	0.35	0.13
Joey Sindelar	13	31	9	16	0.57	0.12	0.31	0.13
Kenny Perry	14	106	21	2	0.57	0.04	0.23	0.23
Lee Westwood	15	59	14	19	0.56	0.08	0.25	0.13
Kris Blanks	16	2	29	38	0.56	0.26	0.18	0.10
David Toms	17	108	10	15	0.55	0.04	0.30	0.13
Paul Casey	18	11	30	14	0.53	0.19	0.18	0.15
Tim Clark	19	41	23	20	0.52	0.10	0.22	0.13
Justin Rose	20	84	27	4	0.51	0.06	0.19	0.20
John Senden	21	16	15	94	0.49	0.16	0.25	0.05
Alex Cejka	22	12	57	26	0.47	0.18	0.13	0.11
Camilo Villegas	23	23	43	42	0.47	0.14	0.16	0.10
Brendon de Jonge	24	121	35	8	0.46	0.03	0.18	0.17
Davis Love III	25	15	54	110	0.46	0.16	0.14	0.03
Steve Stricker	26	28	28	59	0.45	0.12	0.19	0.08
Stewart Cink	27	58	18	95	0.43	0.08	0.24	0.05
Ricky Barnes	28	32	20	58	0.42	0.12	0.23	0.08
Joe Durant	29	22	25	32	0.42	0.14	0.20	0.11
Zach Johnson	30	51	16	45	0.41	0.08	0.25	0.09
Heath Slocum	31	49	45	34	0.40	0.09	0.16	0.10
Trevor Immelman	32	126	52	13	0.40	0.02	0.14	0.15
Retief Goosen	33	56	83	6	0.39	0.08	0.09	0.18
Boo Weekley	34	43	38	81	0.38	0.10	0.17	0.06
Jeff Sluman	35	36	32	54	0.38	0.11	0.18	0.08
Briny Baird	36	46	67	27	0.38	0.09	0.12	0.11
Jason Bohn	37	67	22	114	0.37	0.07	0.23	0.02
Stephen Ames	38	91	33	96	0.37	0.06	0.18	0.05
K. J. Choi	39	52	12	136	0.36	0.08	0.25	0.00
Dudley Hart	40	9	78	62	0.35	0.20	0.10	0.08
				Top 40 average	0.55	0.13	0.24	0.12

Table A-20 shows the top 40 golfers in strokes gained short game (SGS) per round on the PGA Tour from 2004 through 2012 broken down by shot category. Steve Stricker is ranked first in strokes gained for shots starting between 20 and 60 yards from the hole. He's ranked first for shots starting between 60 and 100 yards from the hole. But from zero to 20 yards, the top golfers are Corey Pavin and Luke Donald. From the sand, zero to 50 yards from the hole, the top golfers are Mike Weir and Luke Donald.[29] Average strokes gained of the top 40 golfers in SGS shows that off-green shots from 0 to 20 yards contribute the most to SGS, followed closely by sand shots from 0 to 50 yards.

[29] Both Tables A-19 and A-20 give results per round. For identifying the best golfer in a given shot category, for example from greenside sand, it is better to use strokes gained per shot. However, both stats give nearly identical results. Strokes gained per round is attractive because summing overall shot categories gives a golfer's total strokes gained per round. Strokes gained per shot does not have this additivity property.

Table A-20. Strokes gained short game (SGS) per round broken down by shot category: top 40 golfers in SGS on the PGA Tour from 2004 through 2012. Ranks are out of 240 golfers with at least 200 rounds from 2004 to 2012. Shot categories 0–20, 20–60, and 60–100 do not include putts or sand shots. Sand shots 50–100 yards from the hole are not included for space reasons.

Golfer	Rank					Strokes gained per round				
	Total SGS	0–20	20–60	60–100	Sand 0–50	Total SGS	0–20	20–60	60–100	Sand 0–50
Steve Stricker	1	3	1	1	69	0.63	0.17	0.21	0.18	0.05
Corey Pavin	2	1	14	12	16	0.54	0.23	0.10	0.09	0.12
Chris Riley	3	6	3	59	3	0.52	0.16	0.14	0.04	0.18
Luke Donald	4	2	51	26	2	0.51	0.19	0.06	0.06	0.20
Mike Weir	5	57	9	21	1	0.50	0.08	0.12	0.07	0.24
Pádraig Harrington	6	7	6	7	31	0.50	0.16	0.13	0.12	0.09
Phil Mickelson	7	11	7	27	17	0.46	0.15	0.12	0.06	0.12
Vijay Singh	8	21	12	44	14	0.42	0.12	0.10	0.05	0.12
Justin Leonard	9	10	5	9	92	0.41	0.16	0.13	0.10	0.03
Brian Gay	10	32	43	5	34	0.39	0.11	0.07	0.13	0.09
Ryuji Imada	11	20	18	46	13	0.39	0.13	0.10	0.04	0.12
Jim Furyk	12	12	19	22	38	0.39	0.15	0.09	0.07	0.08
Nick O'Hern	13	54	30	8	20	0.38	0.08	0.08	0.11	0.11
Kevin Na	14	13	16	87	25	0.38	0.14	0.10	0.02	0.11
Shigeki Maruyama	15	75	2	35	23	0.37	0.06	0.14	0.05	0.11
Justin Rose	16	28	60	36	7	0.36	0.11	0.05	0.05	0.14
Stuart Appleby	17	23	8	75	28	0.36	0.12	0.12	0.03	0.10
Todd Fischer	18	9	4	13	168	0.35	0.16	0.13	0.09	-0.03
Rory Sabbatini	19	56	32	37	10	0.34	0.08	0.07	0.05	0.13
Ian Poulter	20	4	80	98	19	0.33	0.17	0.03	0.01	0.11
Ernie Els	21	30	24	20	63	0.32	0.11	0.09	0.07	0.06
Aaron Baddeley	22	19	29	173	24	0.30	0.13	0.08	-0.02	0.11
K. J. Choi	23	14	100	128	5	0.30	0.14	0.02	0.00	0.14
Tiger Woods	24	41	10	30	98	0.30	0.09	0.11	0.06	0.03
Rod Pampling	25	33	94	95	4	0.30	0.10	0.03	0.02	0.15
Kirk Triplett	26	36	142	6	37	0.29	0.10	0.00	0.12	0.08
Arron Oberholser	27	59	15	78	46	0.28	0.08	0.10	0.02	0.08
Retief Goosen	28	16	67	99	36	0.28	0.14	0.04	0.01	0.08
Kevin Sutherland	29	15	79	157	15	0.28	0.14	0.03	-0.01	0.12
Matt Kuchar	30	63	23	66	35	0.28	0.07	0.09	0.03	0.08
Bob Heintz	31	18	138	42	27	0.27	0.13	0.00	0.05	0.10
Brandt Snedeker	32	35	21	29	121	0.27	0.10	0.09	0.06	0.01
Bryce Molder	33	24	145	15	54	0.27	0.12	0.00	0.08	0.07
Jonathan Byrd	34	22	35	63	84	0.27	0.12	0.07	0.03	0.04
Webb Simpson	35	105	42	32	18	0.27	0.03	0.07	0.05	0.12
Geoff Ogilvy	36	58	119	40	11	0.26	0.08	0.01	0.05	0.13
Omar Uresti	37	65	92	34	26	0.26	0.07	0.03	0.05	0.10
Glen Day	38	70	39	17	65	0.26	0.06	0.07	0.07	0.06
Tom Pernice Jr.	39	31	37	132	50	0.26	0.11	0.07	0.00	0.07
Tim Petrovic	40	8	57	81	124	0.25	0.16	0.05	0.02	0.01
Top 40 average						0.35	0.12	0.08	0.05	0.10

Table A-21 compares strokes gained for tournament winners and the top 40 golfers by shot category. Also shown is the PGA Tour average number of shots by shot category. Putts account for 41% of all shots, 34% of strokes gained by winners, and 15% of strokes gained by the top 40 golfers.

Table A-21. Strokes gained for tournament winners, strokes gained for top 40 golfers, and the PGA Tour average number of shots by shot category. Strokes gained for winners are computed for play during the tournament win. Tournament winners gain an average of 3.7 strokes per round versus the field. The top 40 golfers gain an average of 1.1 strokes per round versus an average PGA Tour field. Approach shots contribute 40% of this gain. Putting accounts for 41% of pro shots, but only 15% of the strokes gained of the top 40 golfers. Approach shots account for 26% of shots, but 40% of the strokes gained of the top forty golfers. Putts in the 0 to 6 foot range account for 22% of all shots. Though not shown in the table, putts in the 0 to 2 feet range account for 13%; putts in 3 to 6 feet account for 9%.

	Winners		Top 40		Tour average	
	SG	Fraction	SG	Fraction	Number of shots	Fraction
Drive	0.7	18%	0.3	28%	13.9	20%
Appr	1.3	34%	0.4	40%	18.5	26%
Short	0.5	14%	0.2	17%	9.4	13%
Putt	1.3	34%	0.2	15%	29.2	41%
Total	3.7	100%	1.1	100%	71.0	100%

		Winners		Top 40		Tour average	
		SG	Fraction	SG	Fraction	Number of shots	Fraction
	Drive	0.7	18%	0.32	28%	13.9	20%
Approach	100–150	0.3	9%	0.10	9%	5.0	7%
	150–200	0.5	14%	0.18	16%	7.0	10%
	200–250	0.3	7%	0.10	9%	3.6	5%
	Other appr	0.2	4%	0.06	5%	2.9	4%
Short	0–20	0.2	7%	0.05	5%	4.0	6%
	20–60	0.1	3%	0.04	4%	2.1	3%
	60–100	0.1	2%	0.04	3%	1.4	2%
	Sand 0–50	0.1	2%	0.05	5%	1.7	2%
	Other short	0.0	0%	0.00	0%	0.2	0%
Putt	0–6 ft	0.3	8%	0.06	5%	16.0	22%
	7–21 ft	0.7	19%	0.07	6%	7.9	11%
	22+ ft	0.3	7%	0.05	4%	5.4	8%
	Total	3.7	100%	1.13	100%	71.0	100%

Figures A-2 and A-3 compare the median leave of pros and amateurs on approach shots. Figure A-4 compares the green hit performance of pros and amateurs on approach shots. Figures A-5, A-6, and A-7 compare the short-game performance of pros with amateurs. All of these figures show that the gap between pro and amateur performance is huge. An individual golfer can compare his performance to the benchmarks in these figures to determine relative strengths and weaknesses.

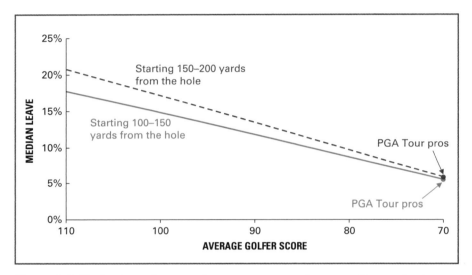

Figure A-2. Median leave (in percent) versus average golfer score. The median leave is the distance from the hole that half of shots fall within. PGA Tour pros hit half of their shots from 100 to 150 yards to within 5.5% of the initial distance to the hole; a typical 90-golfer hits half to within 12%. From 150 to 200 yards, PGA Tour pros hit half of their shots to within 5.9% of the initial distance to the hole; a typical 90-golfer hits half to within 14%. The gap between pros and amateurs increases with longer shots.

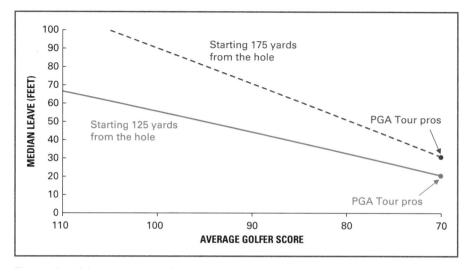

Figure A-3. Median leave (in feet) versus average golfer score. The median leave is the distance from the hole that half of shots fall within. PGA Tour pros hit half of their 125-yard shots to within 21 feet of the hole; a typical 90-golfer hits half within 45 feet. From 175 yards, PGA Tour pros hit half of their shots to within 31 feet of the hole; a typical 90-golfer hits half to within 71 feet. The gap between pros and amateurs increases with longer shots.

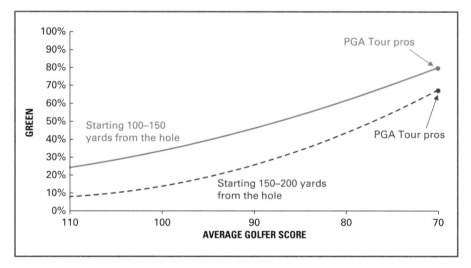

Figure A-4. Green hit fraction versus average golfer score. "Green" refers to the fraction of shots that finish on the green or the fringe of the green. PGA Tour pros hit the green or fringe 80% of the time starting from 100 to 150 yards from the hole; a typical 90-golfer hits the green or fringe 46% of the time. Starting from 150 to 200 yards from the hole, PGA Tour pros hit the green or fringe 67% of the time; a typical 90-golfer hits the green or fringe 26% of the time.

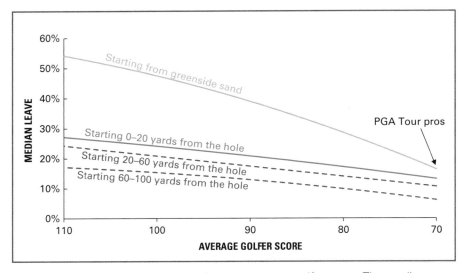

Figure A-5. Median leave (in percent) versus average golfer score. The median leave is the distance from the hole that half of shots fall within.

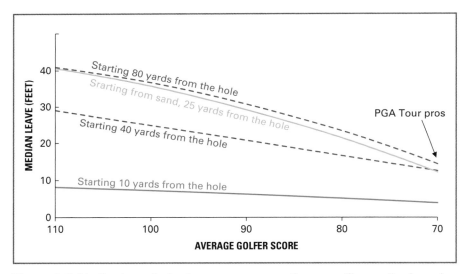

Figure A-6. Median leave (in feet) versus average golfer score. The median leave is the distance from the hole that half of shots fall within.

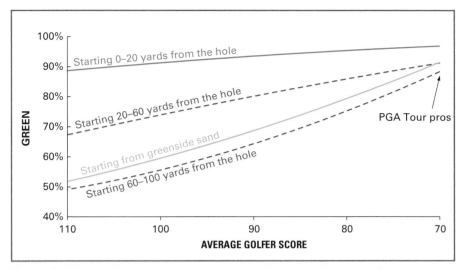

Figure A-7. Green hit fraction versus average golfer score. "Green" refers to the fraction of shots that finish on the green or the fringe of the green.

Chapter 7. Putting Strategy

Figures A-8 and A-9 show the targets set by PGA Tour pros for a range of putt distances and putt angles, on greens with average slopes of 0.7 degrees and 2.3 degrees.

Table A-22 provides details of the putt importance results for pros and amateurs. For pros, the single most important putt distance is five feet; for amateurs, it's four feet. Figure A-10 shows strokes gained putting skill differences. Putt frequency results are displayed in Figure A-11.

Table A-22 gives useful information for setting goals. Imagine practicing 10-footers with the goal of sinking 55% of these putts. There's nothing wrong with setting your sights high, but the best putters in the world only sink 45% from this distance. Time is precious and spending too many hours working toward a goal that might not be achievable means there's that much less time to practice in other areas.

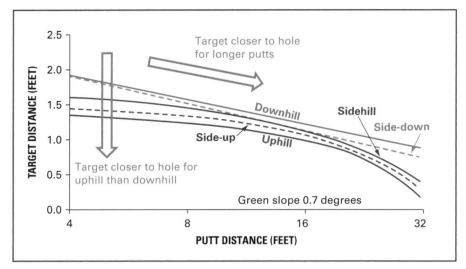

Figure A-8. Target distances for PGA Tour pros as estimated by the middle of scatter patterns of missed putts. Greens have slopes between zero and one degrees at the hole, with an average slope of 0.7 degrees. The target is farther from the hole on downhill putts than on uphill putts. The target is farther from the hole on shorter putts than on longer putts.

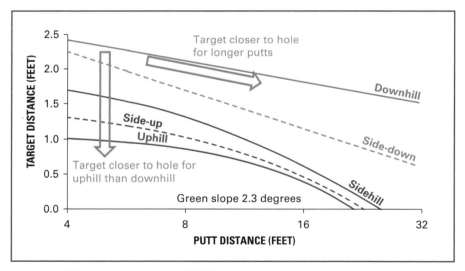

Figure A-9. Target distances for PGA Tour pros on greens with slopes greater than two degrees at the hole and an average slope of 2.3 degrees. The target is farther from the hole on downhill putts than on uphill putts. The target is farther from the hole on shorter putts than on longer putts. For long uphill, side-up, and sidehill putts, the target is slightly short of the hole and pros leave 50% to 60% of these putts short.

Table A-22. Putt importance results. One-putt probabilities by distance are given for the best tour putters, average tour putters, and 90-golfers. The putt importance is proportional to the product of the skill difference and the number of putts per round. For clarity, skill differences are measured using one-putt probabilities. The correct way to measure the skill difference is by using strokes gained, but the two measures give very similar results. For both pros and amateur golfers, short putts are the most important. For pros, the single most important putt distance is five feet; for amateurs, it's four feet.

Putt distance	Golfer group		Best-Tour difference	Putts per round	Putt importance
	Best	**Tour**			
3	98%	96%	1%	2.8	0.037
4	91%	88%	3%	1.8	0.058
5	82%	77%	5%	1.3	0.064
6	72%	67%	6%	1.0	0.057
7	63%	58%	5%	0.9	0.046
8	55%	50%	5%	0.8	0.038
9	50%	45%	5%	0.7	0.039
10	45%	40%	5%	0.7	0.035
11	39%	35%	4%	0.6	0.025
12	36%	31%	5%	0.6	0.027
13	33%	28%	5%	0.5	0.025
14	29%	25%	4%	0.5	0.019
15	27%	23%	3%	0.5	0.016
16	24%	21%	3%	0.4	0.015

Putt distance	Golfer group		Tour-90 difference	Putts per round	Putt importance
	Tour	**90-golfer**			
3	96%	87%	10%	2.8	0.27
4	88%	67%	21%	1.8	0.39
5	77%	51%	26%	1.3	0.34
6	67%	41%	26%	1.0	0.27
7	58%	33%	25%	0.9	0.22
8	50%	28%	22%	0.8	0.18
9	45%	24%	20%	0.7	0.15
10	40%	21%	19%	0.7	0.13
11	35%	18%	16%	0.6	0.10
12	31%	16%	15%	0.6	0.09
13	28%	14%	14%	0.5	0.08
14	25%	13%	13%	0.5	0.06
15	23%	11%	12%	0.5	0.06
16	21%	10%	11%	0.4	0.05

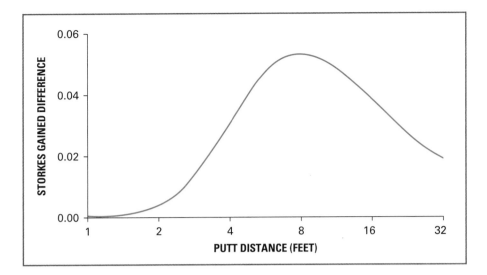

Figure A-10. Difference in strokes gained per putt between the best and average PGA Tour putters by putt distance (shown in log scale for clarity). The largest difference in strokes gained is for five- to 10-foot putts, where the difference is about 0.05. This is consistent with a 5% difference in one-putt probability. For example, the best tour putters sink about 55% from eight feet while the PGA Tour average is about 50%.

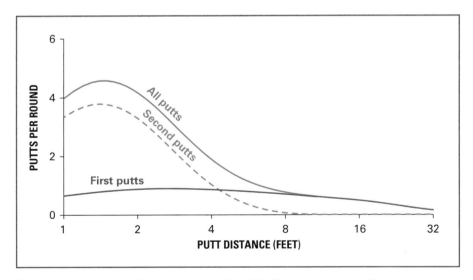

Figure A-11. Number of putts per round for PGA Tour pros by putt distance (shown in log scale for clarity). One-and-a-half-foot putts happen the most often and most of those are second putts. There are almost no second putts longer than 10 feet.

Figure A-12 shows one-putt probabilities for three- to five-foot putts. The putt angle matters less on very short putts. Figure A-13 shows one-putt probabilities for nine- to 11-foot putts.

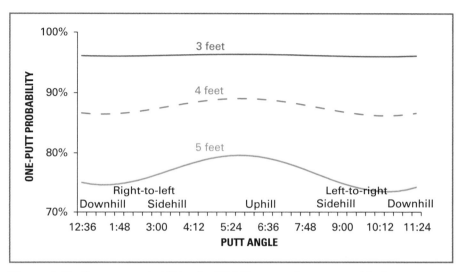

Figure A-12. One-putt probabilities for PGA Tour pros for greens with slopes between one and two degrees at the hole (54% of hole locations are in this range), with an average slope of 1.4 degrees.

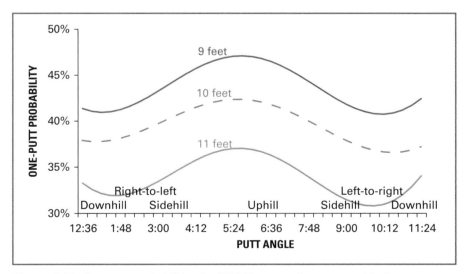

Figure A-13. One-putt probabilities for PGA Tour pros for greens with slopes between one and two degrees at the hole (54% of hole locations are in this range), with an average slope of 1.4 degrees.

Chapter 8. Tee-to-Green Strategy

Table A-23. Up-and-down fraction and average strokes to hole out by distance for PGA Tour pros.

Distance to hole	Fraction of shots	Up-and-down fraction			Average strokes to hole out		
		Fairway	Rough	Sand	Fairway	Rough	Sand
10	35%	79%	66%	55%	2.17	2.34	2.47
20	27%	63%	47%	50%	2.37	2.57	2.53
30	12%	52%	37%	40%	2.50	2.69	2.65
40	5%	44%	31%	30%	2.59	2.77	2.79
50	3%	39%	26%	18%	2.65	2.86	2.99
60	2%	36%	23%	10%	2.69	2.90	3.17
70	3%	34%	21%	10%	2.71	2.93	3.19
80	3%	32%	19%		2.74	2.96	
90	4%	30%	18%		2.76	2.98	
100	6%	28%	16%		2.79	3.01	
	Fraction of off-green shots inside 100 yards				69%	19%	12%

GLOSSARY

ACCURACY IN DEGREES. The average degrees offline of a set of tee shots. More precisely, accuracy in degrees is the standard deviation of directional error, measured in degrees. PGA Tour golfers have accuracies between 2.7 and 4.4 degrees and the tour average is 3.4 degrees. Almost all 90-golfers have accuracies between four and 10 degrees and the 90-golfer average is 6.5 degrees.

AIM OR AIMLINE. A golfer's intended initial direction of a shot or putt.

APEX. The point on a putt's trajectory that is farthest from the line connecting the initial ball position to the hole.

APPROACH SHOT. A shot that starts outside of 100 yards from the hole, excluding tee shots on par-four and par-five holes. This differs from standard golf terminology in that it includes tee shots on par-three holes, layup shots, and recovery shots that start outside of 100 yards from the hole.

AWFUL SHOT. Any shot with a strokes gained between -0.8 and -1.3. These are poor shots where a single swing makes almost no progress to the hole, or even loses ground.

DEGREES OFFLINE. The angle, in degrees, from the final position of a tee shot to the middle of the fairway as measured from the initial tee shot position. For example, a 300-yard tee shot that is four degrees offline finishes 21 yards from the middle of the fairway. Degrees offline is a measure of directional error.

DIE-IT STRATEGY. The strategy of hitting a putt so softly that the ball falls into the hole near its last revolution before stopping.

DOUBLE-AWFUL SHOT. Any shot with a strokes gained less than -1.3. These shots are so poor that a single swing loses significantly more than one stroke, as in hitting a shot out of bounds.

DRIVING ACCURACY. The fraction of fairways hit on tee shots on par-four and par-five holes.

DYNAMIC PROGRAMMING. A mathematical method for finding the best solution to a decision problem with multiple stages.

FAIRWAY HIT. A tee shot on a par-four or par-five hole that finishes in the fairway. A golfer might say that he hit 10 fairways in 14 attempts in his round, or that he hit 71% of his fairways.

FALL LINE. The straight downhill direction on a green in which water would flow due to gravity.

GO FOR IT. A shot hit with the intent of reaching the green.

GOLFMETRICS. A computer program to collect, store, and analyze golf data.

GREEN OR FRINGE IN REGULATION PLUS ONE (GIRP). A hole counts as a GIRP if the golfer reaches the green or fringe of the green on a par-three in one or two shots, a par-four in three or fewer shots, or a par-five in four or fewer shots. A GIRP gives the golfer one more shot to reach the green (or fringe) than a GIR, and is therefore a more useful stat for many amateur golfers to track.

GREEN READING. Assessing the contours, slope, and speed of the green, in order to hit a good putt.

GREEN SPEED. The distance, in feet, a ball travels on a level green when started at a velocity of approximately four miles per hour. Green speeds are usually measured using a Stimpmeter. The average green speed of a municipal course might be seven while the average at PGA Tour events is about 11.

GREENS IN REGULATION (GIR). A hole counts as a GIR, or "greenie," if the golfer reaches the green on a par-three in one shot, a par-four in one or two shots, or a par-five in three or fewer shots. A hole's par includes a nominal two putts, so a GIR is counted if a green is reached in par minus two strokes or less. A golfer might say that he hit five greens in his round, which means that he had five greens in regulation in 18 holes.

JAM-IT STRATEGY. The strategy of hitting a putt so hard that the ball hits, or almost hits, the back of the hole before falling.

LATERAL HAZARD. An area designated as a hazard that typically runs along the side of the fairway, in the direction of play. A variety of rules apply as to where the ball can be dropped when it finishes inside a lateral hazard. Boundaries of lateral hazards are indicated with red stakes and/or red lines.

LAYUP. A shot hit with the intent of finishing short of the green or short of a hazard.

LEVEL GREEN DISTANCE. The distance a ball would travel on a level green (i.e., a flat green without any tilt). For example, a 20-foot downhill putt might have a level green distance of only 15 feet.

LONG GAME. All shots starting outside of 100 yards from the hole.

MEDIAN LEAVE. The value such that half of shots finish closer to the hole and half finish farther from the hole, where distance is measured as the final distance to the hole relative to the initial distance to the hole. For example, a shot that starts 100 yards from the hole and finishes five yards from the hole represents a leave of 5%. If, on five shots, a golfer has leaves of 3%, 8%, 11%, 14%, and 35%, then the median leave is 11%, the middle of the five values. For shots starting 100 to 150 yards from the hole, the PGA Tour average median leave is 5.5% while for 90-golfers it is 12%.

OPTIMIZATION. A procedure for finding the best solution among a set of allowable alternatives in a mathematical model.

OUT OF BOUNDS (OB). An area designated as outside the boundaries of a golf course. When a golfer hits a shot that finishes OB, the golfer hits the next shot from the original position after a penalty of one shot. This is called a "stroke and distance" penalty. OB boundaries are usually indicated with white stakes and/ or white lines.

PUTTING CONTRIBUTION TO SCORES (PCS). The fraction of score differences between two groups of golfers that is due to putting. For example, if the difference in strokes gained putting between two groups is one stroke per round, and the difference in total strokes gained is three strokes per round, then the PCS is 33%. The same concept applies to a single professional golfer relative to the tournament field. In this case, the PCS is the pro's strokes gained putting divided by the total number of strokes gained relative to the field. For example, if the golfer gained 0.2 strokes per round putting, and gained a total of 0.5 strokes per round to the field, then the PCS is 40%.

PUTTING CONTRIBUTION TO VICTORY (PCV). A tournament winner's strokes gained putting divided by the total number of strokes by which the winner beat the field. For example, if the winner beat the field by four strokes per round in a tournament and gained one stroke per round in putting, then the PCV is 25%. The average PCV for a PGA Tour tournament win is 35%.

RECOVERY SHOT. A shot where the direct route to the hole is impeded by trees or other obstacles.

SCATTER PATTERN. The final location of a group of putts taken by a single golfer starting from the same position on the green. Scatter patterns can be used to estimate the golfer's distance control, directional accuracy, and intended target.

SCRATCH GOLFER. A golfer whose handicap is zero, i.e., scratch. Because of the way handicaps are computed, a scratch golfer's average score is about 75, but will vary depending on the difficulty of the courses where the scores are recorded.

SHORT-GAME SHOT. A shot that starts within 100 yards of the hole, excluding shots that start on the green (i.e., excluding putts).

SHOTLINK. The system created by the PGA Tour to collect and disseminate golf scoring and statistical data.

SHOT PATTERN. The final location of a group of shots taken by a single golfer starting from the same position off the green.

SIMULATION. A method, typically implemented in a computer, to mimic the behavior of real-world systems.

STROKES GAINED APPROACH SHOTS (SGA). The total strokes gained for all approach shots per round.

STROKES GAINED DRIVING (SGD). The total strokes gained for all tee shots on par-four and par-five holes per round. A driver is typically used for these shots, but tee shots with other clubs are also included.

STROKES GAINED LONG GAME. The total strokes gained for all long-game shots per round. This is the sum of strokes gained driving and strokes gained approach.

STROKES GAINED OF A SINGLE GOLF SHOT. The decrease in the average number of strokes to hole out minus one to account for the stroke taken. For example, if a stroke starts on a tee where the average score is four, and if it finishes at a position in the fairway where the average strokes to hole out is 2.8, then the tee shot has moved the ball 1.2 strokes closer to the hole with just one stroke. The single tee shot has a strokes gained of 0.2.

STROKES GAINED PUTTING PER HOLE. The average number of putts to hole out from a given distance, minus the number of putts taken. For example, taking two putts from a distance where the average number of putts to hole out is 1.5 gives a strokes gained of -0.5. The average number of putts, or benchmark, is typically computed using data from professional golfers, but the benchmark can also be defined to be the average number of putts taken by scratch (i.e., zero-handicap) golfers.

STROKES GAINED PUTTING PER ROUND (SGP). The sum of strokes gained putting per hole for all 18 holes in a round.

STROKES GAINED SHORT GAME (SGS). The total strokes gained for all short-game shots per round.

TARGET. In putting, the target is the spot where a putt struck on the intended line and at the intended speed would come to a stop if the hole were covered. The target is typically beyond the hole, in order for the ball to fall into the hole when the hole gets in the way of the putt. For shots starting off the green, the target is the intended finishing position of the shot. A golfer might aim away from the target to account for the curved trajectory of a shot or putt.

75TH PERCENTILE DISTANCE. The distance of a group of shots such that one out of four shots travels longer and three out of four travel shorter. For example, if a golfer hits five drives, the distance of the second-longest shot is the 75th percentile distance. With nine drives, the distance of the third-longest shot is the 75th percentile distance (because two are longer and six are shorter than this distance).

80-GOLFER. A golfer whose average score is 80 per round.

90-GOLFER. A golfer whose average score is 90 per round.

100-GOLFER. A golfer whose average score is 100 per round.

ACKNOWLEDGMENTS

My wife, Nancy, laughed out loud the first time my boys and I tuned in to the PGA Tour on our car radio. As the only nongolfer in the family, she's been quite a sport about the role of golf in our lives. I'd like to thank her both for her support and for carefully reading the manuscript and catching mistakes that everyone else missed.

We've always encouraged our boys to follow their own passions, yet both have chosen to become golfers and worked hard on their skills (though to be honest, Daniel's first love is baseball). Christopher is a serious three-handicap golfer, has won the junior championship twice at our club. He has been a big help throughout the years, from creating courses and entering data in the Golfmetrics program to providing insightful feedback on the book and on all aspects of golf statistics and strategy.

Jennifer Freeman did a fabulous job smoothing my words, reorganizing the flow of ideas, and suggesting many changes that greatly improved the readability of the book. Thanks, Jenny!

I am thankful to the editors at Gotham, Jessica Sindler and Brooke Carey, for shepherding the book to its conclusion. I'm especially grateful to Bill Shinker for his support, encouragement, and strong belief in the book from the outset. It's been fun playing golf and learning about the publishing business with my agent, David McCormick. Thanks to Trevor Johnston for creating the beautiful illustrations in the book.

I've benefited from conversations with too many people to mention them all, but I would like to thank longtime friends and fellow golfers Paul Bader, Ted Conover, Tom Couch, Tom Dundon, Bob Grober, John Hellström, Jon Karlsen, Eric Kenworthy, Jahn Levin, Rob Neal, Dan Parks, Tony Renshaw, Ben Shear, Steve Smith, and Frank Thomas (who gets credit for the Driver-Fairyland idea). I also wanted to thank club professionals Mike Diffley, Dennis Hillman, Michael Hunt, Greg Pace and Phil Wildermuth, and golf writers Michael Agger, Connell Barrett, David Barrett, Farrell Evans, Sean Martin, Peter Morrice, John Paul Newport, Bill Pennington, Adam Schupak, Josh Sens, and Mike Stachura. I've enjoyed working on golf research with PhD students Matulya Bansal, Ningyuan Chen, Soonmin Ko, and Dongwook Shin, and fellow academic Dick Rendleman. I'm proud to be associated with TaylorMade, and to have had the pleasure of working with and learning from so many people there: David Anderson, Todd Borjesson, James Cornish, Chuck Presto, Keith Sbarbaro, Andrew Semrad, and Kraig Willett. It's been fun and an honor to work on handicapping issues as part of the USGA Handicap Research Team (HRT). From the USGA and the HRT I'd like to thank Steven Edmondson, Frank Engle, Scott Hovde, Adam Karnush, Kevin O'Connor, Matt Pringle, Lou Riccio, Warren Simmons, Dick Stroud, and the late Fran Scheid.

A fortuitous meeting at the birthday party of a friend was the beginning of a long collaboration with Lou Lipnickey. I can't thank Lou enough for all of his programming wizardry in developing the Golfmetrics program that was used to collect and analyze amateur and pro golf data. Others who helped with the Golfmetrics software include Kivanc Anar, Weiwei Deng, Don Devendorf, Alexsandra Guerra, and Bin Li. Thanks to the many golfers who input data into Golfmetrics.

A big thank-you to the PGA Tour for allowing academics like me to access their incredible ShotLink data. Without this access, strokes gained putting and the entire concept of a statistical approach to golf would have had a hard time getting out of the starting gate. I'd especially like to thank Tom Alter, Steve Evans, Kin Lo, Ken Lovell, Alex Turnbull, Rob Uselman, Mike Vitti, and Don Wallace of the PGA Tour.

I've been fortunate to glean many pearls of wisdom by spending time and having conversations with touring professionals and their coaches. In particular, I'd like to thank golf coaches Sean Foley, Pat Goss, Rickard Lindberg, David Orr, Justin Poynter, Greg Rose, Terry Rowles, Colin Swatton, and Mark Wood, and players Amy Alcott, Jonas Blixt, Mark Calcavecchia, Ben Crane, Jason Day, Luke Donald, Brad Faxon, Sophie Gustafson, Peter Hanson, Nannette Hill, Scott Hoch, Robert Karlsson, David Lingmerth, Edoardo Molinari, Justin Rose, and Bo Van Pelt.

Like all academics' work, mine is a melting pot of ideas resting on the shoulders of those who went before me. When I started research into golf, I didn't even remember that in high school I had picked up from the library the now classic book *Search for the Perfect Swing*. The authors Cochran and Stobbs in the 1960s were the first ones to record and analyze individual golf shots. Clyne Soley recorded and analyzed individual putts by pros and amateurs, and published his results in the late 1970s in the book *How Well Should You Putt?*. Since the PGA Tour began publishing strokes gained putting stats, I've heard from a number of individuals who have had similar ideas.

I received helpful comments on an early draft from Greg Coleman, Mike Johannes, and Tom Kalman. I especially want to thank my friend Edoardo Molinari for his careful reading of a draft of the book, his thoughtful suggestions and probing questions, and the many conversations we've had. Of course, any remaining errors, and I'm sure there are some, are my responsibility. To find my mulligans (updates and errata) and other information related to the book, please go to www.everyshotcounts.com.

Finally, thanks to you for taking the time to read this book. I hope you've learned a few things about golf, picked up at least one idea that will help your game, and enjoyed a story or two along the way.

ART CREDITS

Figures on pages xv, 30, 120, 135, 136, 143, 144, 146, 148, 152, 153, 191, and 195
courtesy of the author

Photographs on pages xvi and 76 courtesy of the author

Photograph on page 29 courtesy of Getty Images/photographer Alfred Eisenstaedt

Figures on pages 35, 68, 81, 87, 97, 166, 167, 169, 170, 171, 172, 173 copyright
© Trevor Johnston/TrevorJohnston.com

Photographs on pages 40 and 70 copyright © Bettmann/CORBIS

Photograph on page 60 copyright © CORBIS

Photograph on page 62 (top) used with the permission of Melanie Jackson
Agency, LLC

Photograph on page 81 (top) courtesy of PGA TOUR Entertainment

Photograph on page 81 (bottom) courtesy of Christopher Broadie

Photograph on page 131 courtesy of Ron Wilkerson